THE WINNING ORAL ARGUMENT

Published by
Thomson/West
610 Opperman Drive
P.O. Box 64526
St. Paul, MN 55164-0527
1-800-328-9352

ISBN: 978-0-314-19885-3

Library of Congress Cataloguing-in-Publication Data
Bryan A. Garner
The winning oral argument — 2nd ed.
    p.   cm.
Includes bibliographical references and index.
1. Law — United States — Methodology.
2. Oral pleading — United States.
3. Appellate procedure — United States.
I. Garner, Bryan A.
II. The Winning Oral Argument.

Layout by Jeff Newman
Copy — Hoefler Text 10/12
Headings — Hoefler Black 12/13

The Winning Oral Argument

Enduring Principles
with Supporting
Comments from
the Literature

BRYAN A. GARNER

"No one can attain a character for wisdom and eloquence without the greatest study, industry, and learning."

—*Cicero*

"The art of persuading human beings — including judges — has remained pretty consistent through the years."

—*Roy L. Steinheimer Jr.*

"You may hear or believe that oral argument is an art. To a degree, that is true, but it is irrelevant. Whatever your experience or inborn skill, the fundamentals count. Observe them, and you will improve your artistry."

—*Gary L. Sasso*

"It is surprising how often counsel, even of mature years, violate the most elementary principles of oral argument."

—*Ben W. Palmer*

"Long experience of sitting as Judge in an inferior court has led me to believe that it is not necessary or convenient that the advocacy should also be inferior."

—*Hon. Edward Abbott Parry*

Books Written or Edited by Bryan A. Garner

Black's Law Dictionary (all current editions)

Garner's Modern American Usage

Making Your Case: The Art of Persuading Judges
(with Justice Antonin Scalia)

Garner on Language and Writing
(foreword by Justice Ruth Bader Ginsburg)

A Dictionary of Modern Legal Usage

The Redbook: A Manual on Legal Style

The Elements of Legal Style

The Winning Brief

The Winning Oral Argument

Legal Writing in Plain English

Guidelines for Drafting and Editing Court Rules

A Handbook of Basic Law Terms

A Handbook of Business Law Terms

A Handbook of Criminal Law Terms

A Handbook of Family Law Terms

The Oxford Dictionary of American Usage and Style

The Rules of Golf in Plain English
(with Jeffrey S. Kuhn)

A New Miscellany-at-Law
(by Sir Robert Megarry)

Texas, Our Texas: Reminiscences of The University
(an anthology of autobiographical essays)

For Judge Thomas M. Reavley
mentor in chief

Preface

Glance first at the bibliography at the back of this book, and then imagine my astonishment, when reading my 250th or so article on oral argument, to find a recent essay beginning with these words: "There is scant literature on the subject of oral argument." In truth, the author merely had scanty knowledge of the copious literature.

This book has its origins in my research for another book, *Making Your Case: The Art of Persuading Judges*, which I coauthored with Justice Antonin Scalia. Before I undertook that joint project, the only major component of judicial persuasion that I'd never written about, and for which I'd never canvassed the literature, was oral argument. And so I began reading every relevant piece I could find.

As in my other research projects, such as *The Winning Brief*, I found great wealth in the literature. But the gems of advice lay buried in dozens of articles and books, many of them little-known, and some of the best advice could be excavated only through tremendous exertion. My goal was to codify the principles and illustrate them with the wisest, pithiest formulations in support of the principles. That's what I've tried to do, in hopes that the book will benefit both those who read it systematically and those who just browse through it from time to time. I like browsable books, and this one seems especially browsable.

As in all my scholarly endeavors, I'm grateful to the late Roy M. Mersky of the University of Texas School of Law, who as director of the Tarlton Law Library generously made the resources and staff of that great institution available to me. Jeanne Price, the library's associate director for patron services, and Leslie Ashbrook, a Tarlton Fellow, arranged to have dozens of articles sent to me in Dallas. Meanwhile, several appellate practitioners sent me their entire files of articles on oral argument as I was preparing the first version of the book, which was privately printed by LawProse, Inc. My sincere gratitude goes to Jordan B. Cherrick of St. Louis, Jeffrey I. Ehrlich of Los Angeles, Benjamin G. Shatz of Los Angeles, and Scott P. Stolley of Dallas. They jump-started my research and made it possible for me to complete this book in the span of seven months. Since then, useful materials have alighted in my mailbox from various friends, including Gideon Kanner of Los Angeles.

If any reader knows of a good source on oral argument not cited here, I'd be grateful to have it: send the article or citation to bgarner@lawprose.org.

At LawProse, my colleagues Jeff Newman and Tiger Jackson were monumentally helpful. Jeff edited the text, designed the pages, and spearheaded the production. Tiger verified the citations and prepared the index. The spadework that goes into producing a sound book is greater than most people imagine, and I'm thankful for the excellent help that Jeff and Tiger have given me. Additionally, Arrissa Meyer and Laurie Velasco of S.M.U. Law School helped in proofreading.

I've been studying appellate arguments for a long time. When I was an undergraduate in Austin, Chief Justice Joe R. Greenhill of the Supreme Court of Texas, the colleague and friend of my late grandfather, Justice Meade F. Griffin, twice had me as his guest at oral arguments in the Supreme Court of Texas. He generously introduced me to the entire Court, including two notable authorities quoted in this book: Justices Jack Pope and Franklin Spears. Later, I was heavily involved in moot-court activities in law school, as both advocate and judge. As law clerk to Judge Thomas M. Reavley of the Fifth Circuit, I was part of an experiment in which the law clerks served also as bailiffs. I saw many oral arguments up close in those days, including some breathtaking performances by Arthur Miller and Michael Tigar. Judge Reavley often talked with me about effective and ineffective advocacy, and we've continued that conversation through the years. In full-time practice in the late 1980s, I had my share of oral arguments, and I've done some since. Over the years, I've continued to watch arguments intently, in courts at all levels throughout the country — and some in England as well.

An oral argument has the potential for magic. It's the thrill of an intellectual and moral competition. Which side has outprepared the other? One usually does. Which side has it right? Often you can't really tell and won't really know for many months. But it's always fascinating to watch and predict.

Bryan A. Garner
Dallas, Texas
July 2008

Table of Contents

Introduction

The Importance of Oral Argument

(a) *Classic statement 1.* "[T]he desirability . . . of a full exposition by oral argument in the highest court is not to be gainsaid. . . . [A]side from cases of exceptional difficulty, the impression that a judge has at the close of a full oral argument accords with the conviction which controls his final vote." Hon. Charles Evans Hughes, *The Supreme Court of the United States* 61, 62–63 (1928).

(b) *Classic statement 2.* "[O]ral argument is the absolutely indispensable ingredient of appellate advocacy. . . . [O]ften my whole notion of what a case is about crystallizes at oral argument. This happens even though I read all the briefs before oral argument; indeed, that is the practice now of all the members of the Supreme Court." Hon. William J. Brennan, *Harvard Law School Occasional Pamphlet No. 9* 22–23 (1967).

(c) *Best chance to engage judges' minds.* "You could write hundreds of pages of briefs, and you are still never absolutely sure that the judge is focused on exactly what you want him to focus on in that brief. Right there at the time of oral argument, you know that you do have an opportunity to engage or get into the judge's mental processes." Hon. William H. Rehnquist (as quoted in Hon. Myron H. Bright, *The Power of the Spoken Word: In Defense of Oral Argument*, 72 Iowa L. Rev. 35, 36–37 (1986)).

(d) *The view from the summit.* "As a justice, I know how very important oral argument is. As an advocate, I wasn't as sure of this." Hon. John Roberts, at the Ninth Circuit Judicial Conference, 13 July 2006.

(e) *Intimacy of direct address.* "[Y]ou may take my word for it, oral address may breed an intimacy between advocate and judge that can never come out of a printed page." Hon. John T. Loughran, "The Argument in the Court of Appeals" (1943), in *Advocacy and the King's English* 570, 576 (George Rossman ed., 1960).

(f) *Judges learning from colleagues.* "How often I have begun argument with a clear idea of the strength or weakness of the decision being appealed, only to realize from a colleague's questioning that there was much, much more to the case then met my eye." Hon. Frank M. Coffin, *On Appeal: Courts, Lawyering and Judging* 133 (1994).

(g) *High skills at a premium.* "[A]t oral argument, even more than in brief writing, high skills are at a premium. Many more cases than you would think are decisively influenced at that point." Hon. Laurence H. Silberman, *Plain Talk on Appellate Advocacy*, 20 Litig. 3, 4 (Spring 1994).

(h) *Changing minds.* "I have known cases in which when the case started I was convinced that the appellant was either right or wrong and during the course of the case a point made either by me or by one of my colleagues has completely changed one's view." Rt. Hon. Lord Guest (as quoted in Alan Paterson, *The Law Lords* 37 (1982)).

(i) *Shifting opinions.* "I think that in a significant minority of the cases in which I have heard oral argument, I have left the bench feeling different about the case than I did when I came on the bench. The change is seldom a full one-hundred-eighty-degree swing, and I find that it is most likely to occur in cases involving areas of law with which I am least familiar." Hon. William H. Rehnquist, *The Supreme Court: How It Was, How It Is* 276 (1987).

(j) *One last chance.* "In oral argument lies counsel's one hedge against misdiagnosis and misperformance in the brief, the one last chance of locating a postern missed in the advance survey. In oral argument lies the opportunity to catch attention and rouse interest among men who must be got to read — or to reread — *this* brief not as a routine duty nor under the undiscriminating press of other business, but with the pointed concentration *this* cause merits. . . . In any but freak situations, oral argument is a must." Karl N. Llewellyn, *The Common Law Tradition: Deciding Appeals* 240 (1960).

(k) *Face-to-face discussion as preventive of wandering.* "The mere fact that oral argument is presented in the face of the court and in the presence of opposing counsel tends to discipline counsel to deal with the issues and not to wander. The real merit of oral argument is that in the cross fire of discussion the issues become crystallized and vivid." John J. Robinette, *A Counsel Looks at the Court*, 53 Can. B. Rev. 558, 558 (1975).

(l) *Breaking the judges' isolation.* "Oral argument is important as a means of giving judges a continuing awareness of their relationship and dependence on others; without it, the judge is isolated from all but a limited group of subordinates." Paul Carrington et al., *Justice on Appeal* 17 (1976).

(m) *Potential decisiveness.* "In the majority of appellate cases, oral argument isn't decisive; the case is won or lost on the briefs. But in a significant minority of cases, oral argument is decisive. Probably somewhere between 10% and 35% of cases on appeal are won or lost on oral argument. Think about these statistics the next time that you are tempted to treat oral argument as an afterthought." Raymond P. Ward, *The Importance of Earnest Oral Argument*, Certworthy (Defense Research Inst. App. Advocacy Comm. newsletter), Summer 1999, at 12.

(n) *What you want the judges to have.* "The lawyer can write hundreds of pages of briefs and you never know whether that judge's mental processes are such that the judge realizes and picks up exactly what you want that judge to have. And it is that oral argument that crystallizes the whole appeal." Hon. William H. Rehnquist, Panel Discussion, *Mastering the Appeal* (31 Mar. 1989).

(o) *Quotidian question-answering.* "Day in and day out, it is the advocate's ability to answer questions effectively and persuasively, not ask them, that is likely to have a major impact on trials, appellate arguments, administrative proceedings, negotiations, pretrial conferences, and the like." Hon. Douglas S. Lavine, *Responding to Questions*, Nat'l L.J., 1 Jan. 2007, at 20.

(p) *Better opinions.* "[A] good oral argument . . . is more likely to result in a better opinion than in a changed vote. . . . [But] there are cases in which the oral argument can change some votes, and you cannot assume that your case will not be one of them." Rex E. Lee, *Oral Argument in the Supreme Court*, 72 ABA J. 60, 60 (June 1986).

(q) *A powerful weapon.* "I should like to leave with you, particularly those of you who are among the younger barristers, the thought that your oral argument on an appeal is perhaps the most effective weapon you have got if you will give it the time and attention it deserves. Oral argument is exciting and will return rich dividends if it is done well. And I think it will be a sorry day for the American bar if the place of the oral argument in our appellate courts is depreciated and oral advocacy becomes looked upon as a pro forma exercise which, because of tradition or because of the insistence of his client, a lawyer has to go through." Hon. John M. Harlan, *What Part Does the Oral Argument Play in the Conduct of an Appeal?*, 41 Cornell L.Q. 6, 11 (1955).

(r) *More than mere tradition.* "Oral argument is more than just a tradition; it can and does influence the decision in your case. No matter how little effect the naysayers claim oral argument has on the outcome of appeals, the potential is always there to change someone's mind. The law clerks might have missed an important issue, or judges might have glossed over a vital aspect of your argument. The bench may have questions about the effect of a ruling in your favor that you satisfactorily answer, but that were not addressed in your brief. While not all appellate judges agree on the numbers, each and every one we asked about the importance of oral argument has stated that his or her mind has been changed by an effective oral argument. Many (if not most) of us can be more persuasive with the spoken word than with the written. Oral argument is our chance to prove it." Hon. Thomas J. Wright & Perry H. Piper, *Oral Advocacy — Some Reminders*, Tenn. B.J., Nov./Dec. 1994, at 28.

(s) *Empirical evidence.* Two Eighth Circuit judges kept track of all the cases that came before them for 10 months, asking themselves: "(1) Was oral argument necessary? (2) Was oral argument helpful? (3) Did it change the judge's mind?" Their answers:

- Hon. Myron H. Bright: (1) 85% yes. (2) 82% yes. (3) 24% yes, 7% maybe.
- Hon. Richard S. Arnold: (1) 75% yes. (2) 80% yes. (3) 15% yes, 2% maybe.

See Hon. Myron H. Bright & Hon. Richard S. Arnold, *Oral Argument? It May Be Crucial!*, 70 ABA J. 68 (Sept. 1984).

(t) *Life and meaning.* "Books, articles, and speeches on appellate advocacy strongly support the oral argument of appeals. It makes the appeal take on life and meaning, highlights the significant issues, brings out the doubtful questions of fact and law, starts the judges thinking in the direction of the ultimate decision by giving them the 'feel' of the case, and makes possible a prompt decision . . . while the matter is fresh in the minds of all." B.E. Witkin, *Manual on Appellate Court Opinions* 45–46 (1977).

(u) *Cutting both ways.* "Oral argument may lift up the fallen or cause the tottering to fall." *TJX Cos., Inc. v. Superior Court*, 104 Cal. Rptr. 2d 810, 815 (Cal. App. 2001).

(v) *A great time-saver.* "[Oral argument] is a great saving of time of the court . . . to obtain the grasp of the case. . . and to be able more quickly to separate the wheat from the chaff. Our records in these days of typing are apt to be full of chaff." Hon. Charles Evans Hughes, *The Supreme Court of the United States* 61–62 (1928).

(w) *Cynical British view about an inverse relationship.* "Generally speaking, the worse the court, the greater the importance of advocacy." Anon., *English Justice* 151 (1932).

The Purpose of Oral Advocacy

(a) *Classic statement 1.* "The ultimate purpose of oral argument, from the point of view of the advocate, is to work his way into the judge's consciousness and make the judge think about the things that the advocate wishes him to think about. One of the best ways to begin this process is to establish eye contact with as many of the judges as possible . . . ." Hon. William H. Rehnquist, *The Supreme Court: How It Was, How It Is* 279 (1987).

(b) *Classic statement 2.* "Oral argument serves two purposes: it gives the lawyers a chance to present their theory of the case in a nutshell, and it allows the judges to ask questions to clear up any doubts that the court might have about the case or the lawyer's approach to it." Hon. Myron H. Bright, *The Changing Nature of the Federal Appeals Process in the 1970's*, 65 F.R.D. 496, 506 (1975).

(c) *Classic statement 3.* "Like their brethren in most appellate courts, the Justices of the Supreme Court view the argument not as an occasion for speeches or a game of 20 questions, but rather as an initial conference convened to decide the case. Counsel is invited into the conference for two purposes: to serve as a resource providing information needed to clarify the thinking of the Justices; and to bring an organizing theme, emphasis, and note of drama needed to marshal the information in a meaningful way." Stephen M. Shapiro, *Questions, Answers, and Prepared Remarks*, 15 Litig. 33, 34 (Spring 1989).

(d) *Inside the court's conference (1).* "It isn't just an interchange between counsel and each of the individual Justices. What is going on is also to some extent an exchange of information among the Justices themselves. You hear the questions of the others and see how their minds are working, and that stimulates your own thinking. I use it . . . to give counsel his or her best shot at meeting my major difficulty with that side of the case: 'Here's what's preventing me from going along with you. If you can explain why that's wrong, you have me.'" Hon. Antonin Scalia (as quoted in Hon. Joseph W. Hatchett & Robert J. Telfer III, *The Importance of Appellate Oral Argument*, 33 Stetson L. Rev. 139, 142 (2003)).

(e) *Inside the court's conference (2).* "[W]ith the oral argument, the appellate advocate is in the main serving as a supernumerary member of the court's conference. Counsel will attempt to stimulate the judges to an appreciation of the client's point of view and to demonstrate the essential fallacy of the opponent's position." Hon. Albert Tate Jr., *Federal Appellate Advocacy in the 1980s*, 5 Am. J. Trial Advoc. 63, 79 (1981).

(f) *Helping the court.* "[T]he purpose of the oral argument is not to enable counsel to display his forensic eloquence. Rather its purpose is to assist and enlighten the court to give sympathetic consideration to the client's view. If questioning assists the court in this primary function of counsel's appearance before it, counsel should not regret unduly the interruption of his prepared remarks even by questions [that] may seem to him to be foolish (and [that] indeed may be)." Hon. Albert Tate Jr., *The Appellate Advocate and the Appellate Court*, 13 La. B.J. 107, 112 (Aug. 1965).

(g) *Common-sense disposition.* "Subject to the discipline of clearly established legal doctrine, the trial or appellate judge's basic instinct is to desire that some common-sense justice be done. What the butcher, the baker, or the candlestick-maker as a rule will regard as the fair disposition of the case, so probably at least ninety percent of the time will the trial or appellate judge." Hon. Albert Tate Jr., *The Appellate Advocate and the Appellate Court*, 13 La. B.J. 107, 107–08 (Aug. 1965).

(h) *The business of persuasion.* "The business of oratory is to persuade people, and to please people is a great step to persuading them." Lord Chesterfield (as quoted in Thomas Edward Crispe, *Reminiscences of a K.C.* 256 (1910)).

(i) *Judges as aural learners.* "[A]n appellate judge who has had trial-court experience has of necessity learned to understand law points made orally, often unaided by a brief. So oral argument gives counsel a chance to appeal to the ear-minded judge." Hon. Herbert F. Goodrich, "In the Matter of Oral Argument" (1955), in *Advocacy and the King's English* 233, 233 (George Rossman ed., 1960).

(j) *Focusing on the bench, not adversary.* "We are not judging a debate, and you get no points for destroying either your opponent, or your opponent's argument. Oral argument is not a contest. Oral argument is not a chance for you to muse, or lecture, or argue, with the justices. It is also not a good idea to plan on showing off for your client, the audience, or the press. None of them have a vote on the outcome of your case. Only we do." Hon. Michael J. Wilkins, *Remember, for Every Case Won at Oral Argument, the Other Side Loses,* 17 Utah B.J. 36, 36 (Sept. 2004).

(k) *Direct connection with judges.* "[O]ral argument gives important service to the imperatives of appellate justice. Specifically, it heightens the judges' sense of personal responsibility. It provides them with an opportunity to test their own thinking in a direct way with counsel available to correct error." Paul D. Carrington et al., *Justice on Appeal* 17 (1976).

(l) *Engaging the court.* "[T]he function of oral argument . . . is to engage the court. By engaging the court, I don't mean keeping the judges awake. I do mean that you get the judges into a discussion with the lawyers about the case and the issues in the case. An argument that does not do that is a failure." Hon. Charles D. Breitel, "A Summing Up," in *Counsel on Appeal* 193, 198 (Arthur A. Charpentier ed., 1968).

(m) *Not a literal argument.* "[T]oo many lawyers actually argue. . . . Instead, the experienced oral advocate converses with the panel, as she and the judges jointly grapple with the difficult legal issues presented by the case that will affect the development of the law." Catherine Valerio Barrad, *Successful Oral Arguments Do Not Involve Any Arguing,* S.F. Daily J., 4 Aug. 2004, at 5.

(n) *The particular purpose.* "The job of an appellate argument is to win a particular case before a particular tribunal for a particular client." Karl N. Llewellyn, *A Lecture on Appellate Advocacy,* 29 U. Chi. L. Rev. 627, 629 (1962).

The Quality of Modern Oral Argument

(a) *Classic statement 1.* "Although appellate argument is a common occurrence and represents the culminating competitive effort in the legal contest, it is probably a fact that this is the least qualitative accomplishment of the bar as a whole." Raymond S. Wilkins, "The Argument of an Appeal" (1947), in *Advocacy and the King's English* 277, 281 (George Rossman ed., 1960).

(b) *Classic statement 2.* "Too many, far too many, lawyers burden courts of appeal with poorly prepared, poorly presented, and thoroughly unhelpful arguments — for which they receive, and clients pay, substantial and not infrequently handsome fees. Even after making due allowance for the frailties of mankind, it is amazing how few good arguments are presented and heard, even in the highest state and federal tribunals. Within the year I have been told by a justice of the Supreme Court of the United States that four out of every five arguments to which he must listen are 'not good.' And comments from judges of other appellate courts give me no reason to suppose that the percentage of good arguments is perceptibly higher elsewhere." Frederick Bernays Wiener, *Oral Advocacy*, 62 Harv. L. Rev. 56, 56 (1948).

(c) *Roscoe Pound on oral degeneracy and its main cause.* "One of the most serious features of appellate practice in the United States is the decadence of oral argument. . . . The rules limiting the time for argument, no doubt rendered necessary to no small extent by the volume of work in reviewing courts, suggest . . . [an] attitude toward oral argument as something in which the bar are to be indulged rather than as an effective aid to correct decision." Roscoe Pound, *Appellate Procedure in Civil Cases* 369–70 (1941).

(d) *Ditto Professor Delmar Karlen of New York University.* "Many observers, including a large number of American judges, believe that the quality of appellate advocacy in the United States is low, and that it is declining. If they are correct, a partial explanation may lie in the fact that rigid time limitations allow little opportunity for its development." Delmar Karlen, *Appellate Courts in the United States and England* 152 (1963).

(e) *Justice John M. Harlan's view.* "[The thing] that has astonished me most is the number of disappointing arguments to which courts have to listen. They seem to be due, in some cases, to lack of preparation; in others to lack of capacity; but more generally, I think, the explanation is to be found in the increasing tendency to regard the oral argument as being of little importance in the decision of appeals." Hon. John M. Harlan, *What Part Does the Oral Argument Play in the Conduct of an Appeal?*, 41 Cornell L.Q. 6, 11 (1955).

(f) *Justice William O. Douglas's view.* "Few truly good advocates have appeared before the Court. In my time, 40 percent were incompetent. Only a few were excellent." Hon. William O. Douglas, *The Court Years, 1939–1975* 183 (1980).

(g) *Justice Thurgood Marshall's view.* "Hardly 1 out of 100 lawyers has filed a case on appeal who is not familiar with that admonition — go for the jugular vein — but when you hear the arguments and read the briefs of so many of those lawyers, you find that in aiming for the jugular vein they have put a pinprick in a small vein of the big toe." Hon. Thurgood Marshall, "The Federal Appeal," in *Counsel on Appeal* 139, 153 (Arthur A. Charpentier ed., 1968).

(h) *Chief Justice Warren E. Burger's view.* "From one-third to one-half of the lawyers who appear in the serious cases are not really qualified to render fully adequate representation." Hon. Warren E. Burger, *The Special Skills of Advocacy*, 42 Fordham L. Rev. 227, 234 (1973).

(i) *Justice Lewis F. Powell's view.* "[N]o one expects a John W. Davis in every case, but I had hoped for greater assistance from briefs and oral arguments than we often receive. I certainly had expected that there would be relatively few mediocre performances before our Court. I regret to say that performance has not measured up to my expectations." Hon. Lewis F. Powell, Remarks at Fifth Circuit Judicial Conference, *The Level of Supreme Court Advocacy*, 27 May 1974, at 1–2 (unpublished ms.).

(j) *A Second Circuit judge's view.* "Chief Judge Lumbard of the Second Circuit, in a recent speech before the New York State Bar, deplored the decline in the performance of the appellate bar, saying that in his experience not more than one out of ten cases is well argued." Samuel E. Gates, "Hot Bench or Cold Bench: When the Court Has Not Read the Brief Before Oral Argument," in *Counsel on Appeal* 107, 110 (Arthur A. Charpentier ed., 1968).

(k) *A D.C. Circuit judge's view.* "Day in and day out, the D.C. Circuit reputedly hears the best appellate advocates in the nation, even better than those who appear in the Supreme Court. But . . . it is astonishing how many cases are argued by lawyers who are simply not up to the task. As might be expected, some of our smaller diversity cases are argued by lawyers who are rather unimpressive. What is more surprising is that this low level of performance can be present even when major corporations are quarreling with government agencies." Hon. Laurence H. Silberman, *Plain Talk on Appellate Advocacy*, 20 Litig. 3, 3 (Spring 1994).

(l) *View of the chief judge of the Federal Circuit.* "I have sensed a growing — and dismaying — divergence between what advocates assume to be effective and what judges know to be effective. . . . [M]uch of the advocacy we see, even by senior lawyers, is surprisingly inept." Hon. Paul R. Michel, *Effective Appellate Advocacy*, 24 Litig. 19, 19 (Summer 1998).

(m) *A state-court judge's view.* "Most oral argument is wasted, in that it adds nothing to the written presentation." Hon. Gordon L. Files, *Oral Argument: Before or After the Decision?*, 54 Cal. St. B.J. 88, 89 (1979).

(n) *A Supreme Court law clerk's view.* "As counsel drones on about some complex statutory scheme better described in previously submitted written briefs, the Justices do not always feign interest. They trade quips and trivia questions with their neighbors or ask desultory questions mainly to stay awake. . . . [M]uch of the advocacy before the Court is mediocre, some downright contemptible." Edward Lazarus, *Closed Chambers* 34 (1999).

(o) *A great journalist's view.* "Considering how important oral arguments can be, it is sad to say that most of them are badly done. Lawyers appearing before the Supreme Court are frequently nervous, unprepared, or, worst of all, overconfident." Anthony Lewis, *The Supreme Court and How It Works* 125–26 (1966).

(p) *How great it can be.* "Nothing can equal the experience of seeing the great advocates at work in the courts and catching the magic of the spoken word, for it is not so much what is said but the manner in which it is said that matters." Rt. Hon. Lord Birkett, *Six Great Advocates* 107 (1961).

(q) *A 19th-century quotation to show it's a perennial problem.* "An eminent law writer, and ex-Judge of the United States Circuit Court, has said that 'not one lawyer in twenty can state a case neatly, logically, compactly. They begin in the middle, then introduce irrelevant or immaterial matters, useless details, and everything bad.'" James M. Kerr, *Hints on Advocacy*, 1 Colum. L.T. 141, 142 (1888).

(1) *The early-20th-century British view.* "[T]he law has little place for trained eloquence, and has remarkably few rhetoricians. On many occasions Judges themselves have admitted that forensic elocution is a sadly neglected and decaying art. The Bar student is under no obligation to make a study of it, and the seasoned practitioner, burdened with other duties, scarcely gives it a thought." Frederick Payler, *Law Courts, Lawyers and Litigants* 34 (1926).

Preparing Yourself Generally as a Public Speaker

I.   **Develop a clear, strong, pleasant voice.**

Your voice is your most important tool as an oral advocate. To use it effectively, you must practice. Try recording yourself a few times to learn exactly how you sound — you can't really tell until you hear a recording of your voice.

(a) *Classic statement 1.* "Look into the lives of all the great lawyers, both in this country and abroad, and you will discover that every one of them was a good speaker; they may not have been orators, but they at least possessed the power to express their thoughts clearly and forcibly. . . . [A] lawyer may be called upon for a speech at any time. He may suddenly have to answer an unexpected argument of an adversary in an open court, or he may have to respond to a toast at a banquet, or he may be thrust forward to harangue the crowd at a political meeting, and if at such a time he fails to acquit himself creditably his reputation is likely to be seriously impaired. As Shakespeare says, 'The readiness is all.' And if we would be ready in the future we ought to prepare while we have the opportunity." Anon., *Oratory and the Law — A Plea*, 7 W. Va. Bar 219, 219–20 (1900).

(b) *Classic statement 2.* "One should be as careful as possible to speak in a clear and distinct voice with as little harshness or discordancy as possible. At the same time a certain amount of rise and fall by way of contrast and emphasis is most desirable. These things usually do not come naturally. They require practice and experience." Hon. Harold R. Medina, *The Oral Argument on Appeal*, 20 ABA J. 139, 139–40 (1934).

(c) *Classic statement 3.* "[T]he advocate . . . should count himself exceedingly fortunate if he has been endowed with a good voice. But he must use it. He must speak so that he can be heard, and he must articulate clearly. He must try to acquire tone and modulation, so that his every sentence is pleasant to the ear. To the advocate, the spoken word is the breath of his life, and it is quite astonishing to me that so little thought is given to it. I would like to see it made a part of the training of the young advocate that he should be taught how to speak, and how to produce his voice to the best advantage. Go into any of the courts of law today, and you will see the distressing spectacle of men addressing judges or juries who quite obviously know nothing of voice-production . . . ." Rt. Hon.

Lord Birkett, "Advocacy" (1954), in *Advocacy and the King's English* 3, 12 (George Rossman ed., 1960).

(d) *Like spoken singing.* "The perfect voice for the courtroom is loud without being too loud, full and rich, easy to listen to. When a trial lawyer who possesses the perfect voice stops speaking, the jurors miss hearing it, for that voice sounds remarkably like spoken 'singing.' The perfect male voice is a wonderful voice; it is deep, booming, resonant, and all masculine; in a female the perfect voice is low in pitch, loud and resonant, while at the same time it is all feminine. Such a voice is a healthy vocal instrument, giving charisma to the fortunate trial lawyer." Celia W. Childress, *Persuasive Delivery in the Courtroom* 297 (1995).

(e) *Straining to hear.* "[T]here are few more tiring tasks than straining to hear what is being said or having your eardrums assaulted by a flood of words delivered in a piercing monotone." Hon. Newell Jennings, "The Argument of an Appeal from the Judge's Point of View" (1946), in *Advocacy and the King's English* 551, 553 (George Rossman ed., 1960).

(f) *Ignoring monotones.* "[A]fter we have perceived a monotonous stimulus, we are able because of its monotony to ignore it almost altogether." Wayne C. Minnick, *The Art of Persuasion* 60 (2d ed. 1968).

(g) *Importance of fluency.* "The advocate must of necessity be a good and fluent speaker; the man whose ideas do not flow quickly, who halts in speech, can never succeed at the Bar." Thomas Edward Crispe, *Reminiscences of a K.C.* 254 (1910).

(h) *Irritating whispers, mumbles.* "[T]here is no surer way to irritate the mind of any listener than to speak in so low a voice or with such indistinct articulation or in so monotonous a tone as to make the mere effort at hearing an unnecessary burden." John W. Davis, *The Argument of an Appeal*, 26 ABA J. 895, 896 (Dec. 1940).

(i) *Distracting your listeners.* "Such matters as . . . voice modulation are extremely important. Some lawyers deliver their arguments shouting incessantly at the tops of their voices. This creates an atmosphere of extreme discomfort for their hearers. It becomes literally impossible for the judges to concentrate on what such lawyers are saying, so great is the distraction caused by the noise." Hon. Harold R. Medina, *The Oral Argument on Appeal*, 20 ABA J. 139, 139 (1934).

(j) *Inflections.* "Use inflection when you speak. Nothing puts a listener to sleep faster than a monotone, and sleeping judges are unlikely to rule in your favor." John T. Gaubatz & Taylor Mattis, *The Moot Court Book* 84 (3d ed. 1994).

(k) *Conversational tone.* "The tone of voice should be neither loud nor dull, and the voice pitch should be conversational rather than ora-torical. Variations of tone will lend contrast and interest." Jason L. Honigman, *The Art of Appellate Advocacy*, 64 Mich. L. Rev. 1055, 1067 (1966).

(l) *A common sin.* "One of the worst things an advocate can do in court is to speak in a voice which cannot be comfortably and effortlessly heard and understood; yet in every court building there are advo-cates who sin against this obvious and basic rule." Keith Evans, *The Language of Advocacy* 63 (1998).

(m) *Not a soap box.* "Listeners of today dislike speakers who 'make speeches.' Demosthenes is dead! If you want to please your listen-ers when you take the platform, *talk with the same conversational inflections that you use in your home.* You are mounting a platform, remember, not a soap-box. You are wearing a business suit, not a toga." Richard C. Borden, *Public Speaking as Listeners Like It* 103 (1935).

(n) *Courtroom as sepulcher.* "I am always in awe of my brothers and sisters of the bar who can, by simply opening their mouths, trans-form a courtroom into a sepulcher. Their arguments are dead. They themselves are so unalive that they cannot hear the dreadful scraping sound their instruments are making. . . . [T]o choke some boring blatherer to death rather than to listen to him another second might be successfully defended as justifiable homicide." Garry Spence, *How to Argue and Win Every Time* 154 (1995).

(o) *Overcoming bad acoustics.* "The acoustics in the Supreme Court room, particularly in Philadelphia, are bad. Obviously no attor-ney can persuade the Court if it cannot hear his argument. The first thing to remember, therefore, is to speak loudly enough to be heard." Hon. John C. Bell Jr., *Oral Arguments Before the Supreme Court of Pennsylvania*, 24 Pa. B. Assn. Q. 133, 133 (1953).

(p) *An effective orator.* "Upon the manner of delivery he [Rufus Choate] bestowed no less attention: His own voice was deep and musical, of good carrying power and ample variety of tone. 'Trilling it can be a fife, but it often has a plaintive cadence' said a keen critic. . . . [H]is voice had volume enough to fill the most spacious halls. . . . [B]ut he did not depend altogether upon his natural endowment. Day after day he practiced intonation and expression, reading aloud from Blake, trying to make his voice 'flexibly express all the changes of pitch and time appropriate to the fluctuations of the thought,' and striving constantly to make the tones 'strong and full.' In great moments his voice could be extremely loud, so that it could be heard in the corridors of the Court House. 'Elocutionary training I most highly approve of,' he said, and again and again he reiterated his conviction that good public speaking demands practice. 'With fair natural gifts,' he declared, 'there's many a man who could make himself an orator.'" Charles M. Fuess, *Rufus Choate: The Wizard of the Law* 221–22 (1928).

(q)   *A famous British judge's diary entry from the Nuremberg trials.* "[W]ith complete murder in my heart I am compelled to sit in suffering silence, whilst the maddening, toneless, insipid, flat, depressing voice drones on in endless words which have quite lost all meaning." Lord Birkett (as quoted in H. Montgomery Hyde, *Norman Birkett: The Life of Lord Birkett of Ulverston* 506 (1964)).

2.   Consciously lower the range of your pitch.

High-pitched voices, which often reflect stress, tend to irritate listeners and make them less receptive to what's being said. You can learn to control your pitch, even if your voice is naturally high, with practice and perhaps the aid of a voice coach.

(a)   *Classic statement 1.* "Some voices are naturally higher pitched than others. If the voice is too high and lacks variety, it can become annoying to your audience. Good breath control and a relaxed throat will help. If you are tone-deaf and have been told your voice pitch is too high to be effective, you may want to seek the help of a professional speech teacher." Jean Johnson Spearman, "General Communication Skills," in *Master Advocates' Handbook* 285, 297 (D. Lake Rumsey ed., 1986).

(b)   *Classic statement 2.* "Don't whine. This applies to both sexes. Nervous tension seems to raise voices by octaves. Take a deep breath and lower your register." Hon. Yvonne Kauger (as quoted in Ruggero J. Aldisert, *Winning on Appeal* 325 (1992)).

(c) *Classic statement 3.* "Deeper voices sound more persuasive — why is a mystery, but they just do. Tinny, light voices can sound plaintive, weak, sometimes desperate, appear to be shouts, sound out of control, and finally and most importantly, are difficult to listen to, and so in the end they can be ignored." Iain Morley, *The Devil's Advocate: A Short Polemic on How to Be Seriously Good in Court* 46 (2005).

(d) *Irritating tone.* "High-pitched voices irritate more people than you can imagine. If you have a naturally low-pitched voice [that] is full and rich, count yourself blessed." Celia W. Childress, *Persuasive Delivery in the Courtroom* 346 (1995).

(e) *A bad postadolescent habit.* "[S]ome people continue to talk at a childish or early-adolescent pitch level long after their matured vocal mechanism has become suited to a lower pitch." James H. McBurney & Ernest J. Wrage, *Guide to Good Speech* 184 (2d ed. 1960).

(f) *Gradual pitch corrections.* "There is no doubt that people prefer to listen to low-pitched voices and ascribe stronger personality qualities to the low-pitched speaker. I hasten to add here that you should not abnormally and suddenly change your pitch to a lower one, for there are physical as well as perceptual problems associated with the lawyer who chooses to abnormally lower his or her pitch. . . . [But you can] gradually lower your pitch several notes." Celia W. Childress, *Persuasive Delivery in the Courtroom* 320 (1995).

(g) *Power of a pleasant voice.* "Counsel should appreciate that a pleasing, well-modulated voice is a powerful factor. A squeaky, nasal, or raspy voice is a great handicap to the public speaker and the advocate. To a lawyer who contemplates the trial and argument of cases, a pleasant voice is as indispensable as the ability to read and write." Hon. Edward D. Re, *Brief Writing and Oral Argument* 197 (6th ed. 1987).

(h) *Lowering the tone.* "[T]he higher the court, the lower the pitch of the argument, the less strident its tone, the smaller the role of the brasses and drums. If I were to put it in mathematical terms, I would say that the pitch of argument varies in inverse proportion to the altitude of the court." Hon. Simon H. Rifkind, "Appellate Courts Compared," in *Counsel on Appeal* 163, 169 (Arthur A. Charpentier ed., 1968).

(i) *Women's lowered pitches.* "[W]e unconsciously associate a deep voice with power or strength. More and more female professionals, fearing that their usual voice pitch undermines their power and potential, have decided to try for a lower pitch." Laurie Schloff & Marcia Yudkin, *Smart Speaking* 19 (1991).

(j) *Ideal female tones.* "The most pleasing female lawyer's voice is certainly a few notes lower in register than the ordinary female voice, but the best way to obtain that pleasing yet strong voice is *not* to artificially lower the voice and *not* to force the throat to produce a louder, hard-edged tone. The best way to obtain that strong yet low but entirely female voice is to strengthen the vocal folds by practicing, practicing, practicing, and lower the pitch of the speaking voice naturally over a period of months and years with gentle practice in the lower registers. Truly all voices can be lowered a few notes by expanding the vocal range slowly and carefully." Celia W. Childress, *Persuasive Delivery in the Courtroom* 348–49 (1995).

(k) *The example of Eleanor Roosevelt.* "Many people . . . feel that the voice is a gift of nature that is fixed and cannot be changed, like the color of hair, or flat feet. This is a faulty notion, for voices can be rebuilt, and modified, even among the middle-aged. Mrs. Franklin Roosevelt, when she first entered the White House, was the laughingstock of the nation because of her peculiarly high-pitched voice. People in the moving-picture theaters roared with laughter when she appeared on the screen. Mrs. Roosevelt was embarrassed by this public reaction. She engaged an expert voice teacher and proceeded to rebuild her voice. In a short time the miracle was accomplished. A few years later, national broadcasting chains and advertisers hired her to speak on radio programs." E.C. Buehler, *You and Your Speeches* 129–30 (1949).

(l) *The whiny monotone.* "Many speakers soon after starting reach a monotone pitched about three notes above the ordinary talking key and hold the pitch without variation until the end of the address. This has the most soporific effect upon the court and the jury and makes them wish for a bed where they might attain to a state of unconsciousness." Henry S. Wilcox, *Foibles of the Bar* 135 (1906).

3.   Purge your speech of "ums," "ers," and "ahs."

"Ums," "ers," and "ahs" are speech tics that provide slight interruptions to give the speaker time to think of what to say next. When they become habitual, they draw adverse attention by distracting listeners from the substance of what you're saying. The awkward pauses make speakers sound less confident, break up the flow of speech, and impede comprehension.

(a) *Classic statement 1.* "Avoid mumbling. 'This — ah — case, turns on the — ah — validity of the — ah — Gadget Restriction Act of — ah — 1958. We — that is, the petitioners — ah — contend — ah — that the measure — ah — clearly transcends — ah — the powers vested in the — ah — Congress.' And so on, and on, and on." Frederick Bernays Wiener, *Briefing and Arguing Federal Appeals* § 95, at 285 (2d ed. 1967).

(b) *Classic statement 2.* "A distressing habit possessed by some speakers is the filling in of a pause by 'ah' or 'er.' Such a sound destroys the benefits of the pause. During the pause the speaker should think — silently. The 'er' evidences a lack of self-control, and creates the impression that the advocate is unprepared and groping for ideas." Hon. Edward D. Re, *Brief Writing and Oral Argument* 198 (6th ed. 1987).

(c) *Linguistic fungi.* "Vocalized pauses are used by speakers to fill the air when they don't know what to say. There are hundreds of them. 'Ahhh . . . .' 'Ummm . . . .' Whether they are guttural sounds repeated frequently — or random obscenities — or phrases that have attached themselves to language like fungi — all vocalized pauses can be eliminated without being missed." Ron Hoff, *Say It in Six* 25–26 (1996).

(d) *The hairy voice.* "When you pause — pause cleanly. The worst foe of vocal composure is the pause whisker — the deadly 'Er-r-r.' . . . Recognize clearly that listeners will never like you as long as you 'er.' . . . An 'er' may seem like a little thing, but listeners loathe it out of all proportion to its apparent importance." Richard C. Borden, *Public Speaking as Listeners Like It* 111 (1935).

(e) *Disfluencies.* "The filled pause is a very common disfluency used to fill what would be a silent interval in the flow of words. Usually that sound is 'uh,' sometimes 'um' or 'er.' . . . Researchers say that some people use 'uh,' 'um,' or 'er' as many as 900 times per hour, a sickening thought to professional speakers. As the habitual 'uh-um-er speaker' grapples for the next thought, the filled pause becomes the easiest way to fill the speech gap. Unplanned vocalization of other sounds and words will also clutter your otherwise persuasive address. Below are other words [that] creep into language and become bad habits:

- 'And . . . uh . . . .'
- 'You know . . . .'
- 'OK . . . .'
- 'Things like that . . . .'
- 'Stuff like that . . . .'
- 'See?'

How do you stop filling a pause? Some lawyers are literally unable to speak without uttering one of these unneeded words or sounds. Checking this frustrating habit can be grueling." Celia W. Childress, *Persuasive Delivery in the Courtroom* 331–32 (1995).

4. **Master the preferred pronunciations of English words, legal terms, and proper names — certainly all the ones that might arise in a given argument.**

Pronunciation is a key element of persuasive speech. Mispronunciations reflect badly on the speaker. Before you set foot in the courtroom, make sure you know how to pronounce the names and words you plan to use and also any others that might come up. If you're uncertain, use a dictionary to learn the preferred pronunciation of words or, in the case of a name, ask a person familiar with that person's preference.

(a) *Classic statement 1.* "It should be obvious, but apparently isn't entirely so, that nobody's name should be vocalized if counsel doesn't know how to pronounce it. That includes, besides jurists, the names of cases, legal doctrines (I suspect there must be 1136 different pronunciations of 'rationale' and 'res ipsa loquitur'), and other materia of the lawyer's argot." Edward L. Lascher, *Oral Argument for Fun and Profit*, Cal. St. B.J., Jul./Aug. 1973, at 398, 401–02.

(b) *Classic statement 2.* "Poor pronunciation, like poor grammar, makes you sound poorly educated. Make sure you know the correct pronunciation of every word you use in your argument." Alan L. Dworsky, *The Little Book on Oral Argument* 44 (1991).

(c) *The findings of empirical research.* "While articulation refers to the speaker's skill in forming sounds accurately, pronunciation is a matter of knowing how the sounds and stresses should be combined to say the word correctly. 'Correct' pronunciation is determined by the accepted standard of the educated people of that area. . . . Research shows that listeners perceive a speaker who uses the 'general American' dialect to be more intelligent than one who speaks with an accent, even by listeners who themselves speak in a regional dialect." Joe Ayres & Janice Miller, *Effective Public Speaking* 142 (1983).

(d) *Taking adverse notice.* "When it comes to pronunciation, there are two types of people: those who don't give the subject a second thought and those who do. . . . The sad fact is that lots of people mispronounce words every day and plenty of other people notice." Charles Harrington Elster, *The Big Book of Beastly Mispronunciations* x (2d ed. 2006).

(e) *An embarrassing error.* "[K]now the proper pronunciation of words. As simple as this may seem, there are probably many case names, names of judges, and even subjects involved in litigation you have seen in print, but have never heard properly pronounced. I am always reminded of one of my team members stating, quite loudly, that Justice Scalia had written on a particular point. The only problem was that he pronounced Scalia as 'Skale-ya.'" Ronald J. Rychlak, *Effective Appellate Advocacy: Tips from the Teams*, 66 Miss. L.J. 527, 539 (1997).

5.   Speak with deliberation and force. Avoid speaking too fast, too loudly, or too quietly.

If you speak rapidly, your listeners will have trouble understanding what you've said. You also risk getting ahead of your own thoughts. If you speak hesitantly or softly, you may inadvertently signal that you're not confident about what you're saying. With practice, you can learn to speak at a steady pace and at an appropriate volume for your audience.

(a) *Classic statement 1.* "[T]he arguments of an advocate fit into place in his own mind, but they are less readily intelligible to those to whom the whole business before the court is unfamiliar. One of the earliest rules for an advocate therefore is not to speak too fast. You want the members of the bench . . . to remember your facts and to understand your arguments. Make it as easy as you can for them to do these things." Leo Page, *First Steps in Advocacy* 72 (1943).

(b) *Classic statement 2.* "[I]t is said that the brain comprehends only one-fourth of the words that the ear hears. Sometimes, it may be only one-tenth, then counsel from his great familiarity with the subject speaks too rapidly." Hon. Albert Tate Jr., *On Questions from the Bench*, 7 La. B.J. 128, 128 (Aug. 1959).

(c) *Classic statement 3.* "It is hard to follow one who speaks with extreme rapidity, even if he does articulate well. The listener likes a chance to ponder and to savor, and the effect of the argument is likely to be lost if the person being addressed must strain to keep up with the new thoughts as they tumble forth, helter skelter, one after another, in a never-broken stream." Erwin N. Griswold, *Appellate Advocacy with Particular Reference to the United States Supreme Court*, N.Y. St. B.J., Oct. 1972, at 375, 376.

(d) *Overexcitement.* "[A]n effective oral advocate must concentrate on vocal quality. The most frequently encountered mistake is getting excited and speaking too quickly." Ronald J. Rychlak, *Effective Appellate Advocacy: Tips from the Teams*, 66 Miss. L.J. 527, 536 (1997).

(e) *Annoying vocal tricks.* "[T]he lawyer sometimes talks so loud that he can be heard for a block. . . . Sometimes he strikes the key of the donkey's bray, or whines like the mourning whang-doodle. At others he howls like a hound on a fox's trail. Sometimes he lifts his voice to the roof of his mouth and croons a lullaby and then lets it fall until it seems to issue forth from a cellar. Often a sing-song semi-quaver lulls the jury to momentary repose from which they are aroused by a rasping guttural squeak that grates upon their ears and nearly sets them crazy." Henry S. Wilcox, *Foibles of the Bar* 135 (1906).

(f) *No mumbling.* "The oral advocate . . . should pronounce his words clearly and distinctly. And, above all, he should never mumble. The dictionary says that the word 'mumble' means 'to speak with the lips partly closed, so as to render the sounds inarticulate and imperfect; to utter words in a low, confused, indistinct manner.' There is nothing so destructive of an effective argument, I think, as to present such obstacles between the thought and the listener." Erwin N. Griswold, *Appellate Advocacy with Particular Reference to the United States Supreme Court*, N.Y. St. B.J., Oct. 1972, at 375, 376.

(g) *Practice as a help.* "In some cases, the advocate's mind works so fast that his tongue cannot keep up, no matter how hard he tries. This leads to clipped and omitted words, and to slurring several words together. In my observation, this may be particularly a problem of younger lawyers. It is something which I think can be overcome by experience." Erwin N. Griswold, *Appellate Advocacy with Particular Reference to the United States Supreme Court*, N.Y. St. B.J., Oct. 1972, at 375, 376.

(h) *Embarrassing interruption.* "Speak audibly, clearly, and at a reasonable speed. Often attorneys will become so involved in the proceedings that they begin speaking too quickly, necessitating an unwanted, and sometimes embarrassing, interruption by the judge — or more often the court reporter — asking that they slow down." Michael Paul Thomas, *The Rites and Rights of Oral Argument*, Cal. Law., Sept. 2004, at 40, 42.

(i) *No stentorian tones.* "Any form of delivery [that] bears a resemblance to shouting is almost as bad as to be inaudible, because the speaker who has so little knowledge of how to use his voice as to shout will rapidly reduce himself to the uselessness of a sore throat. Moreover, few things are less pleasant for any audience than to be forced to listen to a speaker who talks too loudly. Clear articulation and reasonable force will enable an advocate to be heard without undue strain upon either his vocal cords or the good nature of his listeners, however bad the acoustics of a courthouse." Leo Page, *First Steps in Advocacy* 77 (1943).

(j) *A bold apology for being too loud.* "Mr. [Lloyd Paul] Stryker quoted [Justice Holmes] with approval. 'Dirty, dirty business,' he said, and, finding the phrase sweet to his lips, he kept repeating it with mounting enthusiasm until the courthouse shook and one of the judges, managing somehow to make himself heard, called down, 'Don't make so much noise; I can hear you.'

"This rebuff was followed by one of those moments of aching silence during which no one in the courtroom breathed. Then, ever so quietly, Mr. Stryker made answer, thereby having the last word. . . .

"'I am very sorry,' he said, 'that the tone of my voice should have been such as to annoy Your Honor. I regret it. Perhaps my fault lies in the fact that I have never yet been able to encounter outrage with complacence. Nor have I yet attained that poise which would enable me to strip an American citizen of his liberty by perjured testimony. And yet I have one consolation. As I think back to little Boston State House in February 1761, when Justice Otis before a hostile court thundered against the Writs of Assistance, I am satisfied that he too on that occasion raised his voice.'" Alexander Woollcott, "Knight with the Rueful Countenance" (1939) (as reproduced in Lloyd Paul Stryker, *The Art of Advocacy* 287, 296 (1954)).

(k) *Easy on the ears.* "The voice of the advocate should be easy to hear but not too difficult to bear. It is remarkable how a low but audible voice will draw a concentration of attention while a shouting, noisy advocate will close the ears of the court to what he says. . . . [A]n overshouting advocate who beats too loudly at the ears of the court drowns out much of the merit of what he says. What a sign of inadequacy it is for an advocate to be told by the court to raise — or worse, to lower — his voice. These are, of course, obvious matters. They should hardly be spoken. Yet the fact is that violation of these simple requirements of deportment goes on every day." Abraham L. Freedman, *On Advocacy*, 1 Vill. L. Rev. 290, 303 (1956).

6.   Learn the value of pausing occasionally, at appropriate points.

You needn't fill every instant of your speaking time. A pause can serve many purposes. It can give your audience a moment to consider what you just said; it can signal a transition from one point to the next; it can invite questions in response to the point you just made; or it can give you a chance to gauge how the audience is reacting to your message.

(a) *Classic statement 1.* "Use the pause. The only way that an oral statement can be punctuated is by a pause — a short one for the commas (which, after all, are simply signals for a breath), a longer one at the end of sentences, and a still longer one when you reach the end of a paragraph. If more emphasis is desired, as to mark the taking up of an entirely new point, underscore the pause and make it longer by taking a sip of water." Frederick Bernays Wiener, *Oral Advocacy*, 62 Harv. L. Rev. 56, 62 (1948).

(b) *Classic statement 2.* "[E]nunciation is of great importance. The oral advocate should speak in sentences and in paragraphs — with suitable pauses and occasional emphasis." Erwin N. Griswold, *Appel-*

late Advocacy with Particular Reference to the United States Supreme Court, N.Y. St. B.J., Oct. 1972, at 375, 376.

(c) *Strategic pauses.* "The period of silence — the strategic pause — should be just long enough to attract the attention of the court. Similarly, it should be followed by the statement of a proposition of major importance to the advocate's position. Having attracted the court's attention, one ought not to squander it on unimportant details." Alan D. Hornstein, *Appellate Advocacy in a Nutshell* 260–61 (1984).

(d) *Disheveled words.* "[T]he rapidity of his words was such, and his oration was winged with such speed, that, though I perceived its force and energy, I could scarcely see its track and course; and [it was] as if I had come into some rich and well-furnished house, where the furniture was not unpacked, nor the plate set-out, nor the pictures and statues placed in view, but a multitude of all these magnificent things laid up and heaped together." Cicero, *Cicero on Oratory and Orators* 45 (45 B.C.; J.S. Watson trans., 1986).

(e) *Inviting questions.* "Good appellate lawyers intentionally slow down the pace of their remarks. A pause is not a bad thing and can be used very effectively for emphasis. It can also invite questions — an important part of any conversation. During your pauses, scan the bench. Be alert to any body language that suggests that a judge wants to put a question to you." Talbot D'Alemberte, *Oral Argument: The Continuing Conversation*, 25 Litig. 12, 15 (Winter 1999).

(f) *An undervalued tool.* "Perhaps the rhetorical device most undervalued and indeed ignored by lawyers is the pause. A strategic pause after an appropriate lead-in can add emphasis to whatever phrase or sentence immediately follows. It can also highlight the divisions of your argument. Instead of following the last sentence of your previous point with an immediate 'I'd like to turn now to . . . ,' insert a brief pause between the two. It will prepare your listeners for the transition to follow. It will also clarify the organization of your thoughts." Hon. Antonin Scalia & Bryan A. Garner, *Making Your Case: The Art of Persuading Judges* 146 (2008).

7. Express facts in plain words — and in chronological order.

The best speech, like the best prose, uses plain words. The old advice is invaluable: prefer one-syllable over two-syllable words (hence *send* over *transmit*), common words over jargon (hence *here* over *the instant case*), and Anglo-Saxon words over Latin and Greek derivatives (hence *before* over *prior to*). When telling a story, heed the timeline and tell the events in order. But for simplicity's sake, omit irrelevant dates.

(a) *Classic statement 1.* "Ready lawyers learn to express plain facts in plain words. They will learn from carpenters about buildings, farmers about farming, merchants about business, and of each class about the facts in the line of their own study." Hon. J.W. Donovan, *Tact in Court* 106 (6th ed. 1915).

(b) *Classic statement 2.* "It is the simple, direct, incisive speech that wins the great victories. And so it is in the Court. . . . My experience has always been with . . . . the great advocates that I have known that it was the element of direct, forceful, lucid, vivid speech, in all its simplicity that gave them their strength." Rt. Hon. Lord Birkett, "The Art of Advocacy: Character and Skills for the Trial of Cases" (1948), in *Advocacy and the King's English* 919, 926 (George Rossman ed., 1960).

(c) *Classic statement 3.* "The advocate . . . will stock the arsenal of his mind with tested dialectical weapons. He will master the short Saxon word that pierces the mind like a spear and the simple figure that lights the understanding. He will never drive the judge to his dictionary. He will rejoice in the strength of the mother tongue as found in the King James version of the Bible, and in the power of the terse and flashing phrase of a Kipling or a Churchill." Hon. Robert H. Jackson, *Advocacy Before the Supreme Court: Suggestions for Effective Case Presentations*, 37 ABA J. 801, 863–64 (Nov. 1951).

(d) *The three Cs.* "In making your statement of facts, always keep in mind the three Cs: chronology, candor, and clarity. Begin at the beginning and trace the facts as they developed. Be objective lest your adversary point out an obvious omission. Never be guilty of misleading the court. Simplicity is an absolute essential; avoid details, and if dates or figures are involved, use only years and round numbers unless exactness is critical to the case. The ear can take in only so much, and the brain will retain only part of that. If a court is submerged in details, it will remember next to nothing and the value of the oral argument will be lost. Most important, you must make the facts live for the court.'" Samuel E. Gates, "Hot Bench or Cold Bench: When the Court Has Not Read the Brief Before Oral Argument," in *Counsel on Appeal* 107, 129 (Arthur A. Charpentier ed., 1968).

(e) *Straight from beginning to end — in brief compass.* The masterly advocate J. Condie Sandeman, K.C., "began at the beginning. He assumed that, so far as knowledge of the subject was concerned, you were an infant in arms, even though you were a Lord of Appeal. He told you a simple story from its beginning to its end. . . . [T]he speaker should make his speech as if he were telling a child a story. Every human situation is simple in essence; but it requires hard thinking to disengage it from verbiage and other trash." Archibald Crawford, *Public Speaking* 99 (1935).

(f) *Importance of chronology.* "A jury or judge will generally not understand the case unless the central events and characters are presented in a chronological fashion; start with the past and move forward to the present." John C. Shepherd & Jordan B. Cherrick, *Advocacy and Emotion*, 139 F.R.D. 619, 621 (1991).

(g) *A rare, highly prized skill.* "[T]here is a species of advocacy, which is coming more into demand, and which is growing more essential to successful practice. It cannot be taught in the schools, and is to be acquired only by experience. It is the rare faculty of a clear, logical, and concise statement of the facts of one's cause. It is a faculty, or perhaps more properly speaking, an art, which is more rarely mastered than is the art of presenting the law applicable to the given case. . . . [I]n courts of last resort, in which the time for oral argument is limited by rule, the importance of this faculty cannot be overestimated." James L. High, *Advocacy v. Oratory*, 1 Advocate 190, 191 (1888).

(h) *A witty judicial response to an ineffable argument.* "There was also a third point, which [counsel] said was difficult to express in words, but which, as he never made me understand what it was, I cannot deal with." *Tolley v. J.S. Fry & Sons, Ltd.*, [1930] 1 K.B. 467, 473 (per Scrutton, L.J.).

8.   Treasure simplicity in presenting your arguments.

Eloquence doesn't mean using highfalutin words and long, complex sentences. Old-fashioned speechifying of that kind tires and irritates listeners. It makes them work too hard to follow you, if they even bother. By contrast, plain English delivers the goods quickly and easily. It helps the listener think about your ideas, not your words.

(a)   *Classic statement 1.* "The simplicity of presentation desired is that which avoids prolixity, verbosity, and repetition; which omits theoretical disquisitions on abstract principles of law, needless presentation of questions of fact as to which the action of the trial court is final, the citation of innumerable authorities indicative of an examination of the subject which has never passed the digest stage, etc." *Bell v. Germain,* 107 P. 630, 631 (Cal. App. 1910).

(b)   *Classic statement 2.* "[The great lawyer] spoke to juries and to judges in exactly the same manner, using the same methods. Gradually it dawned on me that it was surely but right to express your ideas (apart from necessary legal technicalities) so that they would be acceptable to men and women, no matter of what position, standing, or education. This conception drove me nearer and nearer to the seeking of simplicity in thought and expression." Archibald Crawford, *Public Speaking* 87 (1935).

(c)   *Classic statement 3.* "[I]n every court there is nothing so necessary to an advocate as the ability to state a case in an orderly, plain, uncolored fashion." Hon. Henry T. Lummus, "How Lawyers Should Argue Cases on Appeal" (1943), in *Advocacy and the King's English* 348, 349 (George Rossman ed., 1960).

(d)   *The progress of the young Daniel Webster (1782–1852).* "Observing others, he realized the importance of clarity and simplicity, and his style began to acquire a tenseness [that] had special value in legal arguments, where the subject was likely to be abstruse but where he had to be persuasive. Succinct sentences, repetition of pivotal words or phrases, pithy expressions graced his elocution." Maurice G. Baxter, *Daniel Webster and the Supreme Court* 10 (1966).

(e)   *Effectiveness of simplicity.* "Simplicity of presentation and expression, you will find, is a characteristic of every effective oral argument. In the instances where that quality is lacking, it is usually attributable to one of two reasons — lack of preparation or poor selection of the issues to be argued." Hon. John M. Harlan, *What Part Does the*

Oral Argument Play in the Conduct of an Appeal?, 41 Cornell L.Q. 6, 8 (1955).

(f) *The paradox of simplicity.* "Simple expression rarely reflects simple thinking. Usually the reverse is true: Those who can explain a concept simply usually understand it thoroughly, while those with imperfect understanding stumble around in windy, turgid generalities. And simplicity has its own rewards: When the text makes it easy for a judge to appreciate a difficult proposition, he will thank the advocate for the favor, sometimes in the form of a favorable ruling." John E. Nelson III, "Building a Brief," in *Appellate Practice Manual* 228, 231 (Priscilla Anne Schwab ed., 1992).

(g) *Standing out from the crowd.* "[P]erhaps because of the unbelievably bleak tenor of most appellate argument today, the lawyer who can do even a middling job of presenting a short, pithy, well-delivered, and resourceful urging of his best points — and responses to the court's questions — will stand out so conspicuously that his case is bound to get a few extra points, subconsciously or otherwise." Edward L. Lascher, *Oral Argument for Fun and Profit*, Cal. St. B.J., Jul./Aug. 1973, at 398, 400–01.

(h) *Reaching all listeners.* "The argument should be comprehensible to the unsophisticated and ill-prepared judge as well as to the judge who is both very sophisticated and very well prepared on the particular issue." Alan D. Hornstein, *Appellate Advocacy in a Nutshell* 245 (1984).

(i) *Complexity the poisonous serpent.* "Be careful first that your subject is clear to yourself — that you see clear through it, as it were, in all its bearings and details, and comprehend all the surroundings; you will then be able to eliminate it from all the surrounding and connecting circumstances — to go at once to the heart of the matter and take the jury with you. Shun technicalities, foreign phrases, and uncommon words as you would a viper in your path, for they will serve but the single purpose of stinging your hearers and divide between yourself and the mystifying word, that attention which you want concentrated on you and your cause, and thereby, in a measure at least, defeat your object. Be natural, be easy, be plain, be yourself; conceive clearly and express forcibly." James M. Kerr, *Hints on Advocacy*, 1 Colum. L.T. 141, 143 (1888).

(j)   *Getting lost in details.* "Do not become enmeshed in details. Stay with the material and controlling facts." Hon. James R. Norvell, *The Case on Appeal*, 1 So. Tex. L.J. 229, 237 (1954).

(k)   *Justice Ginsburg on legalese.* "Any profession has its jargon. Sociologists have lots of fancy words and they think somehow it puts them on a higher plane. I can't bear it. I don't even like legal Latin. If you can say it in plain English, you should." Hon. Ruth Bader Ginsburg, interviewed by Bryan A. Garner (13 Nov. 2006).

(l)   *Terms of art.* "The only 'legal' words you should employ are those which have no English translation, or which are universally employed shorthand for concepts." Edward L. Lascher, *Oral Argument*, 7 Cal. Litig. 16, 19 (Winter 1994).

(m) *Confusion vs. clarity.* "It may be heresy to say so, but in my experience, oral argument is not as helpful as it should and could be if the advocates would reach the simple point in the lawsuit and discuss it intelligently. The difficulty with the average advocate is that he succeeds primarily in confusing the court rather than clarifying the issues. Many times the logical answer falls into place with a proper understanding of the facts and the issues. In sum, my answer to your inquiry is that most of the arguments leave me in doubt of the conclusion. I do usually manage to gain a clear-cut understanding of the case, even if it be necessary to pull it out of the lawyers." Frederick Bernays Wiener, *Oral Advocacy*, 62 Harv. L. Rev. 56, 58 (1948) (quoting an "able and distinguished federal judge").

(n)   *The advocate's duty.* "If complex cases have been difficult for counsel to understand, they can be equally difficult for the judges and their staff to comprehend, at least initially. It is counsel's responsibility to reduce all segments of an appeal to understandable terms. I recall a patent attorney jesting that, before presenting a complicated patent case for trial or appeal, she would argue the case before her husband on the assumption that if he could understand it, anyone could, including the judges." Hon. Lawrence W. Pierce, *Appellate Advocacy: Some Reflections from the Bench*, 61 Fordham L. Rev. 829, 836–37 (1993).

(o)   *Fearless easiness.* "[D]on't be afraid to make things too easy for us." Hon. Harley N. Crosby, "Mistakes Commonly Made in the Presentation of Appeals," in Sydney C. Schweitzer, 3 *Trial Guide* 1543, 1545 (1948).

(p) *Moving, thrilling, and delighting.* "Men can be stirred and moved, thrilled and delighted, calmed and assured, stimulated to the high endeavour or encouraged to follow the path of duty by the simple and skilful use of the English tongue. The primary rules are not many and they are easily mastered. They are to seek simplicity, to avoid verbiage, to use familiar words of plain meaning, and to be natural. It is lucidity that makes speech enjoyable to the hearer; it is grace of speech that makes the spoken word memorable; and grace and lucidity come only from the observance of the primary rules and willingness to take pains." Rt. Hon. Lord Birkett, "Advocacy" (1954), in *Advocacy and the King's English* 3, 5 (George Rossman ed., 1960).

(q) *No technicalities.* "Nothing takes so well as common sense. Be reasonable. Never weary a court with technicalities." Hon. J.W. Donovan, *Tact in Court* 67 (6th ed. 1915).

(r) *A gift for encapsulating.* "Edward Bennett Williams . . . had the rare capacity of being able to reduce a complicated record to a few simple capsules that marked the heart of the case." Hon. William O. Douglas, *The Court Years, 1939–1975* 186 (1980).

(s) *Direct conversation.* "Elegant speeches and rhetorical flourishes should give way to direct, persuasive conversation. Convincing the others at your closed conference should be your sole focus; looking polished before a courtroom full of observers should not even cross your mind." Talbot D'Alemberte, *Oral Argument: The Continuing Conversation*, 25 Litig. 12, 12 (Winter 1999).

(t) *An older British view.* "In courts of law, all must use a certain amount of legal phraseology, but I observed that the men who mattered used less than the men who did not." Archibald Crawford, *Public Speaking* 86 (1935).

(u) *A modern British view.* "[M]ost first-class advocates make a point of avoiding 'legalese' as much as they can." Keith Evans, *The Language of Advocacy* 37 (1998).

(v) *Less is more.* "It is difficult to say more of the greatest advocates than that they enjoyed a simplicity, directness, and brevity of approach that merits imitation by those who consider that only lengthy submissions . . . can earn their . . . fee." David Pannick, *Advocates* 227 (1992).

9. Learn to drill straight to the core of a problem. Develop a knack for summarizing. Don't get bogged down in minutiae.

The kernel of your argument will probably boil down to a few central issues. If you set aside the lesser ones, your listeners can focus on the critical ones. There is no more important skill in advocacy than streamlining your issues, reaching the crux of the matter, and stating it succinctly.

(a) *Classic statement 1.* "My advice is that early in an oral argument, after the first sentences, counsel ought to state to the court succinctly and accurately the problem or problems posed by the appeal." Hon. E. Barrett Prettyman, *Some Observations Concerning Appellate Advocacy*, 39 Va. L. Rev. 285, 300 (1953).

(b) *Classic statement 2.* "Too much detail tends to befog or weaken an oral argument." Hon. John C. Bell Jr., *Oral Arguments Before the Supreme Court of Pennsylvania*, 24 Pa. B. Assn. Q. 133, 135 (1953).

(c) *Classic statement 3.* "Self-test: Counsel should answer in 25 words or less, to himself, herself, or a willing listener, the question: 'You know what is really fascinating about this case?' The answer provides a basis for requesting oral argument." Michael B. Tigar & Jane B. Tigar, *Federal Appeals: Jurisdiction and Practice* § 10.02, at 484 (3d ed. 1999).

(d) *Justice Alito's three S's.* "Simplify, summarize, synthesize. Be prepared to understand exactly the point that you want to make, the exact contours of the argument you are making, the borders of your argument. You don't have very much time." Hon. Samuel Alito, interviewed by Bryan A. Garner (2 Mar. 2007).

(e) *A rigorous exercise.* "I had to focus on making my opening statement and my responses to questions as succinct as possible. That effort to distill legal arguments down to their essentials is, in my view, one of the most intellectually rigorous exercises an attorney can perform. It undoubtedly is one of the best uses of an oral advocate's preparation time." Beth S. Brinkmann, *A First Argument in the Tradition of Many*, 5 J. App. Prac. & Proc. 61, 65 (Spring 2003).

(f) *Avoiding the periphery.* "In oral argument there seems to be a psychological fear of coming to grips with the main point. The tendency is to avoid the ultimate issue and instead to approach the problem on its periphery instead of at its center. The better the advocate, the more quickly does he come to the heart of the problem. The less able the advocate, the more does he rotate on the circumference of the problem; and if he is ultimately forced to the real issue it is only by degrees that he approaches from the circumference to the center. It is at basis a fear of facing up to the danger and risk of decision. It is this quality [that] is responsible for so much of the unnecessary protraction of legal argument." Abraham L. Freedman, *On Advocacy*, 1 Vill. L. Rev. 290, 309 (1956).

(g) *Leaving conclusion to the listener.* "Whatever you advance should be laid down as a proposition, and you should show why it is so; and from the same premises, you should sometimes form a conclusion, and sometimes leave it to be formed by the hearer, and make a transition to something else." Cicero, *Cicero on Oratory and Orators* 131 (45 B.C.; J.S. Watson trans., 1986).

(h) *Repeated refinements.* "This process of refinement — taking the essence of the issue and argument presented in the brief — and distilling it even further, to get at its most directly accessible and intuitively appealing formulation, is one that has occurred in each appellate argument that I've done. Each time, I think I've gotten to the essence of the issue and argument during the brief-writing process, and each time the process of preparing for oral argument — and especially the process of successive moots — has caused me to achieve a newer, clearer understanding of the issue and has caused me to express my argument in simpler, more accessible, and intuitively appealing terms." Edward B. Foley, *Learning (and Teaching) from Doing*, 5 J. App. Prac. & Proc. 107, 110–11 (Spring 2003).

(i) *Highlights, please.* "[I]nevitably the subtleties of the oral argumentation of a case a week old will, to a great extent, have been forgotten. This is the reason why the court call out, 'Give us the highlights,' when, for example, the argument is whether there is any evidence to support a finding of fact." Hon. John T. Loughran, *The Argument of an Appeal in the Court of Appeals*, 12 Fordham L. Rev. 1, 5 (1943).

(j) *Overtalking to no good purpose.* "Judge Cochrane was one of the most patient and charitable men that ever graced a Bench. He would listen a full hour to a dry, tedious plea without turning in his chair. But he sometimes remarked aside that he knew of lawyers who could talk a full hour and not make one single point. He believed many attorneys talked their cases to death. While a careful explanation is a good argument, a long-drawn-out talk is likely to lead to the belief that the lawyer is trying to persuade men against their better judgment, and this is sure to react on the speaker." Hon. J.W. Donovan, *Tact in Court* 121–22 (6th ed. 1915).

(k) *A Scottish exemplar.* "[A] neater, shorter, more concise thinker and speaker it would be difficult to find. I refer to the late Mr. J. Condie Sandeman, K.C., who could tell the court in five minutes what most counsels would take half an hour to say. His brain had every proposition boiled down to its bare essentials, and he so stated it to the court. The result for him was a large and influential following and a great judicial respect." Archibald Crawford, *Public Speaking* 86 (1935).

(l) *Lincoln as a model.* As a lawyer, Abraham Lincoln had "a striking capacity in the organization of material to come clearly to the heart of a matter. Coupled with this was his brevity. His concise use of materials must be seen not as an isolated phenomenon but as a part of a general overall approach to the means of practicing law. . . . His words were . . . comparatively few in number and well chosen. His fellow lawyers wrote longer and talked longer than he did." John P. Frank, *Lincoln as a Lawyer* 97 (1961).

(m) *Rufus Choate as a model.* "[Rufus Choate] had a real detestation of riding several horses at once and never quite knowing which he was on. In every case he sought after the real point of the case, and had one central commanding theory. Then in weaving and winding the threads of facts he made his theory the hub around which everything had to revolve. This, too, is an eternal fact of advocacy [that] is apt to be forgotten in these hustled days." Hon. Edward Abbott Parry, *What the Judge Thought* 220 (1922).

10. Master the art of allowing ideas to unfold logically in the listener's mind.

Instead of lecturing to the audience, an effective speaker makes a compelling presentation by logically and sequentially laying out its elements. When you're watching an effective advocate in any situation, notice how one idea lays a foundation for another. Consciously study the flow of thoughts and how you're affected as a listener. It's the only way to develop the knack for allowing ideas to unfold logically when you yourself speak.

(a) *Classic statement 1.* "[W]hen you intend to make a point, *lead up to it*. Prepare the mind of your hearers for that which you wish to impress on them. Their attention must be arrested, their expectation heightened, their imagination quickened, their curiosity excited; nay, you must impart to them something of the pleasurable sensation of a grateful surprise." Richard Harris, *Hints on Advocacy* 325 (17th ed. 1937).

(b) *Classic statement 2.* "[T]he appellate specialist should learn the art of arranging thoughts in logical sequence. Thus if you are writing a brief on behalf of a person who has been run down by a bus, and are trying to secure an affirmance of the judgment in his favor entered upon a jury's verdict, you would not begin with the medical testimony. You would begin with the conduct of the bus driver. You would stress his speed, and factors — heaviness of traffic, or darkness of the street — tending to show it was excessive. Perhaps there was testimony that he had just taken on passengers, and was busy making change when he should have been on the lookout for pedestrians. You would then go on to show the plaintiff's movements and to negative contributory negligence. Only after all this would it be logical to take up the nature of his injuries, and other factors bearing upon the amount of the verdict." Paxton Blair, "Appellate Briefs and Advocacy" (1949), in *Advocacy and the King's English* 788, 791 (George Rossman ed., 1960).

(c) *Advice to neophytes.* "I urge the young advocate to make very little conscious effort at the speaking and to be content if he can lay the essentials of his case simply, clearly, and logically before the court." Leo Page, *First Steps in Advocacy* 70 (1943).

(d) *An obvious but elusive point.* "Clear, concise, logical arguments are naturally much more helpful to the court than those that are rambling, confused, and jumbled." Hon. W.G. Roberds, *Some Suggestions as to Oral Arguments and Written Briefs in the Supreme Court of Mississippi*, 29 Miss. L.J. 403, 407 (1958).

(e) *Context before details.* "The greatest mistake a lawyer can make either in briefing or oral argument is to keep the court in the dark as to what the case is about until after a lengthy discussion of dates, testimony of witnesses, legal authorities, and the like. Few judges, after eventually finding out what the case is about, can back up in their mental processes and give proper consideration and evaluation to such narrative matter." Hon. Luke M. McAmis, *The Lawyer and the Court of Appeals*, 24 Tenn. L. Rev. 279, 281–82 (1956).

(f) *Logic as eloquence.* "Sound logic is the sinew of eloquence." Thomas Edward Crispe, *Reminiscences of a K.C.* 255 (1910).

11. Know what a peroration is — it's the concluding part of a speech — and master its use.

The end of a speech is the time to rally your listeners, issue a call to action, and leave them with something to remember your words. Your wrap-up is your last chance to impress them, so you waste an important opportunity if you just trail off at the end.

(a) *Classic statement 1.* "The object of the peroration is to bring the speech to a climax and to drive home the essential arguments, at the same time arousing the feelings to which the facts of the case naturally give rise." John H. Munkman, *The Technique of Advocacy* 147 (1951).

(b) *Classic statement 2.* "Fashioning a peroration presents a difficult problem in any circumstances . . . . [Y]ou must have some sort of an ending in order not to leave your argument up in the air, and to avoid taking on the purely formal 'We therefore submit that the judgment below should be reversed.' Come up with a conclusion in a nutshell, at the very least. For instance: 'The result is that, without pausing to repeat or even to sum up, the totality of errors in this record, particularly those discussed orally, is such that the conviction now under review simply cannot be permitted to stand.'" Frederick Bernays Wiener, *Briefing and Arguing Federal Appeals* § 126, at 332, 333 (2d ed. 1967).

(c) *Classic statement 3.* "The majority of a speaker's direct suggestions are commonly inserted near the end of the speech, or in the peroration itself. Sound reasons support this practice. Years ago, after extensive study and experimentation, Boris Sidis concluded that of four factors studied — repetition, frequency, coexistence, and last impression — the most effective in inducing suggested action was last impression. If a suggestion is repeated in the position of last impression, Sidis found, its effectiveness is increased." Wayne C. Minnick, *The Art of Persuasion* 75 (2d ed. 1968).

(d) *The challenge of time constraints.* "That an oral argument should conclude with an appropriate peroration would seem axiomatic to any student of public speaking. In the past, leaders of the bar in famous cases have concluded their arguments most persuasively, often in a manner which could not fail to stir the emotions of the listener. The trouble is that now there is hardly ever time for a peroration." Robert L. Stern, *Appellate Practice in the United States* 432 (1981).

(e) *Making it memorable.* "Only that conference comment counts which is remembered fifteen or twenty minutes after it is made — *when the vote is taken.*" Richard C. Borden, *Public Speaking as Listeners Like It* 25 (1935).

(f) *Appealing to the heart and head.* "A really good peroration should combine with the emotion of an appeal to the heart the argument of an appeal to the head: there should be an ending on a high note so as to exhibit most strikingly the essence of a case. It should be delivered slowly and in a way to make every work count. For this reason a peroration should not be too long. . . . The conclusion needs to be especially clear, and sentences therefore cannot be too short or phraseology too simple." Leo Page, *First Steps in Advocacy* 83 (1943).

(g) *Avoiding enfeeblement through preparation.* "A desultory or feeble conclusion detracts from whatever preceded it. An advocate should avoid creating a sense that the argument's urgency subsided in only 20 minutes or that the lawyer's interest persisted through only the memorized opening statement. A carefully prepared closing helps." Hon. Steven D. Merryday, "Oral Argument," in *Florida Appellate Practice* § 17.24, at 17–39 (4th ed. 1997).

Preparing
for Oral Argument

12. Prepare, prepare, prepare.

You can't overprepare, at least if you're preparing in the right ways. Preparation involves more than simply being thoroughly versed in the record and the briefs. It includes many other tasks, such as reviewing and updating your research, deciding which points you should argue, anticipating the judges' questions, finding the answers to those questions, organizing your materials, and rehearsing in moot court. The foundation of an effective 15- to 30-minute oral argument is many hours of preparation.

(a) *Classic statement 1.* "[T]he quality of the oral argument can never exceed the quality of the preparation that has gone into the case. It is axiomatic that every successful speaker must be firmly grounded in his subject, and so the lawyer who argues well in appellate court must know the case, its record, and the briefs thoroughly. It is from such knowledge that he derives a sense of confidence in his own argument. By this means he may check upon those of opposing counsel and fortify himself against unexpected developments." Thorrel B. Fest, *Oral Aspects of Appellate Argument*, 22 Rocky Mtn. L. Rev. 273, 274 (1950).

(b) *Classic statement 2.* "The attorney preparing for argument should discuss the issues in the case with anyone who will listen. Intelligent laymen may raise questions that are highly pertinent, as may attorneys who specialize in other fields of law. Specialists in the field, of course, can provide sophisticated insights into potential difficulties. If the case arises in a field of interest to nonlawyer specialists — such as economists, sociologists, or businessmen — the issues should be discussed with such persons as well. Brainstorming sessions with such persons frequently result in the identification of questions and issues that later arise during the course of oral argument." Stephen M. Shapiro, *Oral Argument in the Supreme Court of the United States*, 33 Catholic U. Am. L. Rev. 529, 534 (1984).

(c) *Preparation is everything.* "[P]roper preparation is the be all and end all of trial success." Louis Nizer, *My Life in Court* 10 (1963).

(d) *Focusing the mind.* "The better prepared a lawyer is, the more likely the attorney is going to get to the heart of a matter." Hon. Paul Turner, *Oral Argument and the Judson Welliver Society*, 14 Cal. Litig. 16, 18 (No. 1, 2001).

(e) *How judges view unprepared lawyers.* "Unpreparedness is obvious and disturbing to good judges, while well-prepared attorneys earn their praise. Indeed, in practice 'well prepared' is a high compliment from a judge." Michael R. Fontham et al., *Persuasive Written and Oral Advocacy in Trial and Appellate Courts* 161 (2002).

(f) *Knowing record, cases, evidence.* "Effective argument requires careful preparation. Among other things, the lawyer should completely review that part of the record bearing on the appeal, reread the key cases, and index the evidence (transcript and exhibits) for ready reference during argument. The old adage for success applies to appellate as well as trial advocacy: 99 percent preparation and 1 percent inspiration." Hon. Myron H. Bright, *The Ten Commandments of Oral Argument*, 67 ABA J. 1136, 1137 (1981).

(g) *Antidote to fear.* "Everything I ever had read about appellate advocacy told me that the best, indeed the only, antidote to fear is preparation. In the end, all the lists of all the rules in all the books on appellate advocacy can be distilled into one word: preparation." Christine Hogan, *May It Please the Court*, 27 Litig. 8, 8 (Summer 2001).

(h) *Lincoln's preparation.* "I am never easy now when I am handling a case until I have bounded it north , bounded it south, and bounded it west." Abraham Lincoln (as quoted in Francis L. Wellman, *Day in Court: Or, the Subtle Arts of Great Advocates* 39 (1910)).

(i) *Only sure road to winning.* "There is only one way to be totally sure of winning, and that is to be always ready, always prepared, and always willing to provide the best weapons of warfare." Hon. J.W. Donovan, *Tact in Court* 125 (6th ed. 1915).

(j) *Eating, sleeping, breathing the case.* "To be a successful advocate, . . . one preparing for oral argument should hear nothing but his case, see nothing but his case, talk nothing but his case." Hon. William O. Douglas, *The Court Years, 1939–1975* 177 (1980).

(k) *Anticipating weaknesses.* "[P]repare until you're ready to drop. Reread the briefs, the record, and all of the caselaw. Figure out your weakest points and anticipate the one question that you would not want to be asked. Then figure out an answer to that question." Timothy Coates, *I Couldn't Wait to Argue*, 5 J. App. Prac. & Proc. 81, 85 (Spring 2003).

(l) *Familiarity, not memorization.* "The best oral arguments are made by those who have made careful preparation, not by having a speech learned by rote, but by becoming fully familiar with all the facts and the legal points in the case, and who then — with perhaps typewritten memoranda to serve as headings and as reminders of their main points — proceed to make the oral argument forcibly and briefly." Hon. Orrin N. Carter, "Preparation and Presentation of Cases in Courts of Review" (1917), in *Advocacy and the King's English* 296, 307 (George Rossman ed., 1960).

(m) *Mastery of facts.* "The effective oral advocate first prepares for the conversation at oral argument by thoroughly learning the record. No case is decided without reference to the facts, and absolute mastery of the facts is essential to every legal issue on which the case may turn." Catherine Valerio Barrad, *Successful Oral Arguments Do Not Involve Any Arguing*, S.F. Daily J., 4 Aug. 2004, at 5.

(n) *Common theme of lost cases.* "Too many lawyers depend on their 'courtroom skills' and downplay the preparation necessary to take advantage of their skills. As an appellate lawyer, I have probably read as many transcripts of losing criminal trials as anyone, and if there is one common theme, it is lack of preparation. Lawyers with great reputations come into the courtroom strutting their stuff but unfamiliar with governing case law, modern DNA technology, and the background of critical witnesses." Alan Dershowitz, *Letters to a Young Lawyer* 109 (2001).

(o) *Scheduling time.* "[S]et aside twice as much time as you judge will be necessary for the preparation of the argument." H. Graham Morison, *Oral Argument of Appeals*, 10 Wash. & Lee L. Rev. 1, 4 (1953).

(p) *Embarrassing comeuppance.* In the mid-1990s, Chief Justice Rehnquist told a lawyer arguing in the Supreme Court that his presentation "made us gravely wonder, you know, how well-prepared you were for this argument." Oral-argument transcript, *Shalala v. Whitecotton*, No. 94-372 (U.S. 13 Mar. 1995).

(q) *Opponent's writings.* "Finding any articles written by your opponent may be helpful, particularly if the article is related to the subject matter of your appeal and expresses a view opposite to the one your opponent is now arguing. A subtle reference to such an article can be quite effective during argument. For example, if your opponent has written an article denouncing the expansion of a particular rule, you might comment that 'Even Mr. Smith joins the chorus of legal scholars in opposing any extension of this rule.' Of course, as with any tactic, such a reference must be handled with delicacy. Be careful of being too personal, or your comments may backfire." Edward L. Lascher, *Oral Argument*, 7 Cal. Litig. 16, 17 (Winter 1994).

13. Know your record from cover to cover, and stay within it.

A thorough familiarity with the record is one of your strongest weapons as an advocate. Nothing substitutes for being able to cite specific facts for the judges to verify. Memory is the best approach, but other strategies, such as outlining or tagging, may also help. Be rigorous when citing the record because an error may seem sloppy at best, misleading at worst.

(a) *Classic statement 1.* "Familiarity with the record is probably the most important aspect of appellate advocacy." Hon. Alex Kozinski, *The Wrong Stuff*, 1992 B.Y.U. L. Rev. 325, 330.

(b) *Classic statement 2.* "Know what's in the record and where it can be found. You don't have to memorize the entire record, but you should memorize critical testimony and be able to precisely describe other critical evidence. You should also memorize or put a note on your outline where such testimony or other evidence can be found. That way you'll be ready if a judge asks you to point out the place in the record that substantiates your claims about the facts." Alan L. Dworsky, *The Little Book on Oral Argument* 9 (1991).

(c) *Classic statement 3.* "Nothing is more effective than, after the other side has stated that the record contains no evidence on a particular point, his opponent can give a couple of record references to the evidence that the other side has overlooked." Hon. Daniel M. Friedman, *Winning on Appeal*, 9 Litig. 15, 19 (Spring 1983).

(d) *Memorizing.* "Learning the trial transcript requires memorization, and there are countless ways to accomplish this. I like to outline the testimony of key witnesses so that I develop a clear picture of the order in which evidence was produced at trial. In doing so, I pay careful attention to where items of interest are located in the transcripts so that I can quickly direct the court to relevant passages if asked to do so during oral argument. The importance of mastering the trial record cannot be overstated. You can never anticipate every question a court may have, but a firm grasp of the facts will allow you to respond in most situations. The more command you have with the record, the more confidence the court will have in your argument." Stephen A. McEwen, *Preparing Yourself for Oral Argument*, L.A. Law., June 2002, at 8.

(e) *Avoiding persuader's arteriosclerosis.* "If I were asked to name the advocate's secret weapon — a weapon [that] remains a secret to many — I should say that it was complete knowledge of the record. No lawyer, no matter how able he may be, can afford to argue any case in ignorance of the record. Such arguments are made, of course, but they are risky, and never really good. Whenever any lawyer comes to believe that he no longer needs to know the record, hardening of the forensic arteries has set in." Frederick Bernays Wiener, *Oral Advocacy*, 62 Harv. L. Rev. 56, 69 (1948).

(f) *Cardinal sin.* "Misstating the record is a cardinal sin that raises the hackles of the justices and totally undermines the credibility of counsel. There is just no way to know for sure whether such a misstatement of the record is blameless, negligent, or intentional." Hon. Jim R. Carrigan, "Some Nuts and Bolts of Appellate Advocacy," in *Appellate Practice Manual* 102, 103 (Priscilla Anne Schwab ed., 1992).

(g) *Indexing and tabbing.* "[K]now your record from cover to cover. If it's a lengthy record that you can't remember, have it indexed and key portions of the transcript and exhibits tabbed or marked so you can quickly find what you want. I know of nothing better calculated to lose the attention of the court and break the pace of your argument than to have a lengthy pause, the silence broken only by the shuffling of a stack of papers, while you try to locate a pertinent part of the record or a misplaced exhibit." Samuel E. Gates, "Hot Bench or Cold Bench: When the Court Has Not Read the Brief Before Oral Argument," in *Counsel on Appeal* 107, 113 (Arthur A. Charpentier ed., 1968).

(h) *Building confidence.* "At any moment you may be called on to correct some misstatement of your adversary and at any moment you may confront a question from the court which, if you are able to answer by an apt reference to the record or with a firm reliance on a well-furnished memory, will increase the confidence with which the court will listen to what else you may have to say. Many an argument otherwise admirable has been destroyed because of counsel's inability to make just such a response." John W. Davis, *The Argument of an Appeal*, 26 ABA J. 895, 898 (Dec. 1940).

(i)   *Knowing the physical layout of the record.* "It is not sufficient merely to know the facts contained in the record cold; it is also necessary to be familiar with the physical layout of the record: to be able to put one's finger on a particular bit of testimony or a particular exhibit with a minimum of fuss. Tab indexing can be of some assistance in achieving this goal, but it cannot replace a thorough familiarity with the physical record." Alan D. Hornstein, *Appellate Advocacy in a Nutshell* 247 (1984).

(j)   *A pitiful excuse.* "Nor is it ever satisfactory for an appellate judge to hear, as I have, the explanation that an appellate lawyer does not know where in the record the particular objection was taken because, 'I didn't try the case below.' Neither did the judges hearing the appeal! We expect you to know the record, backwards and forwards, and certainly far better than we do. If your task is to educate, teach, and persuade us, the very least we can expect is that the foundation of the appeal—that is, the record—is as familiar to you as the back of your own hand." Hon. Leonard I. Garth, *How to Appeal to an Appellate Judge*, 21 Litig. 20, 22 (Fall 1994).

(k)   *Refreshing your grasp of the record.* "If the oral argument comes some time after the preparation of your brief, a rereading of the record may give you a fresh approach to your argument. But most important, it will again familiarize you with the details of the record, without which you ought not to venture into a court of review." Owen Rall, "Persuasive Oral Argument," in *Lawyer's Encyclopedia* 1019, 1021 (1963).

(l)   *The bungling documentarian.* "The advocate must be completely conversant with the record. There is nothing worse than a lawyer who, when asked where something is in the record, fumbles around in the document, desperately turning the pages, and finally answers: 'I know it's there, but I can't put my finger on it.' Similarly distressing is the lawyer who, when asked whether the record shows so-and-so, responds, 'I think it does, but I cannot cite you the page.' Even worse, of course, is the lawyer who is forced to answer the question whether the record shows a particular fact with: 'I don't know.' There is no excuse for an advocate not knowing what is in the record, and inability to answer questions about the record creates a bad impression with the court." Hon. Daniel M. Friedman, *Winning on Appeal*, 9 Litig. 15, 19 (Spring 1983).

(m) *Pinpointing record citations.* "One indispensable requisite to effective oral argument is complete mastery of the case. Know in detail the record, the procedural history, and arguments made at different stages. Nothing impresses me more than to ask for a point of fact and to have counsel answer in substance and add, 'That may be found at page 389 of the record.'" Hon. James L. Robertson, "Reality on Appeal," in *Appellate Practice Manual* 119, 126 (Priscilla Anne Schwab ed., 1992).

(n) *Transcending the record in responding.* "In making an affirmative contention, one should adhere closely to the record. In response to a specific question, however, counsel may transcend the bounds of the record. He or she should first inform the Court that the answer to the question is beyond the record, then provide the answer, and finally state the source of his or her information. In particular, the Court expects lawyers for governmental units to be able to provide information about the government's own operations." Stephen M. Shapiro, *Oral Argument in the Supreme Court of the United States*, 33 Catholic U. Am. L. Rev. 529, 538 (1984).

(o) *Easing the court's burden.* "Ignorance of the record evinces to the court both a lack of effort and a failure of integrity, which require the court, if favorably inclined, to assume an inordinate share of the labor of searching for the truth. No reasonable advocate establishes the objective of increasing the court's burden; no reasonable advocate expects the court's happy assumption of that increased burden. Failure to command the facts of a case diminishes the prospect of success." Hon. Steven D. Merryday, *Florida Appellate Practice Handbook* § 17.4 (2003).

(p) *Three exemplars.* "Charles Alan Wright, Michael Tigar, and Michael Boudin — three brilliant lawyers — knew the importance of the record. All three of them could answer any question you might have about the record, and answer not in generalities but with precision, to get exactly what you were asking answered." Hon. Thomas M. Reavley, interviewed by Bryan A. Garner (19 Feb. 2007).

14. Know all you can about the judges or justices — their names, their past opinions, and whatever else you can possibly learn.

Knowing something about the judges may help you avoid blunders. At the very least, you can learn the judges' names, faces, and professional backgrounds from the capsule biographies on the court's website. You can learn more about them by searching news databases for interviews and public appearances. And of course you should ask other lawyers who've appeared before them for insights.

(a) *Classic statement 1.* "I, for my part, when I undertake a cause of such doubt and importance as is likely to excite the feelings of the judges, employ all my sagacity on the care and consideration of ascertaining, as skillfully as I can, what their sentiments and opinions are, what they expect, to which side they incline, and to what conclusion they are likely to be led, with the least difficulty." Cicero, *Cicero on Oratory and Orators* 134 (45 B.C.; J.S. Watson trans., 1986).

(b) *Classic statement 2.* "It is well . . . for the advocate not only to know his case but to know his judge in the sense of knowing the type of mind with which he has to deal." Rt. Hon. Lord Macmillan, "Some Observations on the Art of Advocacy" (1933), in *Law and Other Things* 200, 202 (1937).

(c) *Classic statement 3.* "You should know your court. It is important that you know each judge by name and can attach the proper face to the name. Every judge, and I don't care how important he is, is pleased when, in response to a question, you address him by name. . . . [K]now the background of each judge. He may have likes or dislikes that he has clearly indicated in the past or he may come from an area where a practice you are arguing has been accepted." Hon. Robert Lee Jacobs, *The Judge's View*, 42 Pa. B.Q. 119, 120 (1970).

(d) *Judges' avocations.* "[I]t is well to know as much as possible concerning the personnel of the court. What hobbies do they pursue? What are their recreational activities? What authors and poets do they read? What judges of the past do they admire? Whose reasoning do they emulate? Whom are they prone to quote? Some of these things one can learn from a study of their opinions, or, in the cases of particularly prominent judges, from biographies. Some of these matters one will learn from social conversations with the judges or with their clerks or secretaries." John Alan Appleman, "Tactics in Appellate Briefs," in *Advocacy and the King's English* 440, 459 (George Rossman, ed. 1960).

(e) *Courtroom reconnaissance.* "Precision is important. When I used to argue cases around the country, I would always go out a day early and sit in on a court session, I'd talk to the bailiff of the courtroom. How do the judges like to be addressed? Do they like to be addressed as 'Your Honor,' do they like to be addressed as 'Judge'? Most times the bailiff would say, 'Oh, they don't care.' Other times they would, saying 'Judge So-and-So prefers that it's "Your Honor this" or "Your Honor that."' When you do it, the judge doesn't notice anything and that's fine: he's listening to your argument. When you don't do it, he notices it, for whatever reason. And it's a distraction, so you want to know that. As a lawyer you have to be prepared. To the extent those little tiny things become distractions, that's not good. You should try to work them out of the argument." Hon. John Roberts, interviewed by Bryan A. Garner (2 Mar. 2007).

(f) *The chagrin of getting names wrong.* "Know the names of the judges and where they sit on the panel. You may or may not want to use last names, but I found it awkward if counsel answering my question would call me by a colleague's name. I was not personally offended, but counsel had introduced a little ratchet in the argument that could have been avoided. Anything counsel can do to facilitate directness of communication is desirable." Hon. Hugh R. Jones, *Appellate Advocacy, Written and Oral,* J. Mo. Bar, June 1991, at 297, 302.

(g) *Judicial dossiers.* "Because judges are public figures, the information on them is more available than it is for jurors, which makes it all the more surprising that lawyers do not collect or use such information systematically." Hon. James L. Robertson, "Reality on Appeal," in *Appellate Practice Manual* 119, 120 (Priscilla Anne Schwab ed., 1992).

(h) *Counteracting oblivion.* "[A]n effective advocate must not be oblivious to the interests of the particular judges before whom he is arguing." Hon. Thurgood Marshall, "The Federal Appeal," in *Counsel on Appeal* 139, 143 (Arthur A. Charpentier ed., 1968).

(i) *Striking harmonious chords.* "[L]earn all you can about the members of the panel before whom you are to appear. Appellate advocacy is the art of persuasion, and it is your job to persuade every member of that panel — three, five, seven, or even nine men — of the justice of your client's cause. The more you know about them and their backgrounds, the more likely it is that you can touch a responsive chord. Believe it or not, appellate judges are human beings. They suffer the infirmities and enjoy the strengths of other people; some are quick, others slow. All have been influenced by their environment and their experiences; they have their predilections and emotions, even as you and I." Samuel E. Gates, "Hot Bench or Cold Bench: When the Court Has Not Read the Brief Before Oral Argument," in *Counsel on Appeal* 107, 112 (Arthur A. Charpentier ed., 1968).

(j) *Skillful use of personal knowledge.* "[I]f the advocate intimately knows the membership of the tribunal, he allows that knowledge to intermingle with and influence his own style. If he is a great advocate, the additional ingredient will homogenize with everything else he brings to the argument. The end product will be, not a sycophantic submission to another's mind, but an artistic expression of the advocate's own personality, sharpened and focused to accomplish its mission of winning the mind of the tribunal to his view of the problem and its solution." Hon. Simon H. Rifkind, "Appellate Courts Compared," in *Counsel on Appeal* 163, 173 (Arthur A. Charpentier ed., 1968).

(k) *Familiar contexts.* "I find it . . . useful to research cases the judges handled as lawyers. Quite frequently, you will find that a member of the appellate court has had a case in at least a general area of the law that you are arguing. Some reference to the earlier case, where appropriate, will remind the judge of a principle of law or a circumstance that the judge knew intimately as an advocate. Placing your client's position in a context familiar to the judge enhances the chances for success." Talbot D'Alemberte, *Oral Argument: The Continuing Conversation*, 25 Litig. 12, 13 (Winter 1999).

(l) *Reading the judges' writings.* "I would advise you to read the opinions of judges who will hear your appeal to learn their inclinations in the broad principles you will espouse. Try to determine their mental attitudes as revealed by what they have done and what they have said in their opinions, speeches, and published articles. Then look at your case in the eyes of each of those mental attitudes."

H. Graham Morison, "Oral Argument of Appeals" (1953), in *Advocacy and the King's English* 288, 290 (George Rossman ed., 1960).

(m) *Through the Court's eyes.* "[B]ecause the facts are not out there somewhere, but are the facts as seen by the Court, you have to study the Court first and see the facts through the eyes of the Court." Karl Llewellyn, *A Lecture on Appellate Advocacy*, 29 U. Chi. L. Rev. 627, 630 (1962).

(n) *An illustration from the judge's perspective.* "[F]or seven years, I taught admiralty law. Each year I spent an hour on early admiralty jurisdiction, particularly on a case called *The Genesee Chief.* Several years ago, our court heard a case in which both parties argued *The Genesee Chief.* It was painfully obvious that neither lawyer knew I was familiar with the case. 'Painfully,' I say, because neither realized I knew *The Genesee Chief* had little to do with the case at bar. Their ignorance did not bias me, of course — equal as it was. But then, I do remember it. And them." Hon. James L. Robertson, "Reality on Appeal," in *Appellate Practice Manual* 119, 121 (Priscilla Anne Schwab ed., 1992).

15. Limit the material you'll try to cover.

Because of time constraints and judicial questioning, you won't be able to discuss the points you've already briefed at any length. You must focus narrowly on just the most important issue or issues. But be prepared to answer questions about anything in your brief.

(a) *Classic statement 1.* "[I]n general it is better to pass by not only that which weakens the cause but also that which neither weakens nor helps it." *Rhetorica ad Herrenium* 27 (1st century B.C.; Harry Caplan trans., 1954).

(b) *Classic statement 2.* The genius of selection is the rarest tact . . . . Select your strong points and rightly urge them; select the right proof and give it orderly; . . . select the right basis of judgment. The gift of selection is the genius of victory." Hon. J.W. Donovan, *Tact in Court* 154 (6th ed. 1915).

(c) *Classic statement 3.* "[T]here is a limit to what the judicial ear or the judicial eye is prepared to absorb. Sometimes the judges plead, sometimes they deplore, sometimes they command. The bar is continuously besought to speak with an eye on the clock." John W. Davis, *The Argument of an Appeal*, 26 ABA J. 895, 895 (Dec. 1940).

(d) *Scoring a palpable hit.* "If the forces are marshaled so as to deliver one good, solid blow, the appellant's chances are greatly enhanced. Naturally, the selection of this point requires considerable skill and judgment. Furthermore, it is not a rule of universal application, as some cases are of such a character as to make it possible and advisable to argue two or more points with almost equal force. In other cases, however, the points are of a more or less contradictory character so that it is absolutely indispensable to decide on one and hammer away at that, leaving the rest to be studied by the members of the court when they read the appellant's brief." Hon. Harold R. Medina, *The Oral Argument on Appeal*, 20 ABA J. 139, 142 (1934).

(e) *Aye, there's the nub.* "[T]he most important single element of successful oral argument is the ability to select the heart of your case — the nub — the core, upon which all else depends. If you have saturated yourself with your case as carefully as I recommend, you should be able to make this decision easily." H. Graham Morison, *Oral Argument of Appeals*, 10 Wash. & Lee L. Rev. 1, 6 (1953).

(f) *Serving meat and potatoes.* "Asking attorneys to highlight the meat and potatoes of the cases does not mean that the spices included in the entree or the dessert that follows should be taken off the menu. But it does suggest that serving eight different vegetables will detract from the main course." Hon. Abner J. Mikva, *Counsel Lack Selectivity in Appellate Advocacy*, Legal Times, Nov. 15, 1982, at 10.

(g) *Going for the capillary.* "To paraphrase John Davis's famous imagery, rather than 'go for the jugular,' many lawyers spend oral argument 'going for the capillary.' They — and their message — get bogged down in a swamp of murky and difficult-to-follow detail. One judge compared such an argument to being cornered at a party by someone from whom you cannot get away who insists on telling a complicated and impossible-to-follow story." "Oral Argument — Through the Looking Glass," in *Appellate Practice for the Maryland Lawyer* Ch. 33, § VI (Paul Mark Sandler & Andrew D. Levy eds., 2001).

(h) *Hitting the peaks.* "The oral argument should only touch the high points in the case — the mountain peaks or possibly the hilltops — of the lawyer's side of the case." Hon. Orrin N. Carter, "Preparation and Presentation of Cases in Courts of Review" (1917), in *Advocacy and the King's English* 296, 306 (George Rossman ed., 1960).

(i) *Courageous selectivity.* "There may be several other sound contentions of comparatively lesser moment. It is good practice to put them in the brief. I skip ahead of the story to say, however, that the same advice does not apply to oral argument. In oral argument stern, courageous selectivity is a necessity, diffusion is fatal." Hon. E. Barrett Prettyman, *Some Observations Concerning Appellate Advocacy*, 39 Va. L. Rev. 285, 294 (1953).

(j) *Danger of overextending.* "[I]t often happens that lawyers who attempt to cover all of the issues in the case find themselves left with the uncomfortable feeling that they have failed to deal with any of the issues adequately. You will find that thoughtful selection of the issues to be argued orally is a basic technique of every good appellate advocate." Hon. John M. Harlan, *What Part Does the Oral Argument Play in the Conduct of an Appeal?*, 41 Cornell L.Q. 6, 8 (1955).

(k) *Going for the jugular.* "There is no doubt in my mind that that argument is best that goes to the jugular of the case. The time limitation forces a verbose advocate to restrain himself and stick to the vitals. He must squeeze into those minutes allowed only those points that are really worth telling the court about. An intelligent selectivity on this score insures presentation of what is really important by both eye and ear attack and leaves the relatively minor matters for the brief." Hon. Austin Leander Staley (as quoted in Hon. John Biggs Jr. et al., "In the Matter of Oral Argument" (1955), in *Advocacy and the King's English* 233, 237 (George Rossman ed., 1960)).

(l) *Tunnel vision.* "By the time of an appeal, the lawyers have been immersed in the case for months or even years. They often seem to assume that the judges are as steeped in the issues as the lawyers are, or worse, that all the facts and legal questions are equally important." Hon. Paul R. Michel, *Effective Appellate Advocacy*, 24 Litig. 19, 19 (Summer 1998).

(m) *Three points at most.* "Because of the short time generally allowed for oral argument, be even more selective in choosing the points to argue than in choosing the points to brief. Select only two or three at most, and tell the court at the outset which you intend to discuss and which you will leave to the briefs. By so doing, the court will be less inclined to interrupt you prematurely about matters that you have explained to them that you will reach." Hon. Franklin Spears, *Presenting an Effective Appeal*, Trial, Nov. 1985, at 95, 99.

(n) *Ditto Judge Harry Pregerson of the Ninth Circuit.* "[F]ocus on two, or at the most three, issues in oral argument. . . . [But] be prepared to answer questions on all issues raised in the briefs." Hon. Harry Pregerson, *The Seven Sins of Appellate Brief Writing and Other Transgressions*, 34 UCLA L. Rev. 431, 440 (1986).

(o) *Ditto Rex E. Lee, former Solicitor General.* "You should select no more than two or three large objectives to accomplish during your allotted 30 minutes, and then build your presentation around those objectives. Your oral argument should put forth the basic goodness of your position: if you win, the world will be a better place, or at least, the intent of those who wrote the Constitution or the statute at issue will have been fulfilled." Rex E. Lee, *Oral Argument in the Supreme Court*, 72 ABA J. 60, 60 (June 1986).

(p) *Better still, one or two points.* "Confine oral arguments to the most basic or critical issues. Most cases involve some subsidiary or minor issues and these can be safely left to the crux of the matter. It seems to be generally agreed that the oral argument is best adapted to one or two points incisively stated and vigorously argued rather than a series of points discussed without emphasis or evaluation." Hon. Frank R. Kenison, *Some Aspects of Appellate Arguments*, N.H.B.J., Jan. 1959, at 5, 7.

(q) *Ditto Judge William J. Bauer of the Seventh Circuit.* "The biggest mistake made by lawyers without much appellate experience is to plan to review their entire case in the 15 or 20 minutes they are allotted. They prepare a written text that they can recite in the allotted time. They expect that if they talk fast enough, they will get it all out. It won't work. You will *never* get to say as much as you think you will, even if the court asks no questions. . . . Figure on getting to say about one-third of what you could say in the same period of uninterrupted presentation. . . . Do not count on being able to cover more than one or two substantive points in your argument, unless you have more than 20 minutes." Hon. William J. Bauer & William C. Bryson, "The Appeal," in *Master Advocates' Handbook* 261, 280 (D. Lake Rumsey ed., 1986).

(r) *Ditto Milton S. Gould of New York.* "Select the one point on which you think the decision should turn and hammer away. By the time the light turns amber, you will have won or lost. Courts inundated with work will not tolerate set-piece arguments. They may impress clients or newspaper reporters, but they are a bore to the courts." Milton S. Gould, "Oral Argument Losing Its Appeal," *Nat'l L.J.*, 23 Mar. 1981, 15, 32.

(s) *Scattered points inducing loss of faith.* "Don't fire a shotgun blast at oral argument. We tend to lose faith in your cause when you gravitate into minor and inconsequential arguments." Hon. Robert Lee Jacobs, *The Judge's View*, 42 Pa. B.Q. 119, 121 (1970).

(t) *Laboriously hacking through a jungle of details.* "We all know the advocate who insists on answering every point the other side has made and who cannot let any point, even the most trivial, go unanswered. He burdens the court or the jury with his laborious efforts and obscures the merits of his case in a jungle of details. A lack of objectivity leads downward to the petty." Abraham L. Freedman, *On Advocacy*, 1 Vill. L. Rev. 290, 301 (1956).

(u) *Taking your best shot.* "Whichever side you represent, you must tighten the focus even more when selecting points to be emphasized in oral argument. You will not have time to say everything that could be said about even two or three grounds for appeal. You may not even have time to address such grounds adequately. Take your best shot; focus your time and attention on the pivotal point or points. Then tell the court that you will rest on your brief on the remaining points, and offer to answer questions on those issues." Gary L. Sasso, *Appellate Oral Argument*, 20 Litig. 27, 28 (Summer 1994).

(v) *Knowing the road.* "[N]o journey can be attempted before we know to what place, and by what road, we have to go." Quintilian, *Quintilian on the Teaching of Speaking and Writing: Translations from Books One, Two, and Ten of the Institution Oratoria* 155 (ca. A.D. 95; James J. Murphy trans., 1987).

(w) *Avoiding diffusion.* "It is a generally recognized principle of emphasis that selection and concentration may be more effective than diffusion. That is especially true when the time available is limited. If the advocate chooses his points wisely, the net effect from the listener's point of view is simplification of the problem and a more meaningful interpretation of what remains. Because of this emphasis, the crucial elements are more likely to be remembered and to play a significant part in the eventual decision." Thorrel B.

Fest, *Oral Aspects of Appellate Argument*, 22 Rocky Mtn. L. Rev. 273, 277 (1950).

(x) *No embarrassing overfertility.* "Counsel simply cannot afford to have a litter of intellectual kittens in the courtroom while he is arguing his case — certainly not if he expects to win it for his client." Frederick Bernays Wiener, *Briefing and Arguing Federal Appeals* 229 (2d ed. 1967).

(y) *The art of condensation.* "Too often we see inexperienced counsel, with his eyes fixed, not on the court, but on his printed brief, drifting along and presenting, with no attempt at condensation, every point covered in the brief. But oral argument requires an art quite different from that employed in writing an argument; and it demands intense preparation; for it must be based upon a rigid discrimination as to what topics will be benefited by oral formulation and what may safely be left to the printed brief." Henry W. Taft, *Legal Miscellanies: Six Decades of Changes and Progress* 167 (1941).

(z) *A typically British way of including a weak point that the client insists on.* "A very able advocate who used to appear before me, when he had exhausted his own ammunition, used to introduce his last point by saying: 'There is another point that my client wishes to put before the Court.' I always understood this to be a delicate and ingenious way of informing the Court that there was nothing in the point, and that the sooner it was overruled the better. Then as the next case was called on, I sometimes heard the learned counsel say to his solicitor in a stage-whisper: 'Didn't I tell you the old fool would see through that at once?' It seemed to me a good procedure. The client's bad point was taken, the judge had not to waste time over it, the learned counsel got the kudos of knowing his business, and everyone was pleased." Edward Abbott Parry, *My Own Way: An Autobiography* 182 (1932).

16. Formulate the rule for which your case stands — and be willing to show how the rule would apply by analogy to other cases.

Appellate-court judges are inherently concerned with the effects of their decision on future cases. If you can show that the rule you're arguing is a reasonable one and will have positive effects in other cases involving similar facts, your chances of success will improve. The narrower the ruling you request, the greater the likelihood that you'll get it.

(a) *Classic statement 1.* "[T]here is in every case a cardinal point around which lesser points revolve like planets around the sun, or even as dead moons around a planet; a central fortress which if strongly held will make the loss of all the outworks immaterial." John W. Davis, *The Argument of an Appeal*, 26 ABA J. 895, 897 (Dec. 1940).

(b) *Classic statement 2.* "Before you put a word on paper, before you utter a word orally, limit your topic in your own mind to one dominant purpose, suited to the material and suited to a particular audience." Hon. Edward S. Dore, "Expressing the Idea" (1954), in *Advocacy and the King's English* 810, 812 (George Rossman ed., 1960).

(c) *Why the rule makes sense.* "Be prepared to tell the court what rule you want and why it would make sense in other cases." Rex S. Heinke & Tracy L. Casadio, *Oral Argument in the Federal Circuit Courts*, 16 Cal. Litig. 36, 40–41 (No. 2, 2003).

(d) *The cardinal issue.* "In choosing the issues that you plan to argue, be selective. In every case there is usually one cardinal issue, and your argument should be directed principally to that issue." Samuel E. Gates, "Hot Bench or Cold Bench: When the Court Has Not Read the Brief Before Oral Argument," in *Counsel on Appeal* 107, 124 (Arthur A. Charpentier ed., 1968).

17. Know the salient facts that invoke the relevant rule that disposes of the case.

Sometimes, different rules could potentially apply to a given set of facts. Once you've decided which rule should control the court's decision, you must succinctly explain to the court which facts in the record make that rule applicable and why.

(a) *Classic statement 1.* "The speaker should clear his mind of cant, or half-knowledge, of assumption and inference, and get down to bedrock with himself." Archibald Crawford, *Public Speaking* 90 (1935).

(b) *Classic statement 2.* "It may sound paradoxical, but most contentions of law are won or lost on the facts. The facts often incline a judge to one side or the other. A large part of the time of conference is given to discussion of facts, to determine under what rule of law they fall. Dissents are not usually rooted in disagreement as to a rule of law but as to whether the facts warrant its application." Hon. Robert H. Jackson, *Advocacy Before the Supreme Court: Suggestions for Effective Case Presentations*, 37 ABA J. 801, 803 (Nov. 1951).

(c) *Classic statement 3.* "Because almost every transaction is susceptible of triggering the application of more than one legal tenet, a competition among legal principles inheres in every case. Therefore, counsel should be mindful that the facts are the force that motivates the court to cling to one principle and reject the others and the law is the implement of ultimate decision." Hon. Steven D. Merryday, *Florida Appellate Practice Handbook* § 17.5 (2003).

(d) *Two prerequisites.* "[T]he prerequisites for effective appellate advocacy are such points as making a concise, sympathetic, yet accurate statement of the facts and phrasing an issue to capture the interest of the court both intellectually and emotionally." Hon. Thurgood Marshall, "The Federal Appeal," in *Counsel on Appeal* 139, 141 (Arthur A. Charpentier ed., 1968).

(e) *Facts make law.* "The maxim frequently repeated by Judge Tuley, one of the greatest trial judges that ever sat in the courts of Chicago, was, 'Out of the facts springs the law.' It is a maxim that cannot be kept too steadily in view by all lawyers in the preparation of briefs." Hon. Orrin N. Carter, "Preparation and Presentation of Cases in Courts of Review" (1917), in *Advocacy and the King's English* 296, 298 (George Rossman ed., 1960).

(f) *Arrangement and proportion.* "[A]s is so often true of legal problems, the correct result depends upon how to give the facts the right order of importance." *Coughlin v. Commissioner of Internal Revenue*, 203 F.2d 307, 308 (2d Cir. 1953) (per Chase, J.).

(g) *Melding facts and law.* "Don't separate the law from the facts. This is deadly. Of course the judges who read the briefs know the facts. By separating the facts from the law, you divide the case in two and each part simply dissolves by itself. You must make them live together. Again and again as the lawyer of ability gets up, he begins to discuss the facts of the case but as he does it, he will also be introducing the questions of law at the same time. They are not separate. The lawyer doesn't give the court a monologue history of the facts and say, 'I shall now discuss the law, points 1, 2, and 3.'" Hon. Charles D. Breitel, "A Summing Up," in *Counsel on Appeal* 193, 217 (Arthur A. Charpentier ed., 1968).

(h) *Running your bases within the base path.* "Emphasize the precise, dispositive evidence. Don't roam the outfield. Get on the base path. Get on the dispositive issue, and the dispositive proof. Advocates try to cover too much territory in their oral arguments. Don't argue anything that distracts the decision-maker from the main issue." Hon. Thomas M. Reavley, interviewed by Bryan A. Garner (19 Feb. 2007).

(i) *Stating the core facts.* "[I]t is impossible to argue almost any case without some reference to the facts, and a mastery of the important facts is vital to every argument. So, do not take the presiding judge literally when he recites the standard introduction, 'Counsel, the court has carefully read all briefs and is familiar with the facts and issues in the case, and we ask that you limit your oral argument to anything new or particularly important.' Do not neglect to state the core facts." Talbot D'Alemberte, *Oral Argument: The Continuing Conversation*, 25 Litig. 12, 15 (Winter 1999).

(j) *A shocking instance of not knowing the record.* "Not long since a case was argued in the Supreme Court of a western state in which the only point at issue was the legal consequence of the failure of the sheriff to attach his signature to a certain document or writ. The case was argued by counsel on both sides of the case on the theory that there was no such signature, and much law was cited. The court met in banc, discussed the case, came to a tentative decision, and a judge was assigned the duty of writing the opinion. He did so and in it held that the failure of the signature rendered the proceedings invalid. The remaining judges then concurred in the opinion and decision. Just before the court was to meet, however, and the decision was to be publicly announced, the judge decided to make a personal examination of the original record and the original paper, and much to his surprise discovered that, after all, *the signature had been attached.*" Andrew A. Bruce, *The American Judge* 155 (1924).

18. Be prepared to say, "This Court should [rule in a certain way] for three reasons."

It's hardly enough to say you're entitled to a judgment "for all the foregoing reasons" or similar language. Judges want to be persuaded *why* this is the correct decision. They want you to articulate those reasons clearly. Reducing your position to a concise, well-reasoned statement tends to sound convincing. And there's something magically attractive about a three-part statement of pithy reasons. Two may not be enough; four become hard to remember. Try a trinity.

(a) *Classic statement 1.* "[A]lways keep steadily in mind that what the judge is seeking is material for the judgment or opinion which all through the case he knows he will inevitably have to frame and deliver at the end. He is not really interested in the advocate's pyrotechnic displays: he is searching all the time for the determining facts and the principles of law which he will ultimately embody in his decision." Rt. Hon. Lord Macmillan, "Some Observations on the Art of Advocacy" (1933), in *Law and Other Things* 200, 201 (1937).

(b) *Classic statement 2.* "[T]he advocate must be conscious of how best to draw the lines around her position and how to express the limiting principles that cabin the proposed rule in a manner that most accurately conveys how the court should articulate its ruling." David C. Frederick, *Supreme Court and Appellate Advocacy* 101 (2003).

(c) *Recognizing the court's constraints.* "Experienced appellate advocates recognize that the court's constraints on appeal — statutes, precedents, rules on appeal, and (most important) standards of review — form the building blocks from which the oral argument is constructed. They couch every point in the context of those fundamental principles (such as, 'The trial court abused its discretion in entering this injunction . . . for the following three reasons.'). Forgetting to do so dooms the appeal." Catherine Valerio Barrad, *Successful Oral Arguments Do Not Involve Any Arguing*, S.F. Daily J., 4 Aug. 2004, at 5.

(d) *Keeping it interesting, simple.* "[T]he most complicated civil matter, whether it is corporate, tax, probate, or any other, can and must be reduced to interesting simplicity. There is no such thing as a dry civil matter. Too often on the civil appeal, the advocate becomes involved in a complex argument before he has told the basis of what happened, why it was wrong, and what relief he is seeking. Simplicity is vital in the art of persuasion." Hon. Milton B. Pollack, "The Civil Appeal," in *Counsel on Appeal* 29, 45 (Arthur A. Charpentier ed., 1968).

19. Develop memorable phrasings — even sound bites — for the issues in your case.

Your goals are to capture the court's attention and to make your issues memorable. A terse, cogent, and perhaps evocative statement of the problem at hand is one of your best tools to achieve these goals. And then work to sharpen and brighten the wording throughout your argument.

(a) *Classic statement 1.* "[I]t is an indispensable condition of success that you secure and retain the attention of the tribunal addressed; otherwise the most powerful argument and the most moving appeal will be but an idle expenditure of breath." Roger A. Pryor, *On Forensic Oratory*, 1 Nat'l L. Rev. 309, 310 (1888).

(b) *Classic statement 2.* "You want to arrest attention from the outset.... To be interesting is almost as important as to be logical." Rt. Hon. Lord Macmillan, "Some Observations on the Art of Advocacy" (1933), in *Law and Other Things* 200, 211 (1937).

(c) *Classic statement 3.* "[G]eneral propositions are generally dull. A catchy restatement in the form of an aphorism, epigram, or slogan wins attention and helps to ensure recollection of the speaker's points." Wayne C. Minnick, *The Art of Persuasion* 65 (2d ed. 1968).

(d) *Setting the theme of the argument.* "Preparation of the opening depends on the theme of the oral argument. The theme must synthesize the heart of the case in perhaps only 15 seconds. It can then lead to the development of sound-bite arguments for its support." Roger D. Townsend, *Browsing the Bookshelf*, Certworthy (Defense Research Inst. App. Advocacy Comm. newsletter), Summer 2005, at 47.

(e) *Stories with hooks.* "It's got to be a good story. Every lawsuit is a story. I don't care if it's about a dry contract interpretation, you've got two people who are trying to accomplish something and they're coming together. That's a story. You've got to tell a good story.... You want it to be a little bit of a page-turner, to have some sense of drama, some building up to the legal arguments.... You're looking for a couple of hooks in the facts that hopefully are going to be repeated in one form or another later on in the legal argument, but also are going to catch somebody's interest. It may not have that much to do with the substantive legal arguments, but you want to catch their eyes." Hon. John Roberts, interviewed by Bryan A. Garner (2 Mar. 2007).

(f) *Making it memorable.* "A good sound bite that sums up your arguments, that you can return to frequently in your argument and in answers to questions, can drive home your arguments faster than a long-winded explanation. Try to find the best (and safest) analogy for your situation, and use it whenever you want to remind the court of the equities or legal realities that drive your arguments to their conclusions.... Do not get too wordy or complicated — think advertising copy, not a treatise discussion." Michael D. Murray & Christy H. DeSanctis, *Adversarial Legal Writing and Oral Argument* 261 (2006).

(g) *Striking analogies and metaphors.* "In oral argument you can use analogies and metaphors much better than in writing." Hon. A. Raymond Randolph (interview), Jeffrey Cole, *An Interview with Judge Randolph*, 2 Litig. 16, 24 (Winter 1999).

(h) *Sloganeering.* "[T]o present your contentions in simplified form, it is frequently useful to employ a striking phrase — a dignified slogan, if you please, but a slogan nevertheless." Frederick Bernays Wiener, *Briefing and Arguing Federal Appeals* § 122, at 328 (2d ed. 1967).

(i) *Pithy quotations.* "Original or quoted statements that find their way into appellate opinions can sometimes draw the attention of the tribunal and advance a cause, e.g., the reference in a patent case to 'excursions into the boneyard of failures and abandoned experiments.'" Richard A. Givens, *Advocacy*, vol. 1, § 18.01, at 583 (1992).

(j) *Being extraordinary.* "Being ordinary is not advocacy. To get the judge interested in your case, you must make it interesting. There are many ways to do this. One way is to use sound bites — a short expression or colorful phrase that clearly encapsulates your message and burns it into the listener's short-term memory. Politicians use sound bites because, like the litigators, they carry a burden of persuasion that must be met in a limited amount of time. Mindful of your burden, instead of arguing, 'The court should grant the attachment in order to secure the plaintiff's expected judgment ...,' the following is likely to pull more weight: 'I need this attachment, Your Honor, or otherwise I'll end up with a million dollar judgment but only a fishcake to show for it.'" Kenneth R. Berman, *Snatching Victory: Arguing to Win*, 21 Litig. 18, 19 (Winter 1995).

(k) *The way to be tedious.* "It is the misfortune of some counsel never to acquire that flexibility of speech which puts the method of delivery in harmony with the subject. Atrocious fraud, simple accident, or humorous episode — it is all the same; they maintain one dreary note, one colourless style of phraseology." Frederick Payler, *Law Courts, Lawyers and Litigants* 37 (1926).

(l) *Avoiding dry holes.* "Brevity, clarity, sincerity — these are the keynotes of first-class advocacy. Cases are lost far more often by people who talk too much than by those who talk too little. Whether facing a jury or a judge, a magistrate or an inspector of the Ministry of Housing and Local Government, a Court Martial or an Agricultural Tribunal, you may be quite certain that your audience will consider its own time to be of great importance. If, then, you bore, you do your client a disservice. The old oilman's saying is worth remembering, 'If you can't strike oil, stop boring!'" Ewan Mitchell, *The Lawyer and His World* 92–93 (1962).

(m) *The cost of boring your listeners.* "Lord Macmillan has told us that to be interesting is as important as to be logical. It is easy to see the truth of this statement. Once we begin to bore those to whom we speak, their attention is apt to wander, and . . . our best points have only half the chance of being appreciated." Leo Page, *First Steps in Advocacy* 73 (1943).

20. Avoid splitting the argument between cocounsel.

Cases can rarely be compartmentalized. When argument is apportioned between two or more lawyers, each lawyer tends to focus on his or her piece and how best to present it without considering how it fits with the rest of the case. Judges may see connections that the lawyers don't and then ask a question for which the lawyer at the lectern is unprepared. Deferring the question to a colleage hardly improves your chances of winning. Despite moot-court tradition to the contrary, real-world practice has always discouraged the division of oral-argument time.

(a) *Classic statement 1.* "I think that they commit an error who, if they ever employ several advocates (a practice which never had my approbation), will have him to speak first in whom they confide least, and rank the others also according to their abilities." Cicero, *Cicero on Oratory and Orators* 175 (45 B.C.; J.S. Watson trans., 1986). [How extraordinary that Cicero opposed having multiple advocates more than 2000 years ago. —B.A.G.]

(b) *Classic statement 2.* "When several lawyers are in a case, it is not usually wise or helpful for more than one on the same side to argue a given case orally. It seems almost impossible for the lawyers to divide the points." Hon. Orrin N. Carter, "Preparation and Presentation of Cases in Courts of Review" (1917), in *Advocacy and the King's English* 296, 309 (George Rossman ed., 1960).

(c) *Classic statement 3.* "Never divide between two or more counsel the argument on behalf of a single interest. . . . When two lawyers undertake to share a single presentation, their two arguments at best will be somewhat overlapping, repetitious, and incomplete, and, at worst, contradictory, inconsistent, and confusing. . . . No counsel should be permitted to take the floor in any case who is not willing to master and able to present every aspect of it." Hon. Robert H. Jackson, *Advocacy Before the Supreme Court: Suggestions for Effective Case Presentations,* 37 ABA J. 801, 802 (Nov. 1951).

(d) *Quadrupling the mistakes.* "Two lawyers on the same side are likely to make four times as many mistakes as one. Each makes one mistake and one for the team." Owen Rall, "Persuasive Oral Argument," in *Lawyer's Encyclopedia* 1019, 1025 (1963).

(e) *Dead time.* "While counsel sometimes ask for divided argument, appellate judges are generally not too happy about it, and it's usually a bad idea anyway. For one thing, it takes time for each lawyer to establish rapport with the court; double the number of lawyers and you double the amount of dead time spent introducing counsel, shedding argument jitters, and getting to the meat of the coconut. For another, legal issues do not always divide neatly into segments: A standing issue may have a lot in common with the merits of the case, for example. Almost invariably, there will be crossover during questioning, and the lawyer must take time explaining that that issue will be addressed by his partner, and by the time the partner stands up, the judge may have forgotten the question. . . . In real life, a good lawyer almost never divides his time with other counsel; rather, he immerses himself in the case and is ready to discuss whatever is on the judges' minds when he stands up to argue." Hon. Alex Kozinski, *In Praise of Moot Court — Not!,* 97 Colum. L. Rev. 178, 193 (1997).

(f) *Unlike moot court.* "The common practice in moot court competitions of having two-person teams on each side with the members of the team sharing the oral argument is highly undesirable. It is exactly contrary to a basic principle of effective advocacy. . . . Some courts have even included in their rules a prohibition against split arguments." Robert J. Martineau, *Fundamentals of Modern Appellate Advocacy* 188 (1985) (citing Second Circuit Rule 34(c) and Vt. R. App. P. 34(3)).

(g) *Disfavored practice.* "Only one attorney will be heard for each side, except by leave of the Court . . . . Divided Argument is not favored." S. Ct. R. 28.4.

(h) *Not a relay race.* "I simply do not think two lawyers can cover a case as effectively in ten or fifteen minutes each as a single lawyer can cover the case in twenty or thirty minutes. It is true that four sprinters can run a mile faster than a single runner. But because of the shortened time requirements, oral argument is more like running a twenty-yard dash with a relay team instead of a single runner." Hon. James L. Robertson, "Reality on Appeal," in *Appellate Practice Manual* 119, 127 (Priscilla Anne Schwab ed., 1992).

(i) *Ineffective for answering questions.* "My colleagues and I believe it to be a great mistake for two advocates to argue for the same party — one to argue some issues, the second to argue the remaining issues. What invariably happens is that the court will question one counsel on an issue that the second counsel intended to argue. It is a lame response to say, 'Ahem, my cocounsel will answer that question.'" Hon. Myron H. Bright, *The Ten Commandments of Oral Argument*, 67 ABA J. 1136, 1138 (1981).

(j) *Increased danger of erring.* "[O]nly one lawyer should argue one side of a case. . . . If two co-parties argue the same position, both clients may be damaged by an incorrect response of one attorney. If the error was committed in the first attorney's argument, the second attorney may spend valuable time correcting the errors of the first." Robert M. Tyler Jr., *Practices and Strategies for a Successful Appeal*, 16 Am. J. Trial Advoc. 617, 689 (1993).

(k) *Difficulty of sublimating pride.* "Regularly, almost defiantly, lawyers divide the argument. Pride accounts for most of this. Lawyers are paid to speak; they learn to speak; they think they speak well; they insist on speaking. Unable to sublimate the urge to speak to the need to win, lawyers divide the argument of an appeal despite the unanimous advice of every authority." Hon. Steven D. Merryday, "Oral Argument," in *Florida Appellate Practice* § 17.22, at 17–36 (4th ed. 1997).

(l) *The advantages of coin-tossing.* "If I were a client I think I would rather toss a coin to determine which of two attorneys should argue in my behalf than to let both of them do it." Owen Rall, *Effective Oral Argument on Appeal,* 48 Ill. B.J. 572, 575–76 (1960).

(m) *Moot court vs. practice.* "Because it is so important to answer a court's questions as they arise, it is bad practice for cocounsel to divide their argument time so that each one argues a separate point and has to refer questions to the other. This is often done in moot court simply so that all team members get a chance to argue, but in real life it results in an ineffective argument. Even in moot court competitions, a team member should be able to answer questions on all issues presented by the case." Ursula Bentele & Eve Cary, *Appellate Advocacy: Principle and Practice* 371 (1998).

(n) *Tennessee judges' perverse instincts.* "Judges of reviewing courts have a highly developed perverse instinct for putting the questions to the other lawyer. If you divide your time so you are talking facts, while your colleague is talking law; inevitably, I say, while you are talking facts the judges will manifest the most amazing curiosity about the law, and while your associate is discussing the propositions of law they will have an insatiable curiosity about the facts, and I have never seen it fail. Therefore, I say, don't divide your time." Hon. Walter V. Schaefer, *Appellate Advocacy,* 23 Tenn. L. Rev. 471, 473 (1954).

(o) *Ditto with Pennsylvania judges.* "If there is more than one attorney on each side of the case most Judges believe the entire case should be argued by one attorney from each side. Theoretically, it would be better for each attorney to argue the part of the case in which he is a specialist — however, in practice it often works out that the Court will not recognize or appreciate this division and will ask the first attorney about matters which he had hoped and expected his colleague would cover. The result is often an overlapping, disorganized, and unconvincing presentation." Hon. John C. Bell Jr., *Oral Arguments Before the Supreme Court of Pennsylvania,* 24 Pa. B. Assn. Q. 133, 135 (1953).

21. Ensure that the lawyer most intimately familiar with the case, and its appellate posture, argues the case.

A well-known or high-ranking advocate might be thought to impress the court to some degree and so to secure an advantage. But that advantage will soon disappear — and may even become a liability — if the advocate has not been deeply involved in preparing the case and doesn't thoroughly understand every aspect of it. An attorney who can draw from a mastery of the facts and issues to answer the judges' questions will be the most effective oral advocate.

(a) *Classic statement 1.* "It is perhaps surprising to know that a considerable number of appeals are bungled because of inadequate preparation. This is sometimes due to the inexcusable practice of having the brief written by some junior assistant and handed to the lawyer as he rushes to court to argue the case. More frequently the lack of preparation is due either to an absence of that careful, general training for advocacy which is indispensable to those doing the work or to a misconception of what is the proper preparation for the argument of a particular case." Hon. Harold R. Medina, *The Oral Argument on Appeal*, 20 ABA J. 139, 139 (1934).

(b) *Classic statement 2.* "The attorney general of a state, the senior partner of a law firm, the head of a department, despite having done no work on the case in the lower court and being too busy to participate in the drafting of the brief, nonetheless 'designates' himself to argue the case. This advocate apparently thinks that an outward air of confidence and experience in a number of oral arguments are substitutes for a thorough understanding of this particular case." Hon. William H. Rehnquist, *From Webster to Word-Processing: The Ascendance of the Appellate Brief*, 1 J. App. Prac. & Proc. 1, 5 (Winter 1999).

(c) *Not star-struck.* "Our Court . . . is not the least bit likely to be influenced by the fact that the brief is signed, or the oral argument is made, by a lawyer who practices in Washington rather than somewhere else . . . [or] by a well-known lawyer from a large firm anywhere in the country as opposed to a little-known lawyer from a small firm anywhere in the country." Hon. William H. Rehnquist, *The Supreme Court — How It Was, How It Is* 282 (1987).

(d) *Familiarity with case over reputation.* "[M]uch too frequently lawyers are retained to argue appeals solely because of their prestige and reputation. Often it is difficult for a lawyer who has not been intimately involved in the preparation and trial of a case, in the time available, to get a complete grasp of all its ramifications. At one time I taught public speaking. I quickly learned that the man who talked on a subject he knew — it might be about his leading a boy scout troop or building a brick wall — usually made a far better and more interesting speech than the one who chose some impressive or erudite subject about which he had only a smattering of information. The same thing is true in an appellate argument. A young man making his first argument who has an intimate knowledge of the facts and applicable law will probably make a more effective argument than the 'name' advocate hired to impress the bench." Samuel E. Gates, "Hot Bench or Cold Bench: When the Court Has Not Read the Brief Before Oral Argument," in *Counsel on Appeal* 107, 114–15 (Arthur A. Charpentier ed., 1968).

(e) *A melancholy illustration in the Supreme Court.* "Once a lawyer friend of mine, who was not only thoroughly familiar with all the intricacies of a complicated case, but also fully able to argue it, was forced by his client to allow the case, in which he had been attorney from the start, to be presented by a very eminent member of the Bar, simply for the purpose of having a noted advocate present it. Listening to the argument, [I found it] pathetic to watch my friend as the new counsel, . . . who was an able veteran in law, but a novice in this particular case, floundered about as he attempted to answer questions put to him by the Court. When the argument was done, in reply to my inquiry as to how he felt while it was being carried on, my friend said: 'Just as any father would feel while someone was strangling his pet baby, and he was tied in a chair and unable to do anything to save the baby.'" Charles Henry Butler, *A Century at the Bar of the Supreme Court of the United States* 115–16 (1942).

(f) *Value of familiarity.* "[A] case was decided in favor of the client of a lawyer who was making his first appearance before the Court in a major matter, and who was opposed by the highest legal officers of the United States. That case was won, in my opinion, because it was presented by an advocate so thoroughly familiar with the facts and the law involved, that he was able to answer every one of the many questions asked by members of the Court." Charles Henry Butler, *A Century at the Bar of the Supreme Court of the United States* 115 (1942).

22. Prepare three arguments: (1) a full argument that takes about 20% less than the full time allotted, (2) an intermediate version that allows for some questions from the bench, and (3) a short-form version that allows for an extremely active bench.

As hard as you may try to anticipate the judges' questions, you can never know how intense the questioning will be — and how much time you'll have to argue your key issues. By preparing arguments of different lengths, you can use the version or parts of more than one version that fit the time available to you. The shortest version is the hardest to prepare because you must think carefully about the core point or points of your argument and how to state them in the fewest, plainest words. But it's also the most important.

(a) *Classic statement 1.* "It helps to imagine how you would argue the appeal in ten minutes, then five minutes, then two minutes. What would you tell the court if you had only one minute to present your case? Imagine that your brief were limited to a one-page letter to the court. What would you write?" Steven F. Molo & Paul P. Biebel Jr., "Preparing for Oral Argument," in *Appellate Practice Manual* 244, 247 (Priscilla Anne Schwab ed., 1992).

(b) *Classic statement 2.* "There are as many variations among courts as there are among panels and even individual judges. Some judges shoot the first question before the advocate has cleared his throat. Others hold their fire until the argument is well under way. The lawyer must be prepared to be told that the panel needs no oral recitation of the facts, to have the argument taken over completely by questions from the bench, and to find that the delivery of an entire argument is without a single question." Hon. Murray I. Gurfein, "Appellate Advocacy, Modern Style," in *Appellate Practice Manual* 256, 256 (Priscilla Anne Schwab ed., 1992).

(c) *Paring it down.* "Time the length of your argument so that you can finish it in no more than two-thirds of the time allotted. As you continue your rehearsal, plan to cover your essential argument in half the time, for the court's questions may prevent you from employing over half the time." H. Graham Morison, *Oral Argument of Appeals*, 10 Wash. & Lee L. Rev. 1, 6 (1953).

(d) *Value of erasure.* "[T]he pen is not the least serviceable when it is used to erase." Quintilian, *Quintilian on the Teaching of Speaking and Writing: Translations from Books One, Two, and Ten of the Institution Oratoria* 147 (ca. A.D. 95; James J. Murphy trans., 1987).

23. Know the cases you've cited in your brief — and the ones your opponent has cited.

Case citations in the briefs can't answer the judges' questions. The judges can reasonably expect advocates to answer questions about the pertinent cases in some detail. You must be thoroughly familiar with those cases and be able to explain why they do or don't bear on the court's decision.

(a) *Classic statement 1.* "Too often, counsel find themselves in the embarrassing position of being unable to answer the court's question, 'Counsel, what were the facts before the court in that case?' A citation without some discussion of the treatment of the issue is not very helpful." Hon. Arthur L. Alarcon, "Points on Appeal," in *Appellate Practice Manual* 95, 99 (Priscilla Anne Schwab ed., 1992).

(b) *Classic statement 2.* "The most prominent lawyers do not always make the most effective arguments. Very convincing presentations are often made by comparative strangers in our court." Hon. O. Otto Moore, *Some Observations on Oral Argument*, 33 Rocky Mntn. L. Rev. 30, 32 (1960).

(c) *Classic statement 3.* "Don't cite any cases in your brief that you are unable to discuss on both the facts and the law. During my days at the bar, I was always careful to reread every case cited in my brief just before oral argument. A judge easily loses confidence in your position when you are unable to discuss a case cited as authority for some proposition you are urging on the court." Hon. Roger J. Miner, "The Don'ts of Oral Argument," in *Appellate Practice Manual* 263, 265 (Priscilla Anne Schwab ed., 1992).

(d) *Indexing the cases.* "You may want an index to the major cases . . . . Presumably, you will know the cases well enough not to need this, but it can be a comforting security blanket for the inexperienced lawyer. Some people list alphabetically the ten or fifteen most important cases, with a one- or two-sentence summary of the holding and facts of each. Other lawyers group the cases according to the points they support. In any event, this list should not be more than a page or two to which you can turn if you get stumped during your argument." Steven F. Molo & Paul P. Biebel Jr., "Preparing for Oral Argument," in *Appellate Practice Manual* 244, 255 (Priscilla Anne Schwab ed., 1992).

(e) *Capacious memory a must.* "[T]o do [lawyerly] work . . . capably, one must have a good memory. Memory is largely a matter of training and experience. If from the first a lawyer accustoms himself to retain in his memory rather than on pieces of paper the different points and references that he thinks may become important, he will find that his argument will greatly benefit from the practice." Hon. Harold R. Medina, *The Oral Argument on Appeal*, 20 ABA J. 139, 140 (1934).

(f) *Knowing cases on both sides.* "As important as knowing the record is knowing your authorities and those of your opponent. This means rereading all of the cases and statutes to ensure that you know the facts and holdings of each and will be able to discuss them intelligently." John T. Gaubatz & Taylor Mattis, *The Moot Court Book* 99 (3d ed. 1994).

(g) *Abstracting the cases.* "It is a good idea for your notebook to contain brief abstracts of all cases both for and against you, particularly where a great many cases have been cited on both sides. The fact is that, unless you have one of those miracle memories, cases and their facts and holdings can become confused in your mind in the give-and-take of oral argument. You should prepare these abstracts yourself so that a brief glance at them can remind you of the information you need to know." E. Barrett Prettyman Jr., *Supreme Court Advocacy: Random Thoughts in a Day of Time Restrictions*, 4 Litig. 16, 20 (Winter 1978).

(h) *An embarrassing example.* "[I]n *Mapp v. Ohio* . . . the Court was concerned with an unlawful search and seizure of certain incriminating evidence and its use in a state-court prosecution. The Ohio court had followed the rule, prevailing in New York and many other jurisdictions, permitting the use of evidence obtained in that manner if it was otherwise relevant and material. Counsel for the appellant in the Supreme Court was arguing with the discouraging knowledge that he was flying in the face of the long-established rule, which a majority of the states had adopted and which had been repeatedly accepted by the Supreme Court in the past. One of the justices leaned forward and asked, 'Aren't you asking us to overrule *Wolf v. Colorado*, counsel?' The lawyer is reported to have replied, 'I am sorry, Your Honor, but I am not familiar with that case.' The *Wolf* case, of course, was the principal obstacle to the appeal. What happened is history. The Supreme Court did reverse in *Mapp*, and in the course of its opinion, and indeed as an indispensable part of the tidying process necessary for that task, it overruled its own prior decision in *Wolf v. Colorado*." Harris B. Steinberg, "The Criminal Appeal," in *Counsel on Appeal* 1, 20–21 (Arthur A. Charpentier ed., 1968).

24. **Do some last-minute research to ensure the soundness of your authorities before oral argument.**

Submitting your brief doesn't draw your research to a close. You may find that a new precedent strengthens or weakens an important point you've made in the brief. So stay informed of any changes in the law that might affect your case. Always assume that your opponent or, more likely, the court will be aware of them.

(a) *Classic statement 1.* "There are many difficult moments in a trial lawyer's life; but one of the bitterest is when a lawyer, unaware of last week's decision by an appellate court which affects or destroys the attorney's theory, cannot respond to a judge's question such as: 'Can counsel explain how it is possible to reconcile your theory with this court's recent decision in *Roe v. Doe?*'" Roberto Aron et al., *Trial Communication Skills* § 14.07, at 14-5 (1996).

(b) *Classic statement 2.* "Do not assume that all the necessary legal research is accounted for in your brief. Before oral argument, research the relevant legal issues again to determine if there have been any new developments. In addition, recheck your authorities to make sure they are still good law. The last thing you want to hear is your opponent arguing for the application of a recent court decision about which you know nothing." Stephen A. McEwen, *Preparing Yourself for Oral Argument*, L.A. Law., June 2002, at 8.

(c) *Checking for good law.* "Always Shepardize your cases. One of the most interesting cases I ever saw argued was a U.S. Sixth Circuit case in which both attorneys were arguing about the application of a case that had been overturned. When Judge Wellford finally asked one of the attorneys (who happened to be representing himself) whether he knew that the case was no longer good law, he responded (with great composure): 'No, Your Honor, but I would point out that opposing counsel didn't know it either.'" Ronald J. Rychlak, *Effective Appellate Advocacy: Tips from the Teams*, 66 Miss. L.J. 527, 530 n.3 (1997).

(d) *Fleshing out arguments.* "An advocate should spend time conducting legal research between the filing of the briefs and the oral argument. Sometimes that research runs to ground issues intentionally left open in the brief; sometimes to close holes that did not seem so wide or significant when writing the brief but now seem much more significant. An advocate who can anticipate a question and provide an answer that conveys additional research builds credibility with the court." David C. Frederick, *Supreme Court and Appellate Advocacy* 196 (2003).

(e) *Updating your research.* "The effective advocate will do some last-minute research shortly before oral argument to make sure that in the time between the filing of briefs and argument none of the cases relied on has been reversed or overruled and that no relevant new cases have been decided. Many lawyers now do a quick computer search for information on the very morning of oral argument. That may be unnecessary, but surely counsel would be embarrassed to learn from the court, at the beginning of the argument, that the precedent on which the case turns was reversed two weeks earlier." Ursula Bentele & Eve Cary, *Appellate Advocacy: Principle and Practice* 366 (1998).

(f) *Notifying the court of new findings.* "If you have cases that you have discovered or which have come up subsequent to the filing of your brief, forward them to the court under the procedures set by the court. Do not wait until the day of the argument." Hon. Ruggero J. Aldisert, *Winning on Appeal* 321 (1992).

25. Know precisely how you want the mandate to read.

You'll save the court much time and effort and also serve your client best by thoughtfully composing your prayer. Too many advocates either make general requests or use the wrong terminology and ask for dispositions they don't really want or aren't entitled to. Some federal judges have suggested that 80% of the advocates before them don't know precisely what relief they want. Don't be one of them.

(a) *Classic statement.* "If you want us to instruct the trial court to do something upon remand, suggest to us the precise direction we should give to serve your client's interests." Hon. Arthur L. Alarcon, "Points on Appeal," in *Appellate Practice Manual* 95, 100 (Priscilla Anne Schwab ed., 1992).

(b) *Basic distinctions for mandates.* "[J]udges should almost make a fetish of the following distinctions: an appeals court affirms, reverses, or modifies *judgments* or *orders*; it agrees with, approves, or disapproves *opinions* or *decisions*; and it remands *cases* (or *causes*) and *actions*. When the lower court lacked jurisdiction, the proper disposition by the appellate court is to *vacate* the judgment of the trial court and *dismiss* the case from the docket of the trial court (or *order* the trial court *to dismiss*). If the trial court had jurisdiction over the case, but entered an order beyond its jurisdiction, the proper disposition is to *vacate* the order and remand the case.... Lawyers as well as judges must be sensitive to these niceties if they are to draft meaningful prayers in their appellate briefs." Bryan A. Garner, *A Dictionary of Modern Legal Usage* 482, 483 (2d ed. 1995).

26. Anticipate questions as best you can.

Judges will invariably have questions about your case; that's a fact of life. You'll find the sources of many questions in the briefs and in the record. But they aren't the only possible sources; sometimes, they're not even the richest. You should talk with your colleagues and friends about the case: they may spot some weakness that you'll be asked to address.

(a) *Classic statement 1.* "When you see a good lawyer handle questions adeptly, it may appear that he is simply thinking well on his feet, but usually that is misleading. He has spent several hours on preparation, anticipating those questions and formulating answers.... A good rule of thumb is: prepare to the point that you feel that no reasonable question will surprise you." Myron Moskovitz, *Winning an Appeal* 59 (3d ed. 1995).

(b) *Classic statement 2.* "The questions you get in oral argument are often ones not squarely covered in the brief . . . so an advocate who has not gone beneath the surface of the brief to understand how its parts fit together into a coherent argument will be at a considerable disadvantage." Hon. William H. Rehnquist, *From Webster to Word-Processing*, 1 J. App. Prac. & Proc. 1, 5 (Winter 1999).

(c) *Classic statement 3.* "I am constantly amazed, during Supreme Court arguments, to hear an attorney vitually dumbstruck by questions from the bench that anyone with any knowledge of the case should have anticipated. It is as if the attorney has become so imbued with the spirit of his cause that he has totally blinded himself to the legitimate concerns that someone else might have in adopting his position." E. Barrett Perryman Jr., *Supreme Court Advocacy: Random Thoughts in a Day of Time Restrictions*, 4 Litig. 16, 18–19 (Winter 1978).

(d) *Mining your adversary's argument.* "The place to start looking for the hard questions is the adversary's brief. It should be read carefully to determine the strongest arguments and the best responses. One should remember, however, that courts are not bound by the arguments made in lawyers' briefs. Judges may have concerns of their own that the adversary did not raise. The advocate must be prepared for these questions as well. It is here that the assistance of colleagues and even nonlawyer friends and relations can be a big help. Often an intelligent lay person's skepticism (Well, what *was* he doing on the roof with a hatchet at 1:00 in the morning?) can pinpoint a problem in the case that the attorney has overlooked. Rather than rehearsing a canned speech, it is far better that an oral advocate practice answering difficult questions clearly and confidently." Ursula Bentele & Eve Cary, *Appellate Advocacy: Principle and Practice* 366 (1998).

(e) *Mining your own arguments.* "One of the most important things in preparing for oral argument is to try to anticipate what questions you might be asked. To do this, you must look far beyond the arguments made by your opponent. You must take your case apart and seek to pinpoint every possible weakness or potential weakness — both factual and legal. You must identify the best possible arguments that can be made in opposition to your case and be fully prepared to rebut them. You must closely scrutinize the case record and be fully prepared to answer any and all questions about that record. . . . If you do all of these things, you should be able to answer any questions thrown at you." Gaele McLaughlin Barthold, *Questions by Appellate-Court Jurists: A Threat or an Opportunity?*, Certworthy (Defense Research Inst. App. Advocacy Comm. newsletter), Winter 2001, at 4.

(f) *Viewing questions as opportunities.* "I remember with great satisfaction being asked by a [Supreme Court] justice during one of those arguments how many jurisdictions had considered a particular issue. Having anticipated this question, I was not only prepared to say how many jurisdictions had considered the issue, but also to specifically identify those jurisdictions and discuss the precise nature of their decisions. Proper preparation for appellate arguments will allow you to have similar satisfaction, even when very difficult questions are posed." Gaele McLaughlin Barthold, *Questions by Appellate-Court Jurists: A Threat or an Opportunity?*, Certworthy (Defense Research Inst. App. Advocacy Comm. newsletter), Winter 2001, at 4, 7.

(g) *The value of role-reversal.* "[L]ist all difficult questions that the court may ask. Put yourself in the court's shoes for this exercise. Keep in mind that the court will be concerned about jurisdictional issues and the procedural posture of the case. It may want to determine the narrowest possible ground on which to dispose of the case. Do not ignore these matters simply because the *parties* have not devoted much attention to them or because you do not intend to raise them in argument. You may not have a choice. . . . Prepare a one- or two-line response to each question, jotting down in your notes a phrase or two. This will take some thought. You should not write out responses word for word. That will be less helpful preparation than key words or phrases." Gary L. Sasso, "Appellate Oral Argument," in *The Litigation Manual: Special Problems and Appeals* 316, 324 (1999).

(h) *Brainstorming.* "[Y]ou should brainstorm by yourself or with colleagues for potential questions, areas of concern, and arguments that require emphasis. As you develop these ideas, preserve them in writing. Predicting questions and concerns from the panel is notoriously difficult, but this exercise is valuable because it will force you to think more actively and critically." Stephen A. McEwen, *Preparing Yourself for Oral Argument*, L.A. Law., June 2002, at 8.

(i) *Knowing your trouble spots.* "For those of us who are not truly brilliant — and likely even for those of use who are — there is only one way to effectively answer questions from the bench, and that is to know what they are going to be in advance. This does not require prescience, but diligence and understanding. If you know the weaknesses of your case, or those areas that at least appear at first blush to be weaknesses, you can expect questions from the bench regarding them. The best way to understand the trouble spots in your case is to know your opponent's argument at least as well as he or she does, for the strengths of your opponent's case are undoubtedly the apparent trouble spots in your own." Timothy A. Baughmann, *Effective Appellate Oral Advocacy: "Beauty Is Truth, Truth Beauty,"* 77 Mich. B.J. 38, 39 (Jan. 1998).

(j) *Getting an edge.* "Attorneys who adequately prepare and anticipate the questions that will likely come from the bench have a distinct advantage." Hon. Stanley Mosk, *In Defense of Oral Argument*, 1 J. App. Prac. & Proc. 25, 28 (Winter 1999).

(k) *Rehearsal dialogue.* "A good way to figure out what evidence you'll need is to anticipate objections and questions. But trying to list all of these one after the other is not the most effective way. The mind doesn't think of as many things when just listing as it does when thinking by associating. It's much more effective to hold a rehearsal dialogue with a friend where you try to sell him your idea, or to hold an imaginary dialogue with yourself where you take both sides: your role as persuader and that of the person you're persuading. In the dialogue, more points come up than you could think of by listing.

"You can think of many more ideas by allowing one idea to lead to another than you can by trying to think of them all in advance. When you've brought up as many points as you can this way, you can figure out what evidence you'll need to handle them successfully." Jesse S. Nirenberg, *How to Sell Your Ideas* 11 (1984).

(l) *Discovering and uncovering questions.* "In your preparation you should attempt to discover and uncover, through analysis of your opponent's brief and discussions with colleagues, all the questions that are likely to be asked." Samuel E. Gates, "Hot Bench or Cold Bench: When the Court Has Not Read the Brief Before Oral Argument," in *Counsel on Appeal* 107, 132–33 (Arthur A. Charpentier ed., 1968).

27. If you represent the appellee or respondent, prepare for the unusual but growing possibility that you might be the first to argue.

In the traditional order of argument, you'll get to hear your opponent's arguments challenging the lower court's decision, and then you can structure your answer to rebut those points. But that order isn't immutable. You must be prepared to go first if the appellant or petitioner uses the shenanigan of suddenly demurring and the court acquiesces. Most courts are likely to view this gambit as inappropriate — as if the appellant were to decline to write an opening brief and "save everything for the reply." There's reason for the order of argument — it reflects the burden of persuasion. You might object to this ploy based on that burden, but you should be prepared to argue first if the court insists.

(a) *Classic statement 1.* "A few years ago, at the beginning of an oral argument, the appellant's counsel deferred the opening portion of his oral argument and expressed his wish to save his argument for 'rebuttal.' Naturally taken aback by this tactic, I was placed in a downright dilemma. . . . [U]ntil recently, it appeared to be just a fluke. But over the course of the past year, it happened to me again, and then again. And, while awaiting my turn to argue, I've observed this new 'strategy' occur in a few other cases in California's Second District Court of Appeal, which sits in Los Angeles." Douglas J. Collodel, *Oral Argument — California Style?*, Certworthy (Defense Research Inst. App. Advocacy Comm. newsletter), Fall 1998, at 11.

(b) *Classic statement 2.* "[P]lanning for an unorthodox move by appellant's counsel at oral argument . . . diminishes the panic generated by a presiding justice's indication that the panel wishes to hear from the respondent first, which generally indicates an uphill battle to save the judgment below." Douglas J. Collodel, *Oral Argument — California Style?*, Certworthy (Defense Research Inst. App. Advocacy Comm. newsletter), Fall 1998, at 11, 12.

28. Practice your argument out loud, preferably in a moot court.

Perfecting your delivery requires practice and attention to your words and style. Notes that you jot down may look great on paper but then fall flat when spoken. You may find that you're trying to say too much in too little time. When others watch and critique your presentation, they can help you by telling you why they were or were not impressed by your arguments and by your manner.

(a) *Classic statement 1.* "Be certain that your practice is aloud. Thinking through your speech is useful, but it isn't good speech practice. Thought, while it is subvocal speech, is a shortcut process. You can think an idea through without ever clearly expressing it in actual language." Keith Brooks, *Practical Speaking for the Technical Man* 20 (1958).

(b) *Classic statement 2.* "Prepare for oral argument the way the President prepares for a press conference. His aides pitch him the hard balls and curves that the press will be throwing. And if such a rehearsal is mandatory for the President, it should be mandatory for you." Hon. Ruggero J. Aldisert, *Winning on Appeal* 319 (1992).

(c) *Classic statement 3.* "Rehearse the argument of the appeal. Have a mock oral argument at which your partners or associates or co-counsel pepper you with the sort of questions that the judges are likely to ask. It is best if the moot panel is as ignorant of the case as the judges are likely to be. Make sure that the panel asks hypothetical questions, since a number of judges like to ask such questions in order to determine the implications of the position being argued. Never say to a judge who asks a hypothetical question: 'You are asking a hypothetical question.'" Hon. Richard A. Posner, *Convincing a Federal Court of Appeals*, 25 Litig. 3, 63 (Winter 1999).

(d) *No extemporaneous speaking.* "No lawyer would dream of filing with the clerk the rough first draft of his brief. But too many lawyers present to the court the first draft of their oral argument. There are, of course, some virtuosos — people who have a flair for the extemporaneous. But unless you are one of those fortunate few, a carefully rehearsed, prepared, and revised presentation will always be better than one that is off the cuff." Frederick Bernays Wiener, *Oral Advocacy*, 62 Harv. L. Rev. 56, 71–72 (1948).

(e) *Involving your colleagues.* "The first piece of advice that I give to anyone asking for recommendations for oral-argument preparation is to participate in two moot courts. Moot courts are part of the rich tradition in the Solicitor General's office which prepares so many advocates for their first arguments. Standing up for an hour or more answering every question that very smart lawyers have concocted after reading the same briefs that the Court will have read ensures that you have done your best to prepare answers to likely questions. The attorneys with whom I had worked on the brief participated, of course. But it was by having other Assistants in the office who had not worked on the brief sit in the role of Justices that I got a sense of what impression the briefs in the case had likely left on the Court." Beth S. Brinkmann, *A First Argument in the Tradition of Many*, 5 J. App. Prac. & Proc. 61, 65 (Spring 2003).

(f) *Conducting a moot court.* "There is nothing like conducting a moot court to polish your oral arguments. . . . [A]n appellate advocate who shuns mock argument is like an actor who skips dress rehearsal." Scott Patrick Stolley, *Consult Your Talking Mirror*, Certworthy (Defense Research Inst. App. Advocacy Comm. newsletter), Spring 1998, at 14 (quoting Charles G. Cole).

(g) *Practicing out loud.* "[E]very oral argument on appeal should . . . be rehearsed out loud at least several times before actual delivery. Even if you are merely rehearsing it to yourself, that is not as 'mere' as it might seem. As a trained lawyer, you will be able to recognize weaknesses, awkward phrases, hesitations, excess wordiness, and other areas needing improvement quite as readily as anyone else can, and you will probably be your own harshest critic in any rehearsal situation anyway." Henry St. John Fitzgerald & Daniel Hartnett, *Effective Oral Argument*, 18 Prac. Law. 51, 60 (April 1972).

(h) *The real meaning of rehearsing.* "I rehearse my argument, standing and speaking each word out loud precisely as I intend to argue in court. I don't mean turning the words over silently in my mind; I don't mean muttering the words as I sit in my chair; I don't mean starting and stopping as I pace around the room. I mean standing upright, arms by my side, with only a one-page outline in front of me, and actually delivering the argument, full-throated and articulate, to the empty room." Mark Herrmann, *The Curmudgeon's Guide to Practicing Law* 84 (2006).

(i) *Practicing for time limits.* "Rehearsal of the argument aloud, whether to oneself or to a moot court of associates, is essential, whether the text is written out or not. This is particularly important now that only 30 minutes are allowed for argument, including questions. Counsel must *know* in advance how much can be said in 20 minutes or less, leaving remaining time for questioning. . . . Listening to a tape of one's rehearsed argument may be very helpful." Robert L. Stern et al., *Supreme Court Practice* 694, 695 (8th ed. 2002).

(j) *Dress rehearsal.* "After mapping out your argument and completing your outline, arrange a moot court. Provide each member of the court with the briefing from your case and encourage the participants to be skeptical and critical. Moot court should be approached as seriously as the real thing — abide by the applicable time limits, avoid scripts, and do not call for a time out when you get stumped. A moot court is an invaluable element of oral argument preparation because it gives you a chance to practice and refine your argument and highlights potential weaknesses in your presentation." Stephen A. McEwen, *Preparing Yourself for Oral Argument*, L.A. Law., June 2002, at 10.

29. Practice stating the facts of your case to nonlawyers.

Nonlawyers can be an excellent resource for improving your argument. They can point out language in your statement that seemed perfectly clear to you because of your familiarity with the case but is confusing or incomprehensible to others. The judge or judges may be more familiar with the case than nonlawyers, but they will never be as informed as you are. If you can present the facts and issues clearly enough for a nonlawyer to understand, judges will be impressed by your clarity.

(a) *Classic statement 1.* "A good way to get training and experience in stating facts is to practice upon one's relatives and friends. The idea is merely to tell someone else that here was a case in which the facts were so and so and to ask him what he thinks about it. If this is tried again and again and again, after a while there will come a certain sense of balance and order of statement from which there naturally evolves a method of telling the story so clearly and above all so briefly that anyone can grasp it. In so far as the facts are concerned, it is not necessary that the listener be a lawyer or have any legal training. If one can describe a complicated set of facts in such a clear and simple fashion as to make them intelligible and plain to a layman, they will be even more intelligible and plain to the trained mind of an appellate judge." Hon. Harold R. Medina, *The Oral Argument on Appeal*, 20 ABA J. 139, 140 (1934).

(b) *Classic statement 2*. "Do not think it beneath you to rehearse for an argument. Not even Caruso, at the height of his artistic career, felt above rehearsing for a hundredth performance, although he and the whole cast were guided and confined by a libretto and a score. . . . Answer the questions that occur to another mind. See what sequence of facts is most effective. Accustom yourself to your materials in different arrangements. Argue the case to yourself, your client, your secretary, your friend, and your wife if she is patient. Use every available anvil on which to hammer out your argument." Hon. Robert H. Jackson, *Advocacy Before the Supreme Court: Suggestions for Effective Case Presentations*, 37 ABA J. 801, 861 (Nov. 1951).

(c) *Classic statement 3*. "Don't give the full argument to a layperson, but take five minutes. In five minutes, if you can't explain what this case is about and why you should win, you've got to go back and practice again. You're too immersed in it. You're too much to the level of jargon. Or you don't understand it. . . . You ought to be able to tell them in simple English that they understand what the case is about and why you should win. If they don't say, 'Oh, I see why. That's *not* fair. That *doesn't* make sense,' you've got to do some more work." Hon. John Roberts, interviewed by Bryan A. Garner (2 Mar. 2007).

30. In the weeks preceding your argument, watch another argument or two in the very court where you'll be arguing.

The chance to see and hear the judges of the court when you are not under pressure is of incalculable value. You can learn, for example, to what degree the court is a "hot" one, how questions are asked, and how attentive each judge is. You can learn from other advocates' mistakes and how the court reacts to them.

(a) *Classic statement 1*. "If you have not been familiar with the particular court in which you are to argue, for heaven's sake, go there the day before you argue to watch and listen. I can't, for example, think of anything that would be more devastating than to appear in the Appellate Division, First Department [of New York], today, ready to argue a case, if you have not been there in the last ten years." Hon. Whitman Knapp, *Why Argue an Appeal? If So, How?*, 14 Record N.Y.C.B.A. 415, 428 (1959).

(b) *Classic statement 2.* "Arrive early and listen to other oral arguments in order to familiarize yourself with the Court." Hon. Robert F. Stephens (as quoted in Hon. Ruggero J. Aldisert, *Winning on Appeal* 307 (1992)).

(c) *Part of your research.* "[D]o some research about an appellate panel before oral argument. Does this panel have a published case in the area you will be arguing? Is one panel member an expert in a particular field of law? If you have time, watch the court in session before you appear." Hon. Patti S. Kitching, *The Last Word*, S.F. Daily J., 30 July 1999, at 6.

(d) *Testing the atmosphere.* "If you have to appear in a Tribunal or Court — in any capacity — familiarize yourself as best you can with its style, procedures, and atmosphere. Take time to sit in on someone else's troubles before your own are reached. And if in doubt about the ways and customs of the court or the idiosyncrasies of the Bench — ask the usher or the clerk. The more humble the official and the more distinguished the questioner, the more flattered he is likely to be." Greville Janner, *Janner's Complete Speechmaker* 128 (1981).

31.   Arrive at court plenty early.

By arriving early, you give yourself time to prepare yourself mentally as well as to arrange and organize your materials. You also give yourself a chance to become familiar with the courtroom's layout and acoustics. Even if you've been in a particular courtroom many times, you'll find it helpful to arrive early enough to reacquaint yourself with it and relax before you argue.

(a) *Classic statement 1.* "Reduce apprehension as much as possible by arriving at the courthouse in ample time to carry out your preparatory chores, such as arranging the materials you will take to the lectern. If you have books or other materials that might have to be referred to, be sure they are arranged so as to be readily available." Henry St. John Fitzgerald & Daniel Hartnett, *Effective Oral Argument*, 18 Prac. Law. 51, 64 (April 1972).

(b) *Classic statement 2.* "Only if you allow enough time to arrive at the courtroom early will you have time to deal with unexpected problems. If nothing goes wrong, you'll arrive at the courtroom with time to spare. Assemble your thought. Summon your powers. Center yourself. You're ready." Alan L. Dworsky, *The Little Book on Oral Argument* 23 (1991).

(c) *Calm state of mind.* "The proper state of mind for making an oral argument is calm consideration. A last-minute, frenetic rush to the courthouse isn't conducive to this attitude. You'll have enough cause for nervousness without adding to it concern about arriving late. So leave with plenty of time to spare. In fact, if you're arguing the second case that day, be there for the first." Hon. Antonin Scalia & Bryan A. Garner, *Making Your Case: The Art of Persuading Judges* 161 (2008).

(d) *How promptitude begets relaxation.* "The focus of your attention should not be getting to court but on making the best oral presentation possible. You will do a much better job if you get to court early, review your materials, and relax." Michael Paul Thomas, *The Rites and Rights of Oral Argument*, Cal. Law., Sept. 2004, at 40, 41.

The Manner
of Your Argument

32. Carry yourself as if you know what you're doing and have done it before.

No matter how nervous you are, try to project a calm, confident image. Doing this will be much easier if you've taken plenty of time to organize your materials and familiarize yourself with handling them before entering the courtroom.

(a) *Classic statement 1.* "There is something psychologically persuasive about a man who comes before an appellate court unburdened by a lot of legal paraphernalia." H. Graham Morison, *Oral Argument of Appeals*, 10 Wash. & Lee L. Rev. 1, 7 (1953).

(b) *Classic statement 2.* "The effective advocate should, I think, evidence an appropriate amount of confidence in his case and in himself — not overconfidence, surely, but an appropriate recognition that he is performing an important function in the adversary system, that he thoroughly understands that he is there to persuade, and that that is what he is trying to do. Of course, he should be respectful and courteous, and adequately deferential." Erwin N. Griswold, *Appellate Advocacy with Particular Reference to the United States Supreme Court*, N.Y. St. B.J., Oct. 1972, at 375, 376.

(c) *Projecting confidence.* "Act as if you have been there before, that you know where you are, and that you are ready to proceed." Robert M. Roach Jr. & Kevin Dubose, Texas Bar CLE Presentation, *Eight Commonly Made Mistakes in Appellate Oral Argument* (Austin, Tex.; 9 Jan. 1998), at M-5.

(d) *Organizing your exhibits.* "Nothing is more discouraging to a judge, a jury, and opposing counsel, than to have a lawyer constantly fumbling through his files or the papers on his table for an exhibit. This type of bungling approach does a disservice to the client and the profession. There is no reason why exhibits should not be organized and analyzed in advance of trial and appropriately indexed. Ability to find the correct exhibit at the appropriate time without wasting the time of the court or the jury should be encouraged." Charles W. Joiner, "The Trial Brief" (1955), in *Advocacy and the King's English* 45, 56 (George Rossman ed., 1960).

(e) *Confidence in a maiden voyage.* "Don't waste precious minutes explaining that this is your first appearance, for the court probably already knows it. Furthermore, your first argument will probably be one of the best of your career." Hon. Jack Pope, *Argument on Appeal*, 14 Prac. Law. 33, 35 (1968).

(f) *The doofus at the bar.* "In the few seconds that it takes after his case is called for the advocate to rise from the counsel table, gather his papers and approach the lectern and utter the magic words, 'May it please the Court,' he will be giving the court a preview of his entire argument. If he stumbles over his chair as he leaves it, if he bundles his books and his papers, his glasses and his pencil in his arms like a schoolboy, if he waddles to the scene of action, if he puts on his glasses and then takes them off before he starts to talk, the court will know just about what it is in for." Hon. Arthur T. Vanderbilt, *Forensic Persuasion* 32–33 (1950).

33. Make a good first impression before you utter a word. Be presentable. Hydrate beforehand.

For both men and women, conservative attire is always appropriate for a courtroom. But merely donning a suit is not enough; you must ensure that neither your grooming nor your accessories detract from your professional appearance. Comport yourself as an officer of the court. And drink water before you approach the lectern. The only thing sillier than taking 7–10 seconds of oral-argument time while sipping water is shaking and spilling it all over yourself.

(a) *Classic statement 1.* "The skilled attorney will always be neatly dressed, will sit properly at counsel table, and will rise resolutely when addressing the court or the jury. The novice will often be slumped in his or her chair the entire time that lawyer is either questioning a witness or arguing a point to the judge. Judges notice this." Roberto Aron et al., *Trial Communication Skills* § 28.18, at 28-22 (1996).

(b) *Classic statement 2.* "Try to dress well for oral argument. Make the judges think that you are a serious person who takes the court seriously." Hon. Richard A. Posner, *Convincing a Federal Court of Appeals*, 25 Litig. 3, 62 (Winter 1999).

(c) *Classic statement 3.* "Don't get slack about your appearance at court. Every day you are on show. So show them. Make sure the clothes you wear make you look fantastic. Looking fantastic makes you feel like a winner. Tribunals can't help themselves — they take people who look like winners very seriously. And you have not opened your mouth yet. Elementary human psychology." Iain Morley, *The Devil's Advocate: A Short Polemic on How to Be Seriously Good in Court* 36 (2005).

(d) *Conservative attire.* "One should of course be dressed appropriately: dark suits and ties for men and similarly conservative attire for women. That is, one's mode of dress ought to reflect the dignity of the occasion and project the respect the advocate ought to have for the tribunal before whom she is appearing." Alan D. Hornstein, *Appellate Advocacy in a Nutshell* 250 (1984).

(e) *Court rules.* "Arrive properly attired. Many courts have rules relating to the proper dress of counsel. Even if they did not, you would want to wear clothing befitting a person engaged in a serious business activity." John T. Gaubatz & Taylor Mattis, *The Moot Court Book* 101 (3d ed. 1994).

(f) *A British view.* "[W]hatever the tribunal, you must give a good impression. Your appearance means a lot. Dress neatly, not slovenly. Be well-groomed." Lord Denning, *The Discipline of Law* 9 (1979).

(g) *A Californian view.* "The Hon. Barbara Gamer, one of San Diego's Superior Court judges, once quipped that in her court 'the attorney who wears polyester has the burden of proof.'" Keith Evans, *The Language of Advocacy* 56 (1998).

(h) *Water in glass, not on pants.* "[W]hen you are pouring water, try to get the water in the glass and not on your pants. Having water on your pants sends a really bad message." Carter G. Phillips, *Advocacy Before the United States Supreme Court*, 15 T.M. Cooley L. Rev. 177, 192 (1988).

(i) *Nightmarish cranking.* "[W]hen you go to the Supreme Court, one of the more interesting elements of their podium is that it has a crank. You can crank it up or down. Most people do not move it because cranking does not seem like such a great thing. However, one person made the interesting decision to crank with a glass of water right in front of the crank. The result was that the glass of water flew right into the bench, breaking the glass. In general, I would not recommend doing that." Carter G. Phillips, *Advocacy Before the United States Supreme Court*, 15 T.M. Cooley L. Rev. 177, 192 (1988).

34. Have the relevant papers in order, and organize them for ready reference.

Judges appreciate orderliness both as a courtesy and as a mark of competence. They dislike having their time wasted as a lawyer riffles through documents instead of promptly answering their questions. Organizing your documents isn't a trivial matter; it's an essential part of preparing your argument. But best of all is being so well prepared that you needn't search for a document at all because you have the reference in your head.

(a) *Classic statement 1.* "[T]ime is . . . lost as well as cogency of effort by referring to books and papers and notes when the facts should have been present in the speaker's mind. This is often the fault of an indolent mind, but safety comes only through systematic preparation." Jesse Franklin Brumbaugh, *Legal Reasoning and Briefing* 598 (1917).

(b) *Classic statement 2.* "Orderliness in the arrangement of the documents in a case has far more importance than is generally realised. Which of us has not seen the discomfort and confusion produced by a paper going amissing just at the moment when it is wanted, or the irritation of the judge when he finds his copy of documents differently paged or arranged from counsel's copy? The thread of the argument is interrupted, tempers are upset, and half the effect of a good speech may be irretrievably lost. All this can be avoided by a little forethought and system. . . . [B]elieve me, it is of real importance. Attention to these apparently trivial details has a much greater effect on the fortunes of a case than is imagined." Rt. Hon. Lord Macmillan, "Some Observations on the Art of Advocacy" (1933), in *Law and Other Things* 200, 205–06 (1937).

(c) *Classic statement 3.* "An attorney who, during argument, fumbles through masses of office files, bundles of books, and court records is usually unprepared. But it is a pleasure to see counsel argue from notes that guide him as he moves from point to point, unimpeded by useless paraphernalia." Hon. Jack Pope, *Argument on Appeal*, 14 Prac. Law. 33, 45 (1968).

(d) *The effect of a frenetic search.* "A judge thinks little of an advocate engaged in a frenetic search of the record and counsel's embarrassment may deleteriously affect the remainder of his presentation."

T.W. Wakeling, *The Oral Component of Appellate Work*, 5 Dalhousie L.J. 584, 606–07 (1979).

(e) *Disorganized papers no small matter.* "I speak from the fullness of my heart when I say that I have seen more trouble in Court over disorderly papers than from any other cause. So I decline to treat as a triviality beneath counsel's notice this matter of the tidiness and accessibility of the documents in the case." Rt. Hon. Lord Macmillan, "Some Observations on the Art of Advocacy" (1933), in *Law and Other Things* 200, 206–07 (1937).

(f) *Wasting precious time.* "Avoid fumbling for documents during the precious few minutes available for oral argument." Michael Paul Thomas, *The Rites and Rights of Oral Argument*, Cal. Law., Sept. 2004, at 40, 41.

(g) *Losing concentration.* "A polished advocate does not waste the court's time wading through the record, with the attendant risk that his and the court's concentration, probably for good, will be lost." T.W. Wakeling, *The Oral Component of Appellate Work*, 5 Dalhousie L.J. 584, 607 (1979).

(h) *Minimalism and what it means.* "I should certainly advise, as an irreducible minimum, [taking to the lectern] a note of the various heads or points of the case, in the order in which it is proposed to treat them. But, of course, it may turn out to be impossible or inexpedient to maintain this order in the argument, and the note ought, therefore, to have such elements of fluidity as to meet this contingency. . . . [T]he tendency of the beginner is to embarrass himself by far too many notes, and . . . he will act wisely if he trains himself by degrees to narrower and narrower limits in this class of assistance." David Dundas, *Observations on the Art of Advocacy*, 3 Can. L. Rev. 171, 178 (1904).

35. Unless local custom is to the contrary, always stand when addressing the bench.

Standing is a gesture of respect. And it makes you more visible to the bench. Even when you aren't required to stand when speaking to the judge, you make a good impression if you do.

(a) *Classic statement 1.* "[T]he court should not be addressed nor a witness asked a single question while you are seated. Failure to observe this rule is a cardinal forensic sin." Hon. S. Tupper Bigelow, *Legal Etiquette and Courtroom Decorum* 68 (1955).

(b) *Classic statement 2*. "The advocate must never address the bench from a seated position. Even for something as simple as responding to the bench's inquiry, 'Is counsel prepared to proceed?' the advocate should always rise before saying 'yes.' It is in such small ways that the advocate makes plain to the bench that she is aware of the deference and respect due the court." Alan D. Hornstein, *Appellate Advocacy in a Nutshell* 251 (1984).

(c) *Classic statement 3*. "[A]lways stand when addressing the bench. You will naturally do this when approaching the podium for your presentation, but may forget at other times. It is common, for example, at the outset of the argument, for the chief judge or justice to ask counsel for both sides whether they are ready to proceed. When asked, you would naturally respond, 'We are, Your Honor.' Remember to stand when you do this." John T. Gaubatz & Taylor Mattis, *The Moot Court Book* 103 (3d ed. 1994).

36. When speaking, position yourself: avoid swaying and shifting and other annoying habits, such as gesturing with your pen.

The variety of ways to distract a court with unpleasant mannerisms is truly vast. The experts have amply noted many of them.

(a) *Classic statement 1*. "Don't forget the physical and mechanical aspects of presenting your oral argument. Try not to talk with your hands; that is distracting and unprofessional. Just clasp them behind you or in front of you, or gently grasp the lectern: Do whatever works to make your hands 'invisible.' Don't walk about; don't move around; don't rock to and fro or from side-to-side." Hon. Jacques L. Wiener Jr., *Ruminations from the Bench: Brief Writing and Oral Argument in the Fifth Circuit*, 70 Tul. L. Rev. 187, 205 (1995).

(b) *Classic statement 2*. "For most people, nervousness manifests itself in ways they are completely unaware of, but ways the court will find distracting . . . fiddling with hair; waving glasses around; sucking on the bow of one's glasses; rubbing the back of one's neck or one's chin. Perhaps the most common habit, and the most distracting, is the tendency of many lawyers, especially men, to put their hands in their pockets and jingle their change or keys. If you are at all prone to do this, try to keep your hands at your side or place them lightly on the podium. Just in case, however, empty your pockets before you enter the courtroom." Bradley G. Clary et al., *Advocacy on Appeal* 127 (2d ed. 2004).

(c) *Not a closing argument.* "Do not sway back and forth or from side to side at the podium. You will make the panel seasick. Do not wander from your spot — this is not a closing argument before a jury where you may want to walk the rail and make eye contact with all of the jurors. Do not grip the podium like a dying man or lean your full weight on it or slouch with your elbows on it as if you are exhausted or lazy." Michael D. Murray & Christy H. DeSanctis, *Adversarial Legal Writing and Oral Argument* 265 (2006).

(d) *The absurdity of overgesticulating.* "The lawyer usually speaks 'off hand' and uses both his hands, arms, and sometimes his feet and legs in so doing. Sometimes he threshes the fleeing air with his clenched fists; at other times he hammers the table in front of him until it groans with discomfort. Often he clasps his hands together and chops the atmosphere between him and the jury, or separates his hands and swings his arms like flails, or works them as pump handles. Sometimes he may cause one hand to skim like a swallow while the other coquettishly caresses his coat tails. Occasionally he bores the palm of his left hand with the index finger of his right or pounds the aforesaid palm with his clenched fist. He often shakes his head like an enraged bull fighting a red flag; or he paces back and forth before the jury, increasing his speed according to the rapidity of his utterances. All these and many other grotesque and absurd gestures are supposed to aid the argument in some way. But they do not." Henry S. Wilcox, *Foibles of the Bar* 134 (1906).

(e) *No fiddling around.* "Don't fold your arms or fiddle with your ears, your spectacles, or anything else." Glanville Williams, *Learning the Law* 202 (A.T.H. Smith ed., 12th ed. 2002).

(f) *A few unfavorite things.* "Playing with a pencil, sticking your hands in front of your face, pacing up and down in front of the podium, and tapping a pen on the microphone are just some of the things that draw our attention from the argument. Avoid these distractions." Hon. Roger J. Miner, "The Don'ts of Oral Argument," in *Appellate Practice Manual* 263, 267 (Priscilla Anne Schwab ed., 1992).

(g) *Antics on the parallel bars.* "The peripatetic advocate who strides back and forth across the courtroom distracts attention from what he says and indicates, even if unjustifiably, confusion in his own mind about his case. He should stand erect on both feet. Nothing but distraction is the result of watching the gymnastic exploits of an advocate, who moves from one kind of embrace of the rail to another; and whose one foot climbs up the other leg and back again." Abraham L. Freedman, *On Advocacy*, 1 Vill. L. Rev. 290, 303 (1956).

(h) *No gesturing for the novice.* "The golden rule for the beginner in court regarding gesture is that he should not make any. . . . A beginner in court will be well advised to abandon all conscious thought of gesture — and also of 'facial expression' — and to confine his mind to his task of addressing the bench . . . with sense, simplicity, and sincerity." Leo Page, *First Steps in Advocacy* 78–79 (1943).

(i) *The potential bad consequences.* "[S]ome judges have difficulty in finding for an advocate who has annoyed or upset them." Keith Evans, *The Language of Advocacy* 75 (1998).

37. Look directly at the judges individually — in the eye, not up into space. Connect with your audience.

When you make eye contact, your listeners will pay more attention to what you're saying. And you can more easily detect clues that tell you how they're receiving your argument. Moreover, eye contact bespeaks confidence and conviction.

(a) *Classic statement 1.* "The first [point] is that the speaker assumes a natural pose. His head is up. His eyes are forward and there is contact with the audience permitting the currents of thought and personality to flow through. Is there anything more discouraging to an audience than to be virtually ignored by the speaker whose head and often astigmatic eyes are buried in papers before him?" Louis Nizer, *Thinking on Your Feet* 39 (1940).

(b) *Classic statement 2.* "You've got a chance to look at them and see whether it's getting across. You've got a chance to answer their particular questions. If you by any chance have, as you may have, a panel that you don't know about ahead of time so that you have to write your brief blind — take the case of the Circuit Courts, who sit in threes, and who knows what three are going to be drawn —

you've got a chance in the oral argument to talk to them. And see what's up. And watch their faces. And answer their questions." Karl N. Llewellyn, *A Lecture on Appellate Advocacy*, 29 U. Chi. L. Rev. 627, 639 (1962).

(c) *Classic statement 3.* "Eye contact may be the easiest means of altering intimacy between people. Researchers tell us that the amount of mutual gazing is a measure of liking or disliking. Strong lovers show more eye contact with each other than do weak lovers, showing that eye contact is a function of liking, affection, and love for each other. Not only do experiments show that people think you like them if you look at them, but, they, in turn, will like you more because they think that you have looked at them because you like them. 'Low gaze' people . . . are seen as nervous and lacking in confidence. The more a person looks around and at others, the more he or she is seen as active, dominant, and self-confident." Celia W. Childress, *Persuasive Delivery in the Courtroom* 253 (1995).

(d) *Exuding confidence.* "Maintaining eye contact as the dialogue develops also allows the speaker to detect some of the listener's reactions to what is being said. It also conveys a sense of interest and persuasion from the speaker to the listener. Moreover, maintaining eye contact allows the listener to assess the speaker's confidence, conviction, and frankness." Charles W. Craven, *Chili Palmer and the Art of Appellate Oral Argument*, Committee News (App. Advocacy Comm. newsletter of the ABA Sec. Tort, Trial, and Ins. Prac.), Summer 2005, at 1.

(e) *A modified view of argument.* "The best impressions are made when the lawyer looks the judges in the eye during his oral argument and engages in what Chief Justice Hughes termed 'oral discussion.'" Hon. George Rossman, "Appellate Practice and Advocacy" (1955), in *Advocacy and the King's English* 241, 254 (George Rossman ed., 1960).

(f) *Making it personal.* "In the conduct of an oral argument counsel should make every effort to keep his eyes fastened on individual judges. Only in this way can he maintain the personal contact [that] is the basis of persuasion." Ralph M. Carson, *Conduct of the Appeal — A Lawyer's View* 36, 91 (1952).

(g) *Connecting with each judge.* "Watch the bench. As much as possible, catch the eye of each member of the court from time to time so as to draw him or her into your train of thought. While one judge may ask most of the questions, each has an equal voice in the opinion. Pay attention to the silent ones. Eye contact may encourage them to listen more closely, and may open them to your arguments." John T. Gaubatz & Taylor Mattis, *The Moot Court Book* 104 (3d ed. 1994).

(h) *No dwelling on a single judge.* "Don't address just one judge. As you speak look up and down the court. You can't afford to run the risk of offending any members of the court by ignoring them. Don't assume that the most loquacious judge will sway the court. Many times the judge who doesn't open his mouth has the best grasp of the case and the most influence when the vote is taken." Hon. Robert Lee Jacobs, *The Judge's View*, 42 Pa. B.Q. 119, 120 (1970).

(i) *Direct eye contact (1).* "Maintain eye contact with the court. Look the judges in the eye (one judge at a time, of course). Don't deliver your argument to one judge, but devote your attention to each of them as you move through your argument. When a judge asks a question, look directly at him during the entire colloquy, not at a nearby window or some spot on the wall behind him." Henry St. John Fitzgerald & Daniel Hartnett, *Effective Oral Argument*, 18 Prac. Law. 51, 66 (April 1972).

(j) *Direct eye contact (2).* "Talk to the court. Shift eye contact from judge to judge frequently, but always have eye contact with one. Naturally, look at the judge whose question you're answering, but don't keep on doing so long afterward." Edward L. Lascher, *Oral Argument*, 7 Cal. Litig. 16, 19 (Winter 1994).

(k) *Importance.* "The importance of eye contact in oral communication is widely acknowledged, and it is no less important when addressing a distinguished panel of judges." Hon. Edward D. Re, *Brief Writing and Oral Argument* 196 (6th ed. 1987).

(l) *Consistency of eye contact.* "When you sheepishly drop your eyes to the floor, *you walk out on your audience.* You transform a legitimate pause for reflection into a confidence-destroying signal of confusion. By observing one simple rule, you can make your enforced pauses assets rather than liabilities. Look at your audience *all* the time." Richard C. Borden, *Public Speaking as Listeners Like It* 94 (1935).

38. Always remain cool, calm, and temperate — never agitated and never smug. Listen to opposing counsel with courtesy and respect, without any gesturing or head-shaking.

Although conviction should show in an advocate's presence and speech, emotional reactions inevitably backfire with judges and can also weaken your effectiveness. An advocate who scoffs or harrumphs during an opponent's presentation seems discourteous and unlikable. Sit with a poker face as your adversary argues.

(a) *Classic statement 1.* "The good debater must avoid the fault of temper. Calmness and coolness are his best equipment, if he is to serve his client well." Rt. Hon. Lord Macmillan, "Some Observations on the Art of Advocacy" (1933), in *Law and Other Things* 200, 213 (1937).

(b) *Classic statement 2.* "Don't assume a derisive smile while opposing counsel is addressing the court; this is very bad manners. The only safe rule, for counsel's weak points as well as for his good ones, is to keep as set a poker face as you can muster. . . . There is one exception: when the court laughs, don't hesitate to laugh right along with them — quite regardless of the quality of the humor." Frederick Bernays Wiener, *Briefing and Arguing Federal Appeals* § 127, at 338 (2d ed. 1967).

(c) *Classic statement 3.* "Nothing gives a person so much advantage over another as to remain always cool and unruffled under all circumstances." Thomas Jefferson, 21 May 1816 letter to Francis Eppes, in 19 *The Writings of Thomas Jefferson* 242 (1903).

(d) *Listening with courtesy.* "A calm and dignified attitude is essential throughout the argument. Whether the argument of opposing counsel is excellent or obviously ineffective and poor, the advocate should always listen with courtesy and dignity." Hon. Edward D. Re, *Brief Writing and Oral Argument* 203 (6th ed. 1987).

(e) *Showing respect.* "The lawyer should listen with respect and refrain from any kind of negative reaction to what the opponent says, through either gesture, expression, or any other nonverbal message. . . . Courtesy is a big part of being — and looking — professional. But confidence, strength, and a positive attitude are also crucial to projecting a credible professional image. Lawyers should show the jurors that they have enough confidence in themselves, their case, and their client that they can be courteous and decent in the courtroom while standing up for themselves and their client. This will gain the respect of the judge and the other lawyer." Roberto Aron et al., *Trial Communication Skills* § 21.17, at 21-22–23 (1996).

(f) *Danger of distracting the judges.* "[A]void body-language commentary. Raising your eyebrows, sighing, and making other such gestures during the opponent's presentation accomplishes nothing except to distract the judges and eradicate their respect for your professionalism." Charles W. Craven, "Posttrial and Appellate Oral Argument: A Curmudgeon's Perspective," in Defense Research Institute, *A Defense Lawyer's Guide to Appellate Practice* 221, 223 (2004).

(g) *Taking notes and then responding in turn.* "When a question is addressed to your opponent, there should be no violent head shaking or grimacing at the answer. Make a note of the question and include the response in your argument when your turn comes." Hon. Sol Wachtler (as quoted in Hon. Ruggero J. Aldisert, *Winning on Appeal* 309 (1992)).

(h) *Good temper, common sense.* "[A]mid all the difficulties that beset the advocate, he will find good temper the best companion, and common sense the surest guide." Richard Harris, *Hints on Advocacy* 329 (17th ed. 1937).

(i) *How listeners regard a speaker's anger and overexcitement.* "Not at all excited themselves, they [the jury] make no allowance for your own excitement, but jump at once to the conclusion that you are nervous or angry because you expect to lose. They may have no very distinct idea why you should lose, but if they once think that you expect to do so they will not be apt to disappoint you. I believe many jurymen pay little, if any attention to the actual argument and evidence, but watch the counsel engaged, and go in favor of the man who appears to be least anxious about the result. The most apparently indifferent careless man that I ever saw in practice was Sir John Holker, and he was the most uniformly successful. In fact, he almost made a specialty of winning rotten cases. The most zealous, nervous, angry advocate that ever came under my observation was Dr. Kenealy, and he was the most uniformly unsuccessful. Yet he was incomparably the better speaker, and the more brilliant man of the two. All his gifts were neutralized by his dreadful temper and his ungovernable zeal." A.M.B., *On Some Common Errors in Advocacy*, 10 Va. L.J. 710, 712 (1886).

(j) *The double whammy of disrespect.* "Since successful advocacy is all about getting your decision-makers to listen to you with sympathy, unpleasantness on the part of the advocate really strikes at the root of the whole thing. Not only are you stressing yourself out: at the same time you are significantly reducing your effectiveness." Keith Evans, *The Language of Advocacy* 4 (1998).

(k) *No provocation great enough.* "Whatever the provocation, whether it be that you feel you are required to spend time on matters which you deem to be irrelevant, or for any other reason, do not show annoyance. . . . No matter what happens, you must be respectful to every member of the court." Owen Rall, *Effective Oral Argument on Appeal*, 48 Ill. B.J. 572, 583–84 (1960).

(l) *Anti-gas tablets if necessary.* "Even Cicero would have had problems persuading a court that there was substance in the grounds of appeal in a California case reported in 1988. A defense lawyer, Mr. Clark Head, was to appeal in the case of a client convicted of breaking and entering because, he contended, the prosecuting attorney 'farted about 100 times' during Mr. Head's closing speech to the jury." David Pannick, *Advocates* 51 (1992).

39. Never read an argument. Remember that your delivery must sound natural. Memorize only the preferred sequence of your ideas, and approach the lectern with no more than a few outlined points.

In the understated words of United States Supreme Court Rule 28.1, "Oral argument read from a prepared text is not favored." Reading suggests that you either don't know your case as well as you should or you don't have enough confidence in it to discuss it with the court. And it's a waste of time: judges can read — they don't need you to read to them.

(a) *Classic statement 1.* "Wearied by the futile consumption of time by a lawyer who was droning through his brief, a helpless judge wrote on a piece of paper, 'A brief reader is the lowest form of living animal,' and then passed it to a colleague. The latter read it, took a pencil, wrote, 'He is a vegetable,' and passed it back." Raymond

S. Wilkins, "The Argument of an Appeal" (1947), in *Advocacy and the King's English* 277, 285 (George Rossman ed., 1960).

(b) *Classic statement 2.* "Over and over again one may hear it said from the appellate bench, 'Please do not read us your brief, Counsel. The court may not be able to think but it can certainly read.' The argument should go along the lines of the brief, but it should be different. . . . The protest against brief-reading goes also to a somewhat lesser extent to the reading of any prepared manuscript. Surely a lawyer doing court work can learn to talk to a court from notes without having to put a paper between himself and his judicial audience." Hon. Herbert F. Goodrich, *A Case on Appeal — A Judge's View* 28 (1952).

(c) *Classic statement 3.* "Half [the judges surveyed] complained about attorneys who read in oral arguments from prepared statements, from precedents, and especially from their briefs. Judges find listening to this tedious and feel it wastes time, since they can read the material themselves." Thomas B. Marvell, *Appellate Courts and Lawyers* 33 (1978) (reporting on an empirical study).

(d) *The imbecility of reading.* "If I ever see you reading an argument to a court, I will never work with you again. Why am I so strident? Because only imbeciles read their arguments." Mark Herrmann, *The Curmudgeon's Guide to Practicing Law* 86 (2006).

(e) *A Rehnquist anecdote.* "The court [the New York Appellate Division] had a rule prohibiting counsel from reading their briefs, and this particular lawyer was not long into his argument before it was apparent that he was violating the rule. The presiding judge cautioned him, reminding him of the rule, but he nonetheless persisted in simply reading his brief, albeit in a rather florid way. The presiding judge finally interrupted to say: 'Counsel, I think you may be sure that we have read your brief.' Whereupon counsel righteously replied: ' Yes, but you have not heard it with gestures.'

"The Supreme Court gets more advocates than it should who regard oral argument as a 'brief with gestures.' Actually, the brief in an appellate court has about the same relation to oral argument as the pleadings in a case do to the arguments before the trial judge or even a jury." Hon. William H. Rehnquist, *Oral Advocacy: A Disappearing Art*, 35 Mercer L. Rev. 1015, 1024 (1983).

(f) *"Raising a curtain."* "Never read your argument. Talk to the court instead. For once you begin to read, whether from a formal, written brief or from an informal brief which constitutes your text for argument, you raise a curtain between yourself and the court." Frederick Bernays Wiener, *Oral Advocacy*, 62 Harv. L. Rev. 56, 60 (1949).

(g) *Tiresome quoting.* "Nothing is more tiresome than the reading of quotations from briefs or from books or from the record. The presiding judges of most appellate courts will immediately stop counsel, and this interruption almost always spoils the effect." Hon. Harold R. Medina, *The Oral Argument on Appeal*, 20 ABA J. 139, 141 (1934).

(h) *Getting comfortable with questioning.* "You should not be tied to any kind of 'script.' Rather, you should be comfortable with the concepts and ideas that you want to get across using a variety of techniques, including responses to the judges' questions." Gaele McLaughlin Barthold, *Questions by Appellate-Court Jurists: A Threat or an Opportunity?*, Certworthy (Defense Research Inst. App. Advocacy Comm. newsletter), Winter 2001, at 4.

(i) *Predictable pacing.* "Many counsel open their briefs in front of them and proceed to read. When a judge finds that counsel is doing that, once he has determined the case in miles an hour at which the lawyer reads, he can go out and stay ten minutes and know the exact place where the lawyer will be on his return." Hon. Henry T. Lummus, "How Lawyers Should Argue Cases on Appeal" (1943), in *Advocacy and the King's English* 348, 351 (George Rossman ed., 1960).

(j) *Just as well to stay home.* "Few lawyers are gifted with memory and composure to argue a case without papers of any kind before them. It is not necessary to try. . . . [Yet] if one's oral argument is simply reading his printed brief aloud, he could as well stay at home." Hon. Robert H. Jackson, *Advocacy Before the Supreme Court: Suggestions for Effective Case Presentations*, 37 ABA J. 801, 861 (Nov. 1951).

(k) *Availability for hint-taking.* "[Counsel] have got to know their stuff and know it backwards and they have got to be a little bit, taking a hint, you know. A man who simply reads out his stuff from his notes and will not take a hint is not a good advocate." Rt. Hon. Lord Reid (as quoted in Alan Paterson, *The Law Lords* 37 (1982)).

(l) *The monotone of recitations.* "Oral argument should be made orally. By force of habit, a judge is used to reading for himself. He is not accustomed to having things read to him. By way of example, when one reads a court opinion, various parts of the text seem to stand out and emphasize themselves. The reader employing his visual senses seems to supply this quality to the text, yet the same opinion when read aloud by another seems to assume a flat monotone aspect that is difficult to escape. This may be the result of the training or experience which judges undergo. Most judges read much and read rapidly. To read to them is generally to use up time that could be better utilized." Hon. James R. Norvell, *The Case on Appeal*, 1 So. Tex. L.J. 229, 237 (1954).

(m) *From the judges' perspective.* "The worst case of the lector is the lawyer who actually reads the brief itself; this behavior is so egregious that it is rarely seen. But milder cases read paraphrases of the brief, although they train themselves to look up from their script occasionally to meet the judges' eyes. Questions from the judges, instead of being used as an opportunity to advance one's own arguments by response, are looked upon as an interruption in the advocate's delivery of his 'speech,' and the lawyer after answering the question returns to the printed page at exactly where he left off; returns, one often feels, with the phrase 'as I was saying' implied if not expressed. One feels on occasion that at the conclusion of his argument the lector will say, 'Thus endeth the lesson for today.'" Hon. William H. Rehnquist, *The Supreme Court: How It Was, How It Is* 278 (1987).

(n) *Read some, read all as punishment.* "If a counselor, in making his oral argument, reads from his printed argument, it might be well, as is done in some courts, to require him to confine himself to it." *Oral Arguments Before Courts of Error*, 2 Cent. L.J. 550, 550 (1875).

(o) *Memorizing opening, closing only.* "The more important passages at the beginning and at the end of a speech (and of important topics) should be carefully written out beforehand and memorized." O.C. Mazengarb, *Advocacy in Our Time* 247 (1964).

(p) *Comfort of knowing opening, closing.* "Although the entire argument should not be written out, many lawyers do find it helpful to write out an introduction and a conclusion. A written introduction can be comforting, even if in the end it is not used, if one is afraid of being struck dumb with nervousness upon approaching the bench. A written conclusion can be helpful at the end of the argument, in which questions have been far ranging, to bring the court back to the main point. Both the introduction and conclusion should be short." Ursula Bentele & Eve Cary, *Appellate Advocacy: Principle and Practice* 368 (1998).

(q) *Whose plan matters.* "[W]e treat lawyers as a resource rather than as orators who should be heard out according to their own desires." Hon. Byron White, *The Work of the Supreme Court: A Nuts and Bolts Description*, N.Y. St. B.J., Oct. 1982, at 346, 383.

(r) *Strenuous objections to rehashing.* "I don't know of a single judge who doesn't strenuously object to the rehashing of a brief. The judge has read the brief. Once you have prepared your brief, use your argument to prepare yourself for the questions. It is not what is in your brief. I have seen instances in which rehashing has been tried. I have seen instances in which it has been done. I have seen no instances in which it has worked." Hon. Thurgood Marshall, "The Federal Appeal," in *Counsel on Appeal* 139, 155 (Arthur A. Charpentier ed., 1968).

(s) *Advocate as a cat's toy.* "I . . . saw a younger lawyer in another case do virtually everything wrong, from attempting to read his argument verbatim from three pages of single-spaced text to constantly equivocating in his position. I remember thinking that Justice Scalia appeared to be batting him back and forth the way a cat toys with a ball of yarn." Timothy Coates, *I Couldn't Wait to Argue*, 5 J. App. Prac. & Proc. 81, 82 (Spring 2003).

(t) *Lord Denning's view.* "You must prepare beforehand what you are to say — otherwise you will muff it. I always prepared carefully. I did research. I made notes. . . . But when I got up to speak, I put my notes aside. I did not look at them. I trusted to my memory. Your speech loses much of its effectiveness if you read it or if you keep looking down at notes. You should aim at a simple, easy presentation — addressing your audience directly — as if in conversation in a room. Above all, speak clearly and distinctly." Lord Denning, *The Family Story* 186 (1981).

(u) *Breaking the habit.* "Do *not* write out your argument. Many lawyers do. If you are wedded to this practice, so be it. But if you have not developed the habit (or superstition), do not start; and, if you have, break it if you can. Scripting your argument will reduce your flexibility." Gary L. Sasso, *Appellate Oral Argument*, 20 Litig. 27, 31 (Summer 1994).

(v) *Danger of memorizing.* "[A] danger exists in memorizing a speech. If the words are well committed, they will probably be recited instead of thought. If they are not perfectly learned there is the anguish of recollection, all too visibly revealed to the audience. I am not sure which is worse. The choice is inevitable." Louis Nizer, *Thinking on Your Feet* 36 (1940).

(w) *Folly of memorizing.* "[T]he folly of a prepared speech, especially a memorized one, is dangerous. The great advocate will memorize his first few sentences and perhaps the concluding lines of his argument where he wants a memorable and unforgettable phrase that will wink into the judicial mind and memory and carry over into the conference room. But in between he will rely on his own formulation of words and phrasing to elaborate on the main headlines and subheadings of his argument. He may memorize the first three sentences since sometimes they are more important than twenty minutes of talk." Ben W. Palmer, *Courtroom Strategies* 205 (1959).

(x) *Outline of key phrases.* "Many attorneys bring with them to the lectern a one- or two-page outline of key points and phrases or quotations. Robert L. Stern observes that he frequently writes out his arguments in advance in order to think through each point clearly, and then distills the written text to an outline containing key headings, words and phrases. A glance at the outline permits him to recall the substance of the points he wishes to convey." Stephen M. Shapiro, *Oral Argument in the Supreme Court of the United States*, 33 Catholic U. Am. L. Rev. 529, 539 (1984).

(y) *Summarizing on index cards.* "Plan your speech under a number of points so that it has definite structure. Write it out in full, reflect on it overnight, and polish it the next day. Then summarize the main headings on a small card or cards about the size of a postcard." Glanville Williams, *Learning the Law* 202 (A.T.H. Smith ed., 12th ed. 2002).

(z) *Radical pruning.* "I suggest that you write out what you propose to say . . . . After you have satisfied yourself with the first draft, cut it in half and when you have done this, go over it again and cut it about one-fourth." H. Graham Morison, *Oral Argument of Appeals*, 10 Wash. & Lee L. Rev. 1, 5 (1953).

40. Avoid the rhetorical, table-pounding orations of jury trials.

Grandiose, gesture-embellished, overemotional preaching and other histrionic styles of oratory may influence juries, but they don't work before judges. Although you needn't be detached from your argument, you must remain in control of it and of yourself.

(a) *Classic statement 1.* "The art of the advocate today is not to charm and enthrall the judgment of the Justices by the graces of old-fashioned oratory, but rather to waken the interest of men, already overstrained, in the subject, to indicate its nature, and to stress the contention upon which the case can be won." James M. Beck, *May It Please the Court* 22 (O.R. McGuire ed., 1930).

(b) *Classic statement 2.* "[M]any lawyers do succeed in adopting a quieter and less demonstrative manner than when arguing to jurors. Of course, this manner is preferable before a supreme court. Logic, reason, conciseness, and clearness of statement are more helpful than physical gymnastics." Hon. W.G. Roberds, *Some Suggestions as to Oral Arguments and Written Briefs in the Supreme Court of Mississippi*, 29 Miss. L.J. 403, 404–05 (1958).

(c) *Classic statement 3.* "Hollywood portrayals aside, the Supreme Court is not swayed by a rousing, emotional sermon, nor do the justices suddenly shift their basic views in response to a brilliant lecturer." David G. Savage, *Say the Right Thing*, 83 ABA J. 54, 56 (Sept. 1997).

(d) *No thumping of tubs.* "As for style, effulgent tub-thumping arguments have largely gone out of fashion. . . . The preferred attitude is competent, confident, matter-of-fact refutation of the appellant's points." Michael B. Tigar & Jane B. Tigar, *Federal Appeals: Jurisdiction and Practice* § 10.11, at 522–23 (3d ed. 1999).

(e) *Out of style.* "Advocates not infrequently come to the Supreme Court or a court of appeals thinking they must be at their most eloquent. They concoct elaborately beautiful phrases and utter them with a kind of nineteenth-century pomp. It is all very unnecessary and can be counterproductive." David C. Frederick, *Supreme Court and Appellate Advocacy* 191 (2003).

(f) *More wind than light.* "The country lawyer who bellows at the Justices as if they were jurors usually makes a great mistake. For then the Bench gets more wind than light." Hon. William O. Douglas, *The Court Years, 1939–1975* 180 (1980).

(g) *The unlawyerly harangue.* "Personal diatribes necessarily disrupt and detract from the orderly flow of argument, indicate vulnerability on the merits, and inevitably result in incredulity toward to perpetrator." Hon. Steven D. Merryday, "Oral Argument," in *Florida Appellate Practice* § 17.20, at 17–32 (4th ed. 1997).

(h) *Drama, but substance.* "The All-American oral advocate . . . will realize that there is an element of drama in oral argument. . . . But she also realizes that her spoken lines must have substantive legal meaning. . . . She has a theme and a plan for her argument, but is quite willing to pause and listen carefully to questions. . . . She avoids table pounding and other hortatory mannerisms, but she realizes equally well that an oral argument on behalf of one's client requires controlled enthusiasm and not an impression of *fin de siecle* ennui." Hon. William H. Rehnquist, *Oral Advocacy: A Disappearing Art*, 35 Mercer L. Rev. 1015, 1024–25 (1984).

(i) *Speaking of unfortunate clients.* "I am surprised by the number of lawyers who try to boost their cases with a visceral approach. Of course, judges get just as emotional as anybody else, but a lawyer who asks whether we would like our grandmothers to be victimized by the kind of conduct demonstrated in a case at bar is marked as a sure loser. Once during the course of a very bad argument, an attorney screamed, 'I have a most unfortunate client!' All three of us nodded in agreement." Hon. Roger J. Miner, "The Don'ts of Oral Argument," in *Appellate Practice Manual* 263, 266 (Priscilla Anne Schwab ed., 1992).

(j) *New judges react to a jury argument.* "[T]he judge's usual reaction to . . . 'jury argument' is to be professionally offended. . . . If the judge has the idea that you are asking for an emotional response, he may conclude that you are admitting that you cannot persuade him intellectually." John K. Larkins Jr., "Oral Argument on Motions," in *The Litigation Manual: Pretrial* 107, 110 (1999).

41. Be conversational but not familiar.

Lectures irritate judges. They'll respond to you better if you invite a dialogue. But remember that there must always be a respectful distance between you and the court. A chummy or chatty attitude is inappropriate.

(a) *Classic statement 1.* "The oral argument is a combination of a speech and a conversation. The precise proportion of each will not be known in advance, and will vary from case to case. The atmosphere, however, is more conducive to a conversational tone than to oratory. Since the audience — or at least the part you care about — is small and not very far away, resounding oratory would not be proper even if there were time for it." Robert L. Stern, *Appellate Practice in the United States* 398 (1981).

(b) *Classic statement 2.* "Be as conversational as possible. Try to be a salesperson, not a lecturer. Lectures invite passive listening, and good sales techniques invite customer interaction. You are selling ideas, and should do so as confidently and comfortably as possible. If you imagine that the judges are sitting on your living-room couch, not on a bench, as you talk to them, you may be able to get the right tone." John T. Gaubatz & Taylor Mattis, *The Moot Court Book* 84 (3d ed. 1994).

(c) *Classic statement 3.* "You are talking *to* an audience, not *at* an audience. Choose plain English over flowery rhetoric, warm and conversational language over rigid and pedantic prose." David J. Dempsey, *Legally Speaking* 86–87 (2002).

(d) *What "conversational" means.* "All aspects of your delivery should promote conversational quality. . . . [E]ffective public speaking has important characteristics of good conversation: directness, spontaneity, animation, and emphasis. . . . While speeches ought to be so delivered that they sound like conversation, they must be more dignified, more eloquent, and more forceful than conversation itself." John F. Wilson & Carroll C. Arnold, *Public Speaking as a Liberal Art* 296 (1964).

(e) *Shunning the stentorian.* "[T]he best oral arguments are made in a conversational rather than a stentorian tone. But the voice should have sufficient volume so that it reaches all of the judges, and it does no harm if it is adequately audible to others in the courtroom, too." Erwin N. Griswold, *Appellate Advocacy with Particular Reference to the United States Supreme Court*, N.Y. St. B.J., Oct. 1972, at 375, 376.

(f) *Conversational, not hortatory.* "[A]n attorney may feel it necessary to use the manner of a speaker at a public meeting. But this is not at all desirable; while there may be several hundreds of people in the audience listening to you, your message is directed to the nine individuals on the bench, and the more you can keep your tone conversational, rather than hortatory, the better your case will fare." Hon. William H. Rehnquist, *Oral Advocacy: A Disappearing Art*, 35 Mercer L. Rev. 1015, 1024 (1983).

(g) *Avoiding references to specific judges' opinions.* "On one trip to the Sixth Circuit last year, a lawyer from a big-dog civil firm . . . continually referred to 'judge so-and-so's opinion in such-n-such a case, and as judge so-in-so wrote in such-n-such case.' This guy kept citing the particular author of opinions of the court. The proper way to refer the court to language in previous decisions is to say, 'as this court stated in *U.S. v. Doe*, 736 F.2d at 193 . . . .' Citing . . . the specific author of the opinion, particularly when that author is on the panel to which we are arguing, is inappropriate and is an obvious attempt to try and impress the judges on the panel. Because we are a cynical bunch, attempts to impress us are usually obvious to us and usually have the opposite result." Hon. Thomas J. Wright & Perry H. Piper, *Oral Advocacy — Some Reminders*, Tenn. B.J., Nov./ Dec. 1994, at 28, 30.

42. **Use correct courtroom terminology. On the federal level, trial and circuit judges are "judges"; only members of the U.S. Supreme Court are "justices."**

It's annoying for justices to be called "judges," and it's perhaps even more annoying for judges to be called "justices." Analogous points hold true for other terms in other courts.

(a) *Classic statement 1.* "Courtesy toward the Court is, of course, an all-important element. Justices should be referred to as 'Mr. Chief Justice,' 'Justice — ,' or 'Your Honor.' Justices should never be referred to as 'Judge'; still more clearly, no present or past Justice ever should be referred to by last name only, without the preceding title 'Justice —.' In speaking to the Justices, counsel always should display the kind of courtesy and respect used in communicating with a senior partner or superior in the government." Stephen M. Shapiro, *Oral Argument in the Supreme Court of the United States*, 33 Catholic U. Am. L. Rev. 529, 541 (1984).

(b) *Classic statement 2.* "In answering questions, address the judge as 'Your Honor.' In referring to members of the court, 'Judge Smith' or 'The Chief Justice' is appropriate. Opposing counsel should be referred to as such, or as 'Ms. Overton' or 'counsel for the defendant' but never as 'my opponent.' Associate counsel is called 'my colleague,' 'my associate,' 'cocounsel,' or 'Ms. Jones.'" Board of Student Advisers at Harvard Law School, *Introduction to Advocacy* 89 (7th ed. 2002).

(c) *The biggest solecism in the Supreme Court.* "[T]he Clerk of the Court, William Suter, . . . explains the drill. We are to address the Chief Justice as 'Mr. Chief Justice.' We are to address the other justices by name, e.g., 'Justice O'Connor.' If we forget the name, 'Your Honor,' is okay. But under no circumstances are we to call one of them 'Judge.' Heaven forbid." Christine Hogan, *May It Please the Court*, 27 Litig. 8, 9 (Summer 2001).

(d) *Gender-neutral formality.* "Avoid 'sir' or 'ma'am' in favor of the more formal (and gender-neutral) 'Your Honor.'" John T. Gaubatz & Taylor Mattis, *The Moot Court Book* 101 (3d ed. 1994).

(e) *Forms of address.* "Refer to the court or individual judges as 'Your Honor,' 'this court,' or 'Justice Brown,' but not as 'you,' 'sir,' or 'judge.'" Hon. Franklin Spears, *Presenting an Effective Appeal*, Trial, Nov. 1985, at 95, 101.

(f) *Second-person vs. third-person (1).* "In answer to a question asked by a judge, counsel should say: 'My answer to Your Honor's question . . .' or 'Your Honor, my answer is . . . .' Counsel should refer to a member of the court other than the one with whom counsel is speaking as follows: 'Justice Jones previously asked . . . ,' or 'I agree with the view expressed by the Chief Justice,' or 'In answer to the question asked by Judge Smith, I stated . . . .' In answer to a question by a member of the court, instead of a categorical or curt 'Yes' or 'No' answer, a 'Yes, Your Honor' or 'No, Your Honor' would seem preferable." Hon. Edward D. Re, *Brief Writing and Oral Argument* 202 (6th ed. 1987).

(g) *Second-person vs. third-person (2).* "Calling the judge 'you' grates on judicial ears. Some years ago, a famously chatty lawyer referred to the California Supreme Court in oral argument as 'you guys.' This caused the court some concern. 'You guys' are the boys at the bar, not a court. Justice Joyce Kennard, who was the only female justice at the time, was not only concerned about the lack of decorum, but she also wondered what the lawyer meant. The judge is always 'Your Honor' or 'the court,' never 'you.'" Douglas G. Carnahan, *Courtroom Clod: Learn How to Talk to a Judge*, S.F. Daily J., 24 Nov. 2000, at 6.

43. Avoid the first-person singular (*I*, *me*) and such constructions as "Appellant contends that . . . ," "It is our position that . . . ," and the like.

Personalizing one's advocacy is seldom effective. It dilutes the argument's impact by focusing attention on the speaker rather than the substance. The judges know that what you are saying is your stand or opinion; pointing that out adds nothing. Still, good advocates often refer to themselves and their clients collectively in the first-person plural (*we*).

(a) *Classic statement 1.* "It is not good practice to personalize the argument one is advancing; phrases of personal belief or feeling should be avoided. An argument couched in terms of 'I think,' 'I believe,' 'I feel' is inherently weaker than the same argument made without the personalized introduction. Avoid the first-person pronouns." Alan D. Hornstein, *Appellate Advocacy in a Nutshell* 263 (1984).

(b) *Classic statement 2.* "You can use first-person pronouns when you're introducing yourself . . . . But once you get into the body of your argument, take yourself out of your sentences. Don't say 'In my opinion,' 'I believe,' 'I think,' or — worst of all — 'I feel.' These make your arguments sound subjective. Strictly speaking, what you as an individual believe or think isn't legally relevant. The judges want to know the facts and the law and how the law applies to the facts. Structure your sentences to give them only that. Make yourself grammatically invisible in your argument." Alan L. Dworsky, *The Little Book on Oral Argument* 26–27 (1991).

(c) *Transparency of opinions.* "Most opinions are transparently personal and need no direct mention of the writer — e.g.: 'Though Einstein is routinely lionized as a great scientific mind, Newton was the most original thinker that science has ever produced.' No moderately sophisticated reader would assume that this statement is anything more than an opinion. And it is much more convincingly stated without inserting the phrase *in my opinion*." Bryan A. Garner, *Garner's Modern American Usage* 349 (2d ed. 2003).

44. Use demonstrative aids if they're helpful, but make them easy to see and understand from a distance of 30 feet or so.

Visual aids can be effective in many types of cases. A simple poster of large-size text can concentrate attention on statutory or contractual language. Maps and photographs may be well suited to cases in which judges would otherwise have to visualize a place. Illustrations can be crucial to trademark and patent cases. But remember that if the visuals don't really aid the judges, they distract. With that in mind, keep them as simple and easy to follow as possible.

(a) *Classic statement 1.* "The presentation is sometimes aided by maps and charts, which counsel is at liberty to use." Hon. Robert H. Jackson, *Advocacy Before the Supreme Court: Suggestions for Effective Case Presentations*, 37 ABA J. 801, 803 (Nov. 1951).

(b) *Classic statement 2.* "Demonstrative evidence can often optically clarify a complex verbal description. A judge can see and locate a disputed line on an enlarged map to which his attention is invited more easily than he can mentally twist and turn at each corner of a tract orally described. An enlarged photo will at once show a ditch down which water flows on to a man's field." Hon. Jack Pope, *Argument on Appeal*, 14 Prac. Law. 33, 41 (1968).

(c) *Classic statement 3.* "Some controversies are explained most lucidly by addressing the judges' eyes as well as their ears. For example, a boundary dispute is explained most easily by an aerial photograph or survey from the record on appeal. A diagram can be used to quickly and lucidly illustrate an automobile accident." Hon. Steven D. Merryday, "Oral Argument," in *Florida Appellate Practice* § 17.18, at 17–28 (4th ed. 1997).

(d) *Using pictures and objects.* "Wherever possible, use visual aids — not charts or tables that the judges will not be able to read, but pictures or objects. In one case that I heard, a trademark-infringement case, the plaintiff won in our court because its lawyer showed us his client's merchandise rather than resting content with a verbal description. Photographs are not as effective in cases in which the object itself is small enough to be exhibited in court. In a recent copyright-infringement case, both sides included photographs in their briefs, and the photographs looked completely different because of different angles and other tricks. When we got to see the items themselves at argument, the case was quickly decided." Hon. Richard A. Posner, *Convincing a Federal Court of Appeals*, 25 Litig. 3, 63 (Winter 1999).

(e) *The persuasiveness of first-rate graphics.* "Presentations with visual support are more likely to be successfully persuasive than are presentations without visual support. They lend an improved perception of the speaker to the audience members. In other words, visual support gives him or her more credibility. Presentations with visual support allow the audience greater comprehension of the material presented, garner a higher attention level from the audience, and make audience members agree more with the verbal matter of the presentation than do presentations with no visual support. [But] having no visual aids at all is better than using badly done or sloppy visuals." Celia W. Childress, *Persuasive Delivery in the Courtroom* 626 (1995).

(f) *A picture's worth.* "One of the fine presentations in our court occurred in a complex patent case in which counsel showed us a two-minute movie of the patent apparatus, a haystack mover, in actual operation. The ancient adage proved true: A picture is worth a thousand words." Hon. Myron H. Bright, *The Ten Commandments of Oral Argument*, 67 ABA J. 1136, 1138 (1981).

(g) *A dearth, not a spate, is the problem.* "In general, lawyers use too few rather than too many visual aids in appellate courts. . . . [V]isual aids should not be planned to entertain the judges, but to enlighten them." Owen Rall, "Persuasive Oral Argument," in *Lawyer's Encyclopedia* 1019, 1030 (1963).

(h) *Statutory or contractual language.* "When you're in oral argument discussing a statutory provision, you might consider blowing up the language on a projector or a piece of foam board that you can put on an easel. But I must caution you: some of us have poor eyesight. I have seen, or more accurately not seen, quite a few exhibits with statutory language or contract provisions blown up so that the advocate and the judges could examine the language together. The only problem was that at a bench long enough for seven judges, the print is rarely big enough for all of us to see. So you can either give us an individual copy or refer to your appendix, to follow along, or you can let us sit there and be annoyed. [But] seeing it and hearing at the same time really enhances our understanding."

Hon. Michael A. Wolff, *From the Mouth of a Fish: An Appellate Judge Reflects on Oral Argument*, 45 St. Louis Univ. L.J. 1097, 1107 (2001).

(i) *Keeping counsel the center of attention.* "[I]f you hand a map or chart or drawing or what-not to each member of the court, to be looked at while you are talking, you are inviting competition with your argument. You are asking the judges to give you only part of their attention and to donate the balance of it to the papers that you yourself have placed before them. . . . But if there is only a single map up there before the bench, counsel is the center of attraction, particularly when he is using his pointer." Frederick Bernays Wiener, *Briefing and Arguing Federal Appeals* § 124, at 330 (2d ed. 1967).

(j) *Time-saving assistance.* "[I]t is permissible to prepare charts and tables and display them . . . so long as they are correctly based upon the evidence in the case. All such devices assist the court in getting a better grasp of the factual situation. Moreover, they conserve the time of counsel in stating the facts, because a picture is proverbially better than a thousand words." Randall B. Kester, *Tailoring Appellate Arguments*, 43 Or. L. Rev. 135, 141 (1964).

(k) *Avoiding distractions.* "Occasionally charts or diagrams will be of help in delivering the oral argument. Be wary of charts lest they provide a distraction rather than an assistance to the presentation of the argument, and be sure that any chart you use is to a high degree self-explanatory." Henry St. John Fitzgerald & Daniel Hartnett, *Effective Oral Argument*, 18 Prac. Law. 51, 62 (April 1972).

(l) *Using an easel.* "[I]t is often helpful in aiding the court to grasp the case to use a chart, a map, or an enlarged photograph which is among the exhibits. Those objects should be placed upon an easel. If a short passage from a statute, deed, or will is the subject of the argument, it may be helpful to have the pertinent words enlarged upon a chart and set the latter upon an easel where all can look at it while counsel centers attention upon the passage." Hon. George Rossman, "Appellate Practice and Advocacy" (1955), in *Advocacy and the King's English* 241, 255 (George Rossman ed., 1960).

(m) *Using an assistant.* "[I]f you plan to use visual aids such as charts, graphs, or enlarged excerpts of documents, you should arrange for co-counsel or some other assistant to stand at the easel and change the exhibits, handle the pointer, and take care of any other such activities as may be required. You may not leave the lectern to perform such functions personally." Hon. Jacques L. Wiener Jr., *Ruminations from the Bench: Brief Writing and Oral Argument in the Fifth Circuit*, 70 Tul. L. Rev. 187, 202 (1995).

(n) *Making it large enough.* "My experience with visual aids has been mixed. When used properly, they can be very effective; when the props are technically insufficient, you run a serious risk. Because some judges have come to the bench equipped with reading glasses only and do not have the eyesight to read at a distance, be certain that your visual aids are large enough to be examined." Hon. Ruggero J. Aldisert, *Winning on Appeal* 336 (1992).

(o) *Creative uses.* "Demonstrative evidence is not restricted to trial court presentations. Creativity in an appellate presentation can capture the judges' attention and help the lawyer in the persuasion process." Roberto Aron et al., *Trial Communication Skills* § 14.08, at 14-16 (1996).

(p) *Keeping the design simple.* "Cut down visual noise by keeping the design simple. . . . Charts, graphs, or time lines should demonstrate a single element. For example, the handwritten anesthesia record usually shows systolic and diastolic blood-pressure values and heart rate on a single graph. In some cases, it may be necessary to create three different graphs so that jurors [and judges] can get a clear view of each value." Jim M. Perdue, *The Art of Demonstrative Evidence*, Trial, May 2005, at 46, 50-51.

(q) *Simplifying complexities.* "[T]here is a great deal that could be done in oral arguments in reviewing courts in the way of use of visual materials. We get charts frequently in real-estate cases and accident cases and that sort of thing, and occasionally we get them in a personal-injury case. They are valuable in other types of cases. You have no idea how difficult it is to sit on a will-contest case or a will-construction case and try to catch correctly in your mind the relationship of John and Mary, the step-children, and the second wife and the third wife. All of that could just as well be put on a chart and you could start at once on the heart of your argument. I have seen a large chart used very effectively even in statutory-construction cases. It can be done and the possibilities of that medium, I think, are quite unexplored by the Bar." Hon. Walter V. Schaefer, *Appellate Advocacy*, 23 Tenn. L. Rev. 471, 473-74 (1954).

(r) *What not to do.* "On [one] occasion a lawyer thoughtfully posted on a blackboard several charts presenting complicated statistics in a case involving an electric utility. Whatever clarity had been achieved from reading the briefs quickly dissipated as the lawyer began to explain the charts, misspeak himself, correct himself, start over, and forever lose himself at the first silly question of an utterly confused judge." Hon. Frank M. Coffin, *A Lexicon of Oral Advocacy* 52 (1984).

The Matter
of Your Argument

45.   Start with "May it please the Court."

The traditional opening is the safest way to begin addressing the court. While many judges may not care if you ignore the tradition, others will. Think of it not as a stuffy formality, but as a pleasant way to signal that you're beginning your argument. Understand that "May it please the Court" is an affirmative statement (in the subjunctive mood), not a question — so your voice falls at the end of the utterance. Don't wait for a response before proceeding.

(a) *Classic statement 1.* "It is a pleasingly brief and ritualistic touch to open with 'May it please the Court'; it is a crashingly boring waste of time to describe sycophantically how happy counsel is to be there." Edward L. Lascher, *Oral Argument for Fun and Profit*, Cal. St. B.J., Jul./Aug. 1973, at 398, 402.

(b) *Classic statement 2.* "Begin all arguments with 'May it please the Court.' Although the practice of law tends to be moving away from antiquated formalisms, this time-honored method of beginning every appellate oral argument is one that unquestionably remains unchanged. Advocates who omit this phrase appear to be either ignorant or disrespectful." Robert M. Roach Jr. & Kevin Dubose, Texas Bar CLE Presentation, *Eight Commonly Made Mistakes in Appellate Oral Argument* (Austin, Tex.; 9 Jan. 1998), at M-8.

(c) *Classic statement 3.* "Most oralists will start their argument with the phrase, 'May it please the Court.' This is a convention, not a rule, in most jurisdictions, but it is a convention followed by the vast majority of oralists. If you decide to buck the convention, you should be aware that from time to time you will encounter a judge who will view your free-spirited thinking as rebellion. You will not necessarily win points for originality; instead, judges will think you started the argument incorrectly." Michael D. Murray & Christy H. DeSanctis, *Adversarial Legal Writing and Oral Argument* 258 (2006).

(d) *Traditional formality.* "Probably the best opening sentence is, 'May it please the Court. Good morning. I am ___, and I represent the appellant ___.' There is some debate about the formality of starting with 'May it please the Court.' Unless you know the court extremely well, I suggest you not deviate from this traditional formality." Henry D. Gabriel, *Preparation and Delivery of Oral Argument in Appellate Courts*, 22 Am. J. Trial Advoc. 571, 582 (1999).

(e) *A civil setting.* "The appellate lawyer is privileged to practice in a very civil setting. Indeed, there are certain traditions of civility in virtually all appellate courts: the opening of the court with all in attendance standing and the opening line 'May it please the Court' are two good examples." Talbot D'Alemberte, *Oral Argument: The Continuing Conversation*, 25 Litig. 12, 12 (Winter 1999).

46. Have your opener down pat — and make every word count. Identify yourself, briefly present the question for decision, and state your position.

It's vital to lay out your main point or points at once, so that the judges begin thinking about them. That way their first questions will probably be on the points you most want to make. Knowing your opener well also gives you confidence as you rise to address the court.

(a) *Classic statement 1.* "Writers on the subject of appellate pleading subscribe to the same principle emphasized in texts on public speaking: special attention should be given to the opening of a speech. . . . If the opening statement is clear, correct, concise, and persuasive, the impression which it creates may reflect favorably on what follows. By contrast, a vague, rambling, ineffectual opening may create an atmosphere of uncertainty which makes the development and acceptance of subsequent points more difficult." Thorrel B. Fest, *Oral Aspects of Appellate Argument*, 22 Rocky Mtn. L. Rev. 273, 276–77 (1950).

(b) *Classic statement 2.* "[A]t the outset you have the undivided and often the fresh attention of the justices. They are eager to find out what the case is about so that they may properly orient themselves and set their minds to the argument. Again and again you may formulate these crucial sentences to make them clear and forceful and interesting, to set the key and tone of your argument and to satisfy the initial curiosity of the court. A great start is long progress toward a successful conclusion." Ben W. Palmer, *Courtroom Strategies* 205–06 (1959).

(c) *The most important part.* "The most important part of the oral argument is the beginning — the first minute. An argument that focuses immediately on the issue and the 'essential reasons' is almost always persuasive. The thematic introduction sets the tone for a strong presentation and provides positive ground from which to parry negative points." Michael R. Fontham et al., *Persuasive Written and Oral Advocacy in Trial and Appellate Courts* 158 (2002).

(d) *Answering opponent's main point first.* "Try to get out your main points. In this court, it's hard to do; there are nine judges. But you want to get the main one out quickly. And probably the best one you can have is to figure out what your opponent's strongest argument is and make sure you get out your answer to that argument." Hon. Stephen Breyer, interviewed by Bryan A. Garner (6 Nov. 2006).

(e) *Chief Justice Roberts's view.* "In your opening in the Supreme Court, you're only guaranteed about a minute or so, a minute and a half, before a justice is going to jump in, so I always thought it was very important to work very hard on those first few sentences. You want to convey exactly what you think the case turns on and why you should win . . . . You've got to frame it in a way that makes your main argument . . . . It's often a way to guide the questioning. You want to do it in a provocative way. Bring out the question that you want to be asked at that point so you can respond to it. And then right away you're out of any kind of memorized presentation. You're responding to a question, but it's a question that you have elicited or planted by the way you opened the case." Hon. John Roberts, interviewed by Bryan A. Garner (2 Mar. 2007).

(f) *Lord Denning's view.* "Always prepare the first few sentences of a speech — it is highly important to start off slowly, clearly, with confidence without fumbling for words." Lord Denning's practice notes (as quoted in Edmund Heward, *Lord Denning* 24 (1990)).

(g) *Starting on the right foot.* "I always believe it is essential that your opening should be so well ingrained in your mind that no matter what happens you get started on the right foot, particularly if you are representing an appellant. Something may happen, particularly if you are an appellee or respondent, that will cause you to change your opening, but you have got it there so you can use it if it is opportune." Samuel E. Gates, "Hot Bench or Cold Bench: When the Court Has Not Read the Brief Before Oral Argument," in *Counsel on Appeal* 107, 135 (Arthur A. Charpentier ed., 1968).

(h) *Telling what and why.* "Mak[ing] a good first impression . . . means starting your argument in a way that favorably grabs the judge's attention, without losing your credibility. . . . Good openings answer two questions, whether or not the judge asks them: What do you want? Why do you want it? The answers, and hence your opening, should be short, on point, and — if possible — stated in a way that appeals to the judge's visceral notions of doing the right thing." Kenneth R. Berman, *Snatching Victory: Arguing to Win*, 21 Litig. 18, 18–19 (Winter 1995).

(i) *Key issue plus outline.* "[A]n effective opening statement must set forth the key issue in the case in a clear, persuasive, and sympathetic light, and provide an outline to the argument as a whole. If this is done well, it can immediately start moving the court toward the desired result. If it is done poorly, it can have a detrimental effect on the case." Jay M. Levin, *The Importance of the Opening in an Appellate Argument: A Case Study*, Certworthy (Defense Research Inst. App. Advocacy Comm. newsletter), Winter 2000, at 4.

(j) *Setting the temper.* "The entire temper of an oral argument may well depend upon the impression you create with the court during the first two or three minutes of argument. As an artist is able to sketch the recognizable outlines of his subject with the first quick strokes of his crayon, your opening statement should sketch, in an understandable and interesting way, exactly how the case arrived in the appellate court and the essential issues involved on the appeal." Roy L. Steinheimer Jr., *Winning on Appeal*, 20 Mich. St. B.J. 16, 20–21 (Oct. 1950).

(k) *Your "lead paragraph."* "The opening should, after the technique of the well-written newspaper account, tell the whole story in the first paragraph, after which it is time to go back and fill in the details. . . . [T]he advocate must never keep his audience in suspense; on the contrary, he must give his secret completely away right at the outset." Frederick Bernays Wiener, *Briefing and Arguing Federal Appeals* § 96, at 287 (2d ed. 1967).

(l) *A "thumbnail epitome."* "High on the list of essentials is the use of a good opening sentence or paragraph to catch the court's interest and attention and effectively to lodge the major points of the case in the court's mind in the critical first two minutes of argument. If counsel is appearing for the appellant, he must give a thumbnail epitome of 'what this case is all about.' If he is arguing for the appellee, he must in the opening sentence seize upon the central feature of his case, and, by driving it home, dispel the impression left by his adversary." Frederick Bernays Wiener, *Oral Advocacy*, 62 Harv. L. Rev. 56, 63 (1948).

(m) *Prepared opener.* "Since the first few moments of the argument are perhaps the most difficult, counsel should have a prepared introduction or preliminary statement [that] generally states the nature of the case and the question presented on appeal. The effective opening must stimulate the court's interest in the case." Hon. Edward D. Re, *Brief Writing and Oral Argument* 209 (6th ed. 1987).

(n) *Orientation, then exposition.* "[T]here are some things to do at the beginning that seem to me to be especially important. The first of these is to orient the court. The second is to present the facts clearly and effectively. Many times I have heard counsel overlook these elementary precepts, and launch into the general theoretical discussion of a whole area of the law. This leaves the court looking perplexed; and the argument made on this basis is almost surely wasted, if not positively harmful. For the court is likely to think that there must be some fatal weakness in your case if you will not tell them quickly and simply what it is about." Erwin N. Griswold, *Appellate Advocacy with Particular Reference to the United States Supreme Court*, N.Y. St. B.J., Oct. 1972, at 375, 377.

(o) *One-sentence summary.* "At the very start, state your theory of the case — what authority compels your result, based on which fact findings, and why. Try to state it in one sentence. (It may be your last uninterrupted moment.) Emphasize the legal as opposed to the evidentiary merit of your position — that is, focus on the merit under statutory, regulatory, or decisional authority." Hon. Paul R. Michel, *Effective Appellate Advocacy*, 24 Litig. 19, 21 (Summer 1998).

(p) *Calm tone.* "A useful thing for stability is a calm tone in the introduction. What is more disagreeable than the full voice in the introduction to a discourse?" *Rhetorica ad Herennium* 195 (1st century B.C.; Harry Caplan trans., 1954).

(q) *Giving a brief introduction.* "Open with a short, simple introduction: Tell the panel your name, the name of your client, your client's role in the appeal (appellant, appellee, intervenor, amicus) and in the trial (plaintiff, petitioner, defendant, respondent, third party), but otherwise refrain from blowing a lot of 'smoke' at the court." Hon. Jacques L. Wiener Jr., *Ruminations from the Bench: Brief Writing and Oral Argument in the Fifth Circuit*, 70 Tul. L. Rev. 187, 203 (1995).

(r) *Avoiding generalities.* "The opening statement should be as specific and concise as human ingenuity will permit. The opening statement should indicate how the case arose and how it came to the appellate court. Wherever possible counsel should deal in specifics rather than generalities. It does not add much enlightenment or increase the sum total of knowledge for an attorney to tell the court: 'This is a case where the plaintiff sued the defendant.'" Hon. Frank R. Kenison, *Some Aspects of Appellate Arguments*, N.H.B.J., Jan. 1959, at 5, 7.

(s) *But also avoiding dreary details.* "There are innumerable lawyers who always start with the dreary details, or who begin the statement of a case by carefully embroidering the periphery." Frederick Bernays Wiener, *Oral Advocacy*, 62 Harv. L. Rev. 56, 68 (1948).

(t) *Not a mystery novel.* "The first 90 seconds are important. Do not make a mystery story of your case. Judges want the basic facts and results below, and they want them now. The first three or four sentences of the opening statement can do much to capture the court's interest. Until it is captured, it is impossible to maintain attention." Hon. Jack Pope, *Argument on Appeal*, 14 Prac. Law. 33, 39 (1968).

(u) *But generating anticipation.* "[M]ost audience members — and jurors and judges too — are more easily persuaded when they have enough knowledge presented to them in the introduction so that they are able to anticipate what is to come in the remainder of your speech." Celia W. Childress, *Persuasive Delivery in the Courtroom* 475 (1995).

(v) *Cicero's advice.* "[Y]ou must not spring at once into the pathetic portion of your speech, as it forms no part of the question, and men are at first desirous to learn the very point that is to come under their judgment." Cicero, *Cicero on Oratory and Orators* 143 (45 B.C.; J.S. Watson trans., 1986).

(w) *A blundering opener recounted.* "I gave out an award last year at the circuit conference for the worst beginning of an oral argument. . . . A fellow from New York came down to argue a case dealing with the end of subsidies for the maritime workers. There are no more Merchant Marine ships being made in the United States, and he was arguing that the subsidy program really hadn't ended. That was his case. Now you have to understand, he had 15 minutes for his argument. But he began his argument something like this: 'I want to take the court back to the days of the Civil War. Sherman has just marched to the sea. Tara has burned to the ground. Scarlett O'Hara is standing among the ruins. A horseman approaches, and she says, "I have always depended on the kindness of strangers."' One of my colleagues interrupted and said, 'That's not Scarlett O'Hara, that's Blanche DuBois in A Streetcar Named Desire.' The attorney responded, 'Maybe so, but my point remains.'" Hon. A. Raymond Randolph (interview), Jeffrey Cole, *An Interview with Judge Randolph*, 2 Litig. 16, 22–23 (Winter 1999).

47. Begin with an overview so that you can signpost your argument.

Demonstrate to the judges at once the logical progression of your argument. With a firm idea of where you're going with your remarks, judges are more likely to follow along and address their questions when you are speaking on that point. The overview may also help them single out one or two points they'd like to spend additional time asking you about.

(a) *Classic statement 1.* "Your very first objective, when you get up on your feet to argue, is to convince the court that you have a program, that you have thought out a logical order for the presentation of your points, and that you are capable of adhering to it. This will diminish the number of questions from the Bench." Paxton Blair, "Appellate Briefs and Advocacy" (1949), in *Advocacy and the King's English* 788, 807 (George Rossman ed., 1960).

(b) *Classic statement 2.* "Generally, an argument that from its very outset shows that it will be well-organized and thorough tends to ward off questions." Hon. Robert H. Jackson, *Advocacy Before the Supreme Court: Suggestions for Effective Case Presentations*, 37 ABA J. 801, 862 (Nov. 1951).

(c) *Classic statement 3.* "I view oral argument as a pebble dropping into a pool with concentric circles radiating outward. I think the way to begin is with a small circle. You start out small so that you don't get interrupted. I always tried to begin by making some statements that would not prompt a question because I wanted the court to start listening to me. Then, I would widen the circles until I got to the ultimate point of the argument. If I didn't do that, I would immediately be diverted into areas that did not fit sequentially in the argument. Statements that invite premature questions make it difficult to use other background or analysis as a foundation for leaping to a particular point." Hon. A. Raymond Randolph (interview), Jeffrey Cole, *An Interview with Judge Randolph*, 2 Litig. 16, 22 (Winter 1999).

(d) *Summarize, then expound.* "To summarize the points of argument before dealing with them individually is the simplest and one of the most effective ways of bringing their cumulative force home to any tribunal." Richard Du Cann, *The Art of the Advocate* 178 (1964).

(e) *Focusing attention.* "You should make an early announcement of the structure of your proposed argument, identifying what issues you will discuss and what issues, if any, you submit on the brief. The latter will tend to evoke from the court any questions that the judges have on those submitted issues, and may also smoke out at an early stage any issues that the court wishes to spend extra time on." Hon. Vincent L. McKusick (as quoted in Hon. Ruggero J. Aldisert, *Winning on Appeal* 308 (1992)).

(f) *Getting to the question.* "At the very beginning, and as quickly as possible, counsel should get before the Court the questions involved on the appeal. Many lawyers make the mistake of proceeding at first to state their conception of the facts, even to detailing the testimony of the proceedings in the lower court, and the errors it is contended were committed there, not the question to be passed upon by this court." Hon. W.G. Roberds, *Some Suggestions as to Oral Arguments and Written Briefs in the Supreme Court of Mississippi*, 29 Miss. L.J. 403, 405 (1958).

(g) *Subtle structure.* "One of the most brilliant performances I ever heard in my life was an argument by Judge Proskauer in the Appellate Division, First Department [New York]. He told the Court at the outset that he had three points. He stated the first point, and then said, 'That was my first point, Your Honors.' Then he recapitulated and went on to this second point. Then he said, 'Those were my first and second points,' and reviewed the two together. Then he stated the third point, and 'By way of summary,' reviewed the three of them. Each point was identical to every other point. But you didn't get that impression as you were listening to him. You got the impression each time that you were hearing something new, and it wasn't until you were all through and were wondering how the court below could have been so stupid, that you recognized the artistic performance you had witnessed." Hon. Whitman Knapp, *Why Argue an Appeal? If So, How?*, 14 Record N.Y.C.B.A. 415, 429–30 (1959).

(h) *Limiting harassing questions.* "I believe that much merely harassing questioning — not all of it, but most of it — can be avoided if counsel shows in the beginning of his argument that he understands clearly and precisely the points he wants to make, and if he shows that he has prepared a line of treatment of those points. The court is then inclined to let him proceed except for real inquiries seeking aid in understanding." Hon. E. Barrett Prettyman, *Some Observations Concerning Appellate Advocacy*, 39 Va. L. Rev. 285, 301 (1953).

(i) *Characterizing the case.* "[F]rom the moment you get on your feet, the judicial mind is groping for the nature of the case, and the points of difference between you and your adversary with respect to each question presented for decision." Hon. Hu C. Anderson, "Briefs and Arguments That Help the Court" (1943), in *Advocacy and the King's English* 312, 328 (George Rossman ed., 1960).

(j) *Danger of overfamiliarity with case.* "A great many lawyers in their oral argument make the mistake of sailing into the middle of the case with a discussion of points of law when this Court doesn't know what it's all about. The best of our Alabama lawyers are guilty of this error and argue principles of law before the Justices are ready or are prepared to consider them. The reason for this type fault is probably due to the lawyer's having become so familiar with the case during months of preparation and trial in the lower courts." Hon. J. Ed Livingston (as quoted in *Words of Advice to Attorneys from Members of Appellate Courts of Alabama*, 4 Ala. L. Rev. 207, 207 (1952)).

48. **If you're an appellant before a "cold" bench, briefly explain the history of the case and the key facts before stating the controlling law and how the lower court erred. If you're the appellee, decide whether you must restate the case in some respect.**

A court that is not familiar with the facts and issues of your case must be introduced to them quickly before you go further into your arguments. Few at the appellate level are truly "cold" courts today, but you must still try to gauge just how strong a grasp of the case the judges have.

(a) *Classic statement 1.* "An appellate advocate may find it necessary in a 'cold' court to present the case's background and the advocate's contentions more thoroughly before expanding on the argument." Hon. Myron H. Bright, *The Ten Commandments of Oral Argument,* 67 ABA J. 1136, 1136 (1981).

(b) *Classic statement 2.* "I realized during my first argument before the Supreme Court of Arizona what I should somehow have found out earlier: that the judges simply did not read the briefs in the case before coming on the bench to hear oral argument. To me this is almost a waste of the time set aside for oral argument, which at its best should be a refinement and a polishing of the issues in the case, not an introduction to the facts out of which the litigation arose. But when in Rome, do as the Romans do: if the appellate court before which you are arguing makes a practice of not reading the briefs before they come on the bench, you had better be prepared to develop the facts in some detail." Hon. William H. Rehnquist, *Oral Advocacy: A Disappearing Art,* 35 Mercer L. Rev. 1015, 1023 (1984).

(c) *Warming up a cold bench.* "In those days, as in the Court of Appeals today, the judges did not acquaint themselves with the record or the briefs, their purpose being to give the arguing attorney an opportunity of addressing them before their minds had even begun the opinion-forming process." Hon. Whitman Knapp, *Why Argue an Appeal? If So, How?,* 14 Record N.Y.C.B.A. 415, 428 (1959).

(d) *Giving a cold bench some background.* "[D]uring my earlier days upon the court, before we adopted the practice of reading the briefs in advance of argument, I must confess that to me the oral argument was in most cases almost completely a waste of time. It was extremely difficult for me to follow the oral presentation of complicated facts with which I had no prior familiarity and when, a month later (as our practice then was), we came to conference and the preparation of opinions, the oral argument had gone almost completely out of my mind, so that my reliance had to be on the briefs alone in most cases." Hon. Albert B. Maris (as quoted in Hon. John Biggs Jr. et al., "In the Matter of Oral Argument" (1955), in *Advocacy and the King's English* 233, 240 (George Rossman ed., 1960)).

(e) *Tabula rasa*. "With a cold bench, you are writing on a clean slate, at least insofar as the facts are concerned. The initiative lies almost wholly with counsel. The lawyer is given the opportunity of drawing the facts and applicable law in a way most favorable to his client; and if he does his job properly, this first impression will not be forgotten. When the judges subsequently read the briefs, which usually occurs at any time up to three weeks after the argument, the reading will take place in light of the impressions formed at oral argument, and those impressions should include an answer for the major contentions raised in your opponent's brief." Samuel E. Gates, "Hot Bench or Cold Bench: When the Court Has Not Read the Brief Before Oral Argument," in *Counsel on Appeal* 107, 118–19 (Arthur A. Charpentier ed., 1968).

49. If you're before a "hot" bench, go straight to the most important deep issue.

When the judges are well prepared for your oral argument, they often have questions already in mind before you start speaking. So it's especially important for you to get your strongest point out as soon as possible before becoming sidetracked on questions about a lesser issue.

(a) *Classic statement 1*. "The hot bench, by the way, wants the argument in order to bring the lawyers into actual conference with the judges so that they can see whether you can help them. They know what is bothering them. They know the level of their own ignorance, the scope of their own difficulties, or the conceit of their own superiorities but would like to test them on you." Hon. Charles D. Breitel, "A Summing Up," in *Counsel on Appeal* 193, 203 (Arthur A. Charpentier ed., 1968).

(b) *Classic statement 2*. "An entirely different type of argument could be had, even in the short time allowed, if all the judges should come to the hearing thoroughly prepared on the facts and the law by previous reading of the record and briefs, and study of the issues and authorities. Then the statement of facts could be omitted or highly skeletonized. The greater portion of time, on both sides, could be given to analysis of issues, discussion on principle, and argument from authority." Hon. Wiley B. Rutledge, *The Appellate Brief*, 28 ABA J. 251, 251 (1942).

(c) *Classic statement 3*. "Most state highest courts, as well as the U.S. Courts of Appeals, are considered 'hot' courts, that is, courts where briefs and appendices or records are furnished sufficiently in advance of the argument to permit time for pre-argument study." Hon. Ruggero J. Aldisert, *Winning on Appeal* 301 (1992).

(d) *Getting questions before you can open.* "[M]ost courts are 'hot,' prepared on the facts and the issues and loaded with questions. Don't be surprised if judges start launching questions even before you open your mouth." Jason Vail, *Oral Argument's Big Challenge: Fielding Questions from the Court*, 1 J. App. Prac. & Proc. 401, 404 (Summer 1999).

(e) *Making your points quickly.* "Some panels are 'hot' and ask many questions, while some ask very few questions. With a hot panel, make your main points quickly before you are interrupted and then, if necessary, come back to them." Hon. Patti S. Kitching, *The Last Word*, S.F. Daily J., 30 July 1999, at 6.

(f) *Effect on preparing.* "The modern norm is a 'hot' bench — one where judges come to the oral argument armed with a great number of questions. The difficulty in preparing for an oral argument before a hot bench is that you do not know whether your case will be one that engages the judges and brings forth a number of questions, or whether you will be left to give your prepared presentation. You must be ready either way." Talbot D'Alemberte, *Oral Argument: The Continuing Conversation*, 25 Litig. 12, 15 (Winter 1999).

(g) *Talking down to a hot bench.* "My experience in the last few decades is that the lawyer who tries to describe the nature of the case or its prior history draws from the court a few indignant snorts and an admonishment to get on with the argument. Of course, the judges are right; the nature of the case and its prior history is set out succinctly in the beginning of any brief. Even if the court were to let you discourse on the subject, it would be improvident to waste the precious minutes allotted to you on superfluous boilerplate." Milton S. Gould, "Oral Argument Losing Its Appeal," Nat'l L.J., 23 Mar. 1981, at 15, 32.

(h) *Difficulty of taking judges' "temperature."* "Don't be too sure about the temperature of the judge. Sometimes judges who might be classified as 'cold' are really 'hot,' but they want to hear without interruption what counsel may reveal as to what she thinks is the real thrust of the case. . . . [O]r perhaps the court, like Columbo, is willing to appear uninformed in order to assess more clearly the bona fides of what counsel is arguing. In that situation, questions by the court mistakenly may be thought to be superficial or misplaced." Hon. J. Thomas Greene, *Don't Forget Your Orals*, 183 F.R.D. 289, 292 (1999).

(i) *Impact of statement of facts in the brief.* "[W]ith a hot bench there is a premium on the statement of the facts in your brief, for at the oral argument the hot bench may take the view that it knows the facts and deny you another opportunity to discuss them. Reading the briefs tends to have much the same effect as discovery procedures at the trial level; the issues, both factual and legal, are narrowed, and some of the initiative of the argument passes to the court." Samuel E. Gates, "Hot Bench or Cold Bench: When the Court Has Not Read the Brief Before Oral Argument," in *Counsel on Appeal* 107, 120 (Arthur A. Charpentier ed., 1968).

50. If you represent the appellee or respondent, don't rehash the facts. But correct any salient errors or omissions in the appellant's or petitioner's statement.

Take time to point out any flaws in the facts as presented by the appellant, or to briefly reframe crucial facts as you see them. But if this is not necessary, use the time to plunge right into your argument and your discussion with the judges.

(a) *Classic statement 1.* "Some lawyers feel that when they argue for the respondent it is necessary for them to go over all the facts again, even though their opponent has already stated them clearly and accurately. This is definitely bad procedure. If the appellant has stated the facts fully and accurately, there is no point whatever in the respondent talking about the facts at all. He should get down to his law and present his side of the case without delay. A long, repetitious rehashing of the facts bores the court to distraction and is apt to put the judges in a frame of mind where they pay very little attention to the really important part of the respondent's argument." Hon. Harold R. Medina, *The Oral Argument on Appeal*, 20 ABA J. 139, 142 (1934).

(b) *Classic statement 2.* "To me, one of the most dramatic moments in the trial of a lawsuit comes when the appellee arises to make his reply. . . . [I]n 50 percent of the cases he does this. He starts out again with a statement of the facts and as he starts out you are on the edge of your chair. You think, well now, this has been all wrong, this difference in the facts as stated by the appellant and as the appellee is now going to state them is going to be crucial; the case will turn on this and you listen eagerly for the first minute and the second and the third and nothing happens and he is repeating the same facts, and that man has lost the attention of the court which he had in a highly sensitized degree when he began. He has lost it and it is even money that he will never get it back." Hon. Walter V. Schaefer, *Appellate Advocacy*, 23 Tenn. L. Rev. 471, 474 (1954).

51. If the issue involves statutory or contractual language, focus quickly and concretely on the words at issue.

In cases that hang on how words are to be interpreted, the text is paramount. Even when complex interpretation requires canons of construction or other types of analysis, the text will be the starting point and will always remain the focal point. The judges should have that language right in front of them, either in a document or on a visual aid.

(a) *Classic statement.* "[L]et the court see — and I mean 'see' — the exact language with which they have to deal. Tell them, right at the beginning: 'The statutory language involved appears at page 4 of my brief. Though the clause is a somewhat long one, the issue turns, I believe, on the proper construction or effect of the words in two lines near the top of the page.' Give the court time to find the two lines, and then read the words to them. At this point, the eye can be as important as the ear in oral argument, and the court will follow all of the rest of your argument much better if you have taken pains to tell them exactly what it is about, and where to find the words if they want to look at them again." Erwin N. Griswold, *Appellate Advocacy with Particular Reference to the United States Supreme Court*, N.Y. St. B.J., Oct. 1972, at 375, 377.

(b) *Less classic, but helpful.* "The oral advocate takes a great step in advancing his cause, I think, if, right at the beginning of his argument, after the procedural setting has been established, he tells the court exactly what the case is about, including specific reference to any statutory language which must be construed or evaluated in bringing the case to a decision. With orientation, the court finds moorings." Erwin N. Griswold, *Appellate Advocacy with Particular*

Reference to the United States Supreme Court, N.Y. St. B.J., Oct. 1972, at 375, 377.

52. Never engage in detailed dissection of caselaw.

In a brief, you can analyze precedents in some detail; in an oral argument, you can't. The judges are *listening*, and the medium of oral presentation is strictly *linear*. Hence an argument must be simpler and more straightforward than a brief can be. Once you start discussing particularities of other cases, you've lost your listeners.

(a) *Classic statement 1.* "[Counsel can be] tempted into a tedious recital of the facts in the cited case, not uncommonly prefaced by the somewhat awkward phrase, 'That was a case where,' etc. Now the human mind is a pawky thing and must be held to its work, and it is little wonder after three or four or half a dozen such recitals that not only are the recited facts forgotten but those in the case at bar become blurred and confused. What the advocate needs most of all is that his facts and his alone should stand out stark, simple, unique, clear." John W. Davis, *The Argument of an Appeal*, 26 ABA J. 895, 898 (Dec. 1940).

(b) *Classic statement 2.* "No judge's memory is good enough to remember a lawyer's minute and detailed line of decisions, and the distinctions among them. A great deal of appellate time is wasted because lawyers do not seem to believe that judges, unlike elephants, can forget." Hon. Herbert F. Goodrich (as quoted in Hon. John Biggs Jr., et al., "In the Matter of Oral Argument" (1955), in *Advocacy and the King's English* 233, 234 (George Rossman ed., 1960)).

(c) *Classic statement 3.* "The less successful appellate lawyer spends his time telling the Justices what their opinions mean, often reading excerpts to them. The preeminent appellate advocate makes a distillation of the facts to show why the case fits neatly between two opposed precedents and why this particular case should follow one rather than the other. It is the education of the Justices on the facts of the case that is the essential function of the appellate lawyer." Hon. William O. Douglas, *The Court Years, 1939–1975* 180 (1980).

(d) *What not to do — and to do.* "[D]o not attempt to run through the precedents, engaging in minute dissection of the distinguishing facts in each case. Instead, concentrate on presenting your theory of the applicable rules of law in brief, general terms, and apply those rules to your case." Hon. Myron H. Bright, *The Changing Nature of the Federal Appeals Process in the 1970's*, 65 F.R.D. 496, 506 (1975).

(e) *The turnoff of dwelling on minutia of past cases.* "The court is not much interested in citation-chopping in argument." Hon. Henry T. Lummus, "How Lawyers Should Argue Cases on Appeal" (1943), in *Advocacy and the King's English* 348, 350 (George Rossman ed., 1960).

(f) *The forgettable nature of oral citations.* "[I]t is almost certain that not a single case cited in argument either by name or volume and page will have been remembered." George R. Currie, *Some Aspects of Appellate Practice Before the Wisconsin Supreme Court*, 1955 Wis. L. Rev. 554, 562.

(g) *Keeping cases unnamed.* "Court opinions should not usually be mentioned by name unless the case names are well enough known, or recent enough in the same court, to need no citation." Owen Rall, "Persuasive Oral Argument," in *Lawyer's Encyclopedia* 1019, 1028 (1963).

(h) *A benighted excuse for violating the rule.* "Justice Van Brunt of the appellate court once interrupted a young lawyer in middle of his long quotation from authorities: 'I suggest that you get down to the merits of your own case.'

"'Presently, Your Honor, presently,' the young lawyer responded, but he continued to expound the law earnestly as he saw it.

"'Let me suggest to you,' Justice Van Brunt interrupted him again, 'that you get down to the merits of your case, and take for granted that the court is familiar with the elementary principles of law.'

"'No, Your Honor,' dissented the sincere young man, 'that was the mistake I made when I argued this case in the lower court.'" Peter Hay, *The Book of Legal Anecdotes* 152 (1989).

53. Never bring a triviality to the court's attention.

Bickering over such things as irrelevant minutiae in an opponent's fact statement or a procedural technicality wastes everyone's time. You can lose sight of your primary issue, and the judges will lose patience with you. Yet it's a common mistake.

(a) *Classic statement 1.* "[Y]ou would be surprised to hear the many arguments and read the many briefs in the Court of Appeals demonstrating that the lawyers involved have become so imbued with petty facts, or wholly inapplicable principles, or their own verbosity, that they had completely lost sight of their objective [inducing a favorable decision]." Watson Clay, "Presenting Your Case to the Court of Appeals" (1952), in *Advocacy and the King's English* 330, 331 (George Rossman ed., 1960).

(b) *Classic statement 2.* "Do not nit-pick your opponent's presentation or whine about insignificant misstatements or mischaracterizations." Hon. Jacques L. Wiener Jr., *Ruminations from the Bench: Brief Writing and Oral Argument in the Fifth Circuit*, 70 Tul. L. Rev. 187, 202 (1995).

(c) *The prejudice of petty points.* "Little and trifling things receive no more respect in a printed argument than they would in an oral one, and they may as well be left out. . . . After hearing a few of them, the court will be apt to think that the grievances are all small and fancied, and the case is of little merit since the party is compelled to resort to petty complaints and small points. Such an impression will naturally tend to prejudice the argument in general." James H. Cartwright, *The Briefs and Argument That Help the Court*, 19 Ill. St. B.J. 15, 18 (1896).

(d) *Courting judges' mistrust.* "Both with respect to the respondent and the appellant, it is very inadvisable to interpolate any irrelevant matter. The judges are quick to sense this irrelevancy and to draw the inference that counsel is trying to draw the wool over their eyes and draw their attention away from the real issues. The effect is frequently disastrous, even though it may be pleasing to one's client or his friends sitting in the courtroom listening to the argument." Hon. Harold R. Medina, *The Oral Argument on Appeal*, 20 ABA J. 139, 142 (1934).

(e) *Lost in irrelevancies.* "Often the argument becomes so clouded in a hodgepodge of basic facts and intricate factual detail, much of it irrelevant, that the judge who has not previously dug out the essential ones cannot see the forest for the trees, the bushes, and the trailing arbutus. For him, this kind of argument is a total loss." Wiley B. Rutledge, *The Appellate Brief*, 28 ABA J., 251, 251 (1942).

(f) *Spreading arguments too thin.* "If, after combing the record, you find thirty-seven errors that range in gravity from minimal to devastating, don't argue with equal vigor and passion that each one, standing alone, was prejudicial. You devalue your argument . . . . Try to limit your appeal to three or four most serious issues in the case that you feel best demonstrate the prejudicial error." Hon. Arthur L. Alarcon, "Points on Appeal," in *Appellate Practice Manual* 95, 99 (Priscilla Anne Schwab ed., 1992).

(g) *No place for full citations.* "[I]t is not good practice, if you are relying upon a particular case or cases, to refer to the case of *Jones v. Smith* (215 A.D. 426, at p. 443) and then interrupt yourself and say, 'No, it is 434,' because none of this is essential to oral argument. It is sufficient to say that you are relying upon the *Jones* case which you have cited, which held thus and so, and you may then proceed to apply its doctrine to your case." Hon. William B. Carswell, *The Briefing and Argument of an Appeal*, 16 Brooklyn L. Rev. 147, 156 (1950).

(h) *Marking seeming trivialities with red flags.* "If a seemingly minor matter is important to your case, hang a red flag on it. Tell the court: 'This date is important.' In some manner you must indicate to the court the importance of pertinent details that might otherwise seem to lack significance. In presenting the facts, avoid unnecessary detail so as not to bury the wheat of your case in the chaff of details." Owen Rall, "Persuasive Oral Argument," in *Lawyer's Encyclopedia* 1019, 1020 (1963).

(i) *No tangential comments.* "[I]n the oral presentation, the parenthetical and diversionary argument or statement should be avoided." Hon. James R. Norvell, *The Case on Appeal*, 1 So. Tex. L.J. 229, 242 (1954).

(j) *Driving with a hammer.* "[A] good appellate lawyer will identify those points on which the outcome is likely to turn. Discard everything else and hammer on those points." David G. Knibb, *Federal Court of Appeals Manual* § 26.5, at 320 (1990).

(k) *The story of an argument poisoned.* "A federal judge in one of the western circuits has before him a motion to dismiss a pleading. After listening to the first point, which was that the paper was not properly folioed, he surprised counsel by announcing: 'The point is overruled and the motion is denied.' 'But Your Honor,' exclaimed the excited lawyer, 'I have eight other points which I wish to present.' 'I think it will hardly be necessary,' replied the judge, 'as I invariably deny a motion that begins that way.' Somewhat arbitrary and abrupt, no doubt, and yet, considered from the view point of common sense, there is much that may be urged in support of the judge's position. It is, to say the least, quite possible that a lawyer who brings such trivialities to the attention of the court has no substantial grievance of which to complain." Hon. Alfred C. Coxe, "Is Brief-Making a Lost Art?" (1908), in *Advocacy and the King's English* 338, 340 (George Rossman ed., 1960).

(l) *Ignoring irrelevant errors.* "[I]f your adversary said something happened on November 23 and it happened on November 22, do not point to the error unless it is material." Herbert Monte Levy, *How to Handle an Appeal* 219 (3d ed. 1990).

(m) *Censure.* "A prefatory complaint about how your adversary did not serve the brief on time is, of course, a total waste of time and may even be worse: the Justices may actually get exercised about it and take away the rest of the time you have for argument." Hon. Simon H. Rifkind, "Appellate Courts Compared," in *Counsel on Appeal* 163, 186 (Arthur A. Charpentier ed., 1968).

54. Never tell a joke. Avoid contrived humor. But if you're extraordinarily adept, allow spontaneous good humor to surface as long as it's at no one else's expense.

Although humor can enliven virtually any human interaction — especially in an otherwise tense or formal situation — for the advocate it carries considerable risk. The best source of humor, from the advocate's perspective, is the judge. Laugh if the judge makes a humorous remark. But the advocate as wiseacre is typically a drag on the proceedings. Worst of all are canned jokes that begin, "It's an old joke, Your Honor, but . . . ." Old jokes tend not to be funny. And in any event, amusement isn't really conducive to persuasion.

(a) *Classic statement 1.* "As in your brief, don't attempt humor unless you are sure that you can pull it off." Hon. Jacques L. Wiener Jr., *Ruminations from the Bench,* 70 Tul. L. Rev. 187, 205 (1995).

(b) *Classic statement 2.* "The use of humor in an inappropriate circumstance or before a judge or panelist who does not appreciate your sense of humor can do great damage to your credibility. As a rule, I would advise against using humor unless you know that your judge has or panelists have a good sense of humor, a particular opportunity presents itself, and you are very comfortable using humor. Even then, you should never use humor that could be considered disrespectful to anyone or seems 'canned.'" Lawrence D. Rosenberg, *Using the Lessons of Aristotle to Present Outstanding Oral Arguments: Part II*, ABA App. Prac. J., Spring 2006, at 15, 22–23.

(c) *Self-defeating entertainment.* "[A]void every attempt at witticism. Crack no jokes; tell no funny stories in the argument of the case to court or jury. You will by your fun and levity undoubtedly entertain the jury — possibly the court; but that is not what you are there for. By your brilliant flashes of wit, and by your delightful humor, and by your really good stories — and they are the dangerous ones — you will excite an expectation in the jury for more fun after a while, and they will be impatiently waiting for something funnier still further on; while it is to the doubtful questions, the questions that need clearing up, that you should address yourself: and you should by your own seriousness impress [your listeners] that to you and to your client that case is a matter of grave and serious concern." S.N. Owen, *Courtroom Oratory*, 60 Albany L.J. 324, 325–26 (1899).

(d) *Not entertainment.* "It is no part of your job to entertain the court. Personal pleasantries or other departures from the business at hand not only consume your time needlessly but also consume the time of the judges, who, whatever else they may do, can hardly look upon oral argument as a form of entertainment, light or otherwise." Owen Rall, *Effective Oral Argument on Appeal*, 48 Ill. B.J. 572, 576 (1960).

55. If the court clearly shows how it will rule on a point, move to another. Don't dwell any further on that one.

Occasionally it becomes obvious how the judges will decide an issue. If the ruling favors your client, it's a poor use of time to continue discussing the point. If the ruling favors your opponent, you're probably wasting your time if you try to change the judges' minds. Use the time instead to argue your next-most-important point.

(a) *Classic statement 1.* "When the court makes clear it is not troubled by a point, move to the next one." Hon. Paul R. Michel, *Effective Appellate Advocacy*, 24 Litig. 19, 22 (Summer 1998).

(b) *Classic statement 2.* "Sometimes judges make clear that they simply do not accept an argument. In this situation, it is better to move on to the next point than to try to convince a court that has already made up its mind on that particular issue. It may be, however, that only one or two judges are unconvinced; be sure that you have gotten your point across to those silent members of the bench who may be on your side." Ursula Bentele & Eve Cary, *Appellate Advocacy: Principle and Practice* 371 (1998).

(c) *Being prepared to move on.* "Your oral argument should not exceed three points. You are not afforded the time to develop more. . . . Ideally, your second and third points should be self-sufficient and not be dependent on the court's acceptance of the first argument. If the first point is rejected by the court, be prepared to shift ground immediately. I have heard too many arguments where the advocate persisted, even though the effort was a manifest failure and even though counsel was losing valuable time by not moving on to a point that might have gotten a more sympathetic hearing." Hon. Ruggero J. Aldisert, *Winning on Appeal* 327, 328 (1992).

(d) *Avoiding comment on court's "agreement."* "Never, in passing from one point to another, make the mistake of seeming to commit the court to your position. Never say, 'Since the court apparently agrees to the correctness of this proposition, I move on to my next point.' The court is agreeing to nothing in oral argument. Anything a judge says is only tentative." Owen Rall, "Persuasive Oral Argument," in *Lawyer's Encyclopedia* 1019, 1028 (1963).

56. Face up to your weak points, but then say why they're not controlling.

It's futile to assume that the weaknesses in your case won't surface. Tackle those weaknesses head-on. If possible, you should be the one who first points them out. Then you're not in a defensive posture after an adversary raises them. Rather, you put your adversary in the position of having to refute your arguments — and by the time this happens the weaknesses should seem like old news.

(a) *Classic statement 1.* "[T]ackle the weak points of your case fearlessly. Handle them and answer them on argument. That is what you are there for, and there is where you can do not only the greatest service to your client, but the greatest service to the court." Samuel Deutsch & Simon Balicer, *How to Take an Appeal* 644 (1931).

(b) *Classic statement 2.* "There is rarely a case, however strong, that does not have its weak points. And I do not know any way of meeting a weak point except to face up to it. It is extraordinary the number of instances one sees where through a question from the court or the argument of one's adversary a vulnerable point is laid bare, and the wounded lawyer ducks, dodges, and twists, instead of facing up to the point four square. Attempted evasion in an oral argument is a cardinal sin. No answer to an embarrassing point is better than an evasive one. With a court, lack of candor in meeting a difficult issue of fact or of law goes far to destroying the effectiveness of a lawyer's argument, not merely as to the point of embarrassment, but often as to other points on which he should have the better of it." Hon. John M. Harlan, *What Part Does the Oral Argument Play in the Conduct of an Appeal?*, 41 Cornell L.Q. 6, 9 (1955).

(c) *Discovering your weaknesses.* "Think of the light in which your opponent may look at the case, what points of law might be involved to help him, what construction might be put upon the law favorable to his side, how the law might be applied to the facts to differ from your own theory.... When you merely pay attention to your own case, you are only considering one side of the controversy, and it is natural for you to look at the case in its most favorable light. But if you look at your opponent's side, you may find that he has just as good reason to feel that his is the more favorable one. Thus, you will avoid any false, unwarranted overconfidence, which is wrought with so much danger." Samuel Weiss, *How to Try a Case* 23 (1930).

(d) *Traipsing over thin ice.* "John W. Davis was, I think, the best expositor of facts that I ever heard in court.... If there was thin ice to be got over, he did not conceal it; but he was over it, and off and away on the other side before you really realized how thin the ice had been." Erwin N. Griswold, *Appellate Advocacy with Particular Reference to the United States Supreme Court*, N.Y. St. B.J., Oct. 1972, at 375, 378.

(e) *Appreciation of candor.* "Ignorance is bliss sometimes, but certainly not when you are standing in front of three appellate judges and your appeal is going down in flames. Being able to identify the weaknesses of your argument and address them will strengthen your argument and credibility. Like all jurists, appellate judges appreciate candor and will lose trust in you if you refuse to acknowledge an obvious weakness." Stephen A. McEwen, *Preparing Yourself for Oral Argument*, L.A. Law., June 2002, at 8.

(f) *What to do if it's a failure.* "Sometimes a point fails — a branch of a suit falls though. It may not be more than the regiment of an army. It is no time to flinch or show color; it is a time to bring out mettle. At such times Mr. Lincoln is said to have coolly remarked, 'We will give them that point; I reckon they were right there.' Proceed with as much coolness as though the value of the loss were less than a shilling. But use the other forces, and see that the whole bottom of the case never falls through a small opening." Hon. J.W. Donovan, *Tact in Court* 117–18 (6th ed. 1915).

(g) *Intellectual honesty.* "Be intellectually honest. Don't try to conceal problems the judge is going to find anyway. Do the best you can to explain why your side should win." Hon. John Paul Stevens, interviewed by Bryan A. Garner (27 Feb. 2007).

(h) *Success by facing weaknesses.* "The successful advocate will recognize that there is some weakness in his case and will squarely and candidly meet it. If he lost in the court below and needs appellate relief, that fact alone strongly suggests some defect in his position. . . . The petitioner should never dodge or delay but give priority to answering the reasons why he lost below. The respondent should ask himself what doubts probably brought the case up and answer them. They will then be covering the questions that the Justices are waiting to hear answered. To delay meeting these issues is improvident; to attempt evasion of them is fatal." Hon. Robert H. Jackson, *Advocacy Before the Supreme Court: Suggestions for Effective Case Presentations*, 37 ABA J. 801, 803 (Nov. 1951).

(i) *Deflating adversary's best shots.* "Cases often have serious problems and difficulties. If your case has them, it is better for you to bring them out and explain them away than for the other side or, even worse, the court, to raise them. The difficulties will not just go away if you ignore them. By bringing them out yourself, you can discuss them in the context and with the emphasis you want, and also take some of the wind out of the other side's sails." Hon. Daniel M. Friedman, *Winning on Appeal*, 9 Litig. 15, 60 (Spring 1983).

(j) *Reputation for rigorous honesty.* "The best Solicitor General as far as advocacy was concerned was Charles Fahy, who served from 1941 until shortly after FDR's death in 1945. His virtue was not only clarity and precision, reflecting a sharp-edged mind, but his complete honesty. He never overstated his case; he never stretched a finding of fact to save his end; he was always frank in stating what the shortcomings of the record were. That is to say, he was meticulous in pointing out the factual weaknesses in the record so far as the merits of his case were concerned." Hon. William O. Douglas, *The Court Years, 1939–1975* 183 (1980).

(k) *Advantage of transparency.* "There are occasions when [the instinct of rescue] is worth enlisting on your side. When you know that your case is confronted with a serious difficulty in the shape of an awkward passage in the evidence or an embarrassing precedent, do not shirk it. Read the awkward passage with all the emphasis or quote the authority without flinching, and point out the difficulty [that] it creates for you. You will almost invariably find that the first instinct of the judge is to assist you by pointing out that the evidence is less damaging to you than you represented or that the precedent is on examination distinguishable. The Court is favourably disposed by the absence of all concealment of the difficulty and is attracted by the very statement of the difficulty to address itself to the task of solving or alleviating it." Rt. Hon. Lord Macmillan, "Some Observations on the Art of Advocacy" (1933), in *Law and Other Things* 200, 203–04 (1937).

(l) *No evasion of facts.* "Every case contains factual matters which are embarrassing and difficult. These must be met head-on, face to face, and without any dodging or straddling. Nothing can ruin an oral argument so completely as the slightest tendency toward evasion, concealment, straddling, or running away from the facts." Hon. Harold R. Medina, *The Oral Argument on Appeal*, 20 ABA J. 139, 141 (1934).

(m) *Effective technique.* "Experienced oral advocates know that one of the most effective techniques for dealing with bad facts is admitting them readily and explaining why those facts do not affect the proposed outcome of the appeal." Catherine Valerio Barrad, *Successful Oral Arguments Do Not Involve Any Arguing*, S.F. Daily J., 4 Aug. 2004, at 5, 6.

(n) *Value of being forthright.* "If a question is embarrassing or exposes a weakness in the case, do not give an evasive answer. Answer it directly, with whatever explanation can best extricate you. Judges are quickly aware when counsel is evading a direct answer, and are likely to call on it. Courts become irked with a lawyer who tries to avoid answering difficult questions. Conversely, they respect a lawyer who faces up to difficult problems questions pose and answers the inquiries forthrightly and directly." Hon. Daniel M. Friedman, *Winning on Appeal*, 9 Litig. 15, 60 (Spring 1983).

(o) *Understanding judges' motives.* "Contrary to what some appellate attorneys might think, the tendency of appellate judges to focus on the Achilles Heel of a case is not motivated by some morbid desire to torment counsel during oral argument, but rather by a desire to reach the right and just result." Hon. Margaret M. Grignon, *The Dynamics of Appellate Oral Argument*, Certworthy (Defense Research Inst. App. Advocacy Comm. newsletter), Summer 2006, at 31, 32.

57. If you have an unanswerable point that is fatal to your opponent's case, consider closing your argument by suggesting to the court that your opponent should answer it.

A challenge to your opponent to answer a devastatingly concrete question can make a tremendously powerful conclusion. Just be sure that it's both concrete and unanswerable.

(a) *Classic statement 1.* "I have found it very useful . . . to end an oral argument by posing a rhetorical question to my opponent. The question is not actually addressed to counsel but is made as a suggestion to the court. It highlights some flaw in the reasoning of your opponent, or some gap in the record, that you want to raise just before you sit down so that the court will have your point uppermost in its mind." Talbot D'Alemberte, *Oral Argument: The Continuing Conversation*, 25 Litig. 12, 14 (Winter 1999).

(b) *Classic statement 2.* "[C]onsider challenging your opponent to explain why you are wrong about a decisive point. This is best done at the end of your own presentation. It makes for a strong ending and almost always forces your opponent to respond. If there is no response, it effectively amounts to a concession that you are right." Rex S. Heinke & Tracy L. Casadio, *Oral Argument in the Federal Circuit Courts*, 16 Cal. Litig. 36, 41 (2003).

58. Never ask how much time you still have on the clock.

It's bad form to ask how much time remains. It can also make judges wonder why you want to know.

(a) *Classic statement.* "Don't ask how much time you have left." Stuart M. Riback, *First Argument Impressions of the Supreme Court*, 5 J. App. Prac. & Proc. 133, 146 (Spring 2003).

(b) *How Justice Scalia reacts.* "Our courtroom is very, very high. Behind the bench there is a clock. Very often you see counsel standing there at the podium addressing the court and he'll get a question from one of the justices. And you see his head going up to look at the clock. And you see going through his mind, 'Oh, this fool is wasting my time. If he hadn't asked me this question I could continue regurgitating my brief.' Very, very foolish. The only time you know for sure that you're not wasting your time in oral argument is when you're responding to a question. You know you're addressing a concern of at least one of the three or of the nine." Hon. Antonin Scalia, interviewed by Bryan A. Garner (2 Oct. 2006).

(c) *Wasting precious time.* "The limitation of time also makes necessary that the lawyer arguing the case use every argument as effectively as possible. A lawyer who mentions the fact that his time is limited, or, worse yet, complains about it, is not using to the best advantage the time that he is allowed. The judges are just as alert to and as cognizant of the time limitation as you are in arguing the case. Use your time to advance your case and not to tell the court how little time it has allowed you." Owen Rall, *Effective Oral Argument on Appeal*, 48 Ill. B.J. 572, 576 (1960).

(d) *Complaints verboten.* "Although the time for your oral argument is short, never mention and certainly never complain about the shortness of time. The court is fully as conscious as you are of the time limitation it has set." Owen Rall, "Persuasive Oral Argument," in *Lawyer's Encyclopedia* 1019, 1029 (1963).

(e) *Saying what must be said in the time available.* "[T]he best advocates before appellate courts in recent years have been able to make arguments of real assistance to the courts and of profit to their cases within the somewhat narrow limits of time which the rules of today commonly allow. It is said of John G. Johnson that 'his greatest characteristic was his ability to say within the time limited by rule of court everything necessary to be said in any case.'" Roscoe

Pound, *Appellate Procedure in Civil Cases* 393 (1941) (quoting Hon.
Hampton L. Carson, *John G. Johnson: A Great American Lawyer*, 3
Cornell L.Q. 100, 111 (1918)).

**59. Even if you still have time, stop when you're finished.
If the judges have no further questions, sit down.**

Keep it short. The judges will appreciate your not wasting their time.
An early finish can project a sense of competence and confidence.
On the other hand, running long with unhelpful side-issues just to
fill your allotted time can backfire if you misstep or, worse, misstate
something. Strike a reasonable balance between tedious amplitude
and mystifying brevity.

(a) *Classic statement 1.* "[W]hen you round out your argument and sit
down before your time has expired, a benevolent smile overspreads
the faces on the bench and a sigh of relief and gratification arises
from your brethren at the bar who have been impatiently waiting
for the moment when the angel might again trouble the waters of
the healing pool and permit them to step in. Earn these exhibi-
tions of gratitude therefore whenever you decently can." John W.
Davis, *The Argument of an Appeal*, 26 ABA J. 895, 898–99 (Dec.
1940).

(b) *Classic statement 2.* "This, above all, remember: Time has been
bestowed upon you, not imposed upon you. It will show confidence
in yourself and in your case, and good management of your argument, if you finish before the signal stops you." Hon. Robert H.
Jackson, *Advocacy Before the Supreme Court: Suggestions for Effective
Case Presentations*, 37 ABA J. 801, 861 (Nov. 1951).

(c) *The idea expressed axiomatically.* "The more inexperienced the lawyer,
the longer will be his brief. The more inexperienced the advocate,
the longer will be his argument." Abraham L. Freedman, *On Advocacy*, 1 Vill. L. Rev. 290, 309 (1956).

(d) *A consciously developed technique.* "John J. Sullivan, who was once
Chief Justice of Nebraska, is credited with having developed an
appellate technique in oral argument that was most effective, and
yet extremely simple. He rarely ever used more than 10 or 15 minutes in presenting a case. He would take one, or at most two, of
the principal points, lay them out clearly and convincingly, and
say to the court: 'On this ground there is error in the record and

the judgment must be reversed. There are other grounds thoroughly covered in brief that Your Honors may consider at your leisure.'" Hon. John B. Fournet, *The Effective Presentation of a Case to the Supreme Court in Brief and in Argument*, 3 La. B.J. 95, 104 (Jan. 1956).

(e) *Having said enough.* "It's not unusual for a lawyer to sit down with time left on the clock, having sensed that he's ahead and can only make things worse by talking." Hon. Alex Kozinski, *In Praise of Moot Court — Not!*, 97 Colum. L. Rev. 178, 182 n.14 (1997).

(f) *The error of random repetition.* "[A] very common error in oral argument is not to sit down when done. I have on innumerable occasions observed a lawyer who, clearly having made all the points intended, but realizing there is time remaining, feels compelled to continue. This invariably results in random repetition of points previously made, but far less effectively than originally, and detracting greatly even from what had been a solid performance." Timothy A. Baughmann, *Effective Appellate Oral Advocacy: "Beauty Is Truth, Truth Beauty,"* 77 Mich. B.J. 38, 40 (Jan. 1998).

(g) *A good example.* "One of the most effective arguments that I have heard was one of the shortest. After the appellant's counsel had argued the case, it had become quite obvious that the members of the court disagreed with appellant's views on the merits of the appeal. A prominent Arkansas lawyer representing the appellee stood up, corrected one misstatement of fact by appellant's counsel, and stated, 'If it please the Court, I should be glad to answer any questions; otherwise, I am satisfied that the court clearly understands the issues in this case.' There were no questions, he sat down, and the court reached a decision in his favor. I am told that he collected a magnificent fee for his effort." Hon. Myron H. Bright, *The Ten Commandments of Oral Argument*, 67 ABA J. 1136, 1138 (1981).

(h) *Sage advice.* "In an earlier court generation one youthful counsel, who asked how much time he was permitted, was told, 'You have half an hour to talk, but you do not have to talk half an hour.'" Raymond S. Wilkins, "The Argument of an Appeal" (1947), in *Advocacy and the King's English* 277, 285 (George Rossman ed., 1960).

(i) *Backfiring garrulity.* "A famous judge used to express his impatience with arguments [that] exceeded their persuasion point by saying to the attorney, 'I agree with you now, counselor, but if you continue

I may change my mind.'" Louis Nizer, *Thinking on Your Feet* 40 (1940).

(j)   *The court's appreciation.* "If you say all that needs to be said before your red light comes on, relinquish your unused time to the court and sit down, saying something like 'unless the court has further questions, that completes my remarks.' There has never been a panel that resented an advocate's using less than all of his or her allotted time." Hon. Jacques L. Wiener Jr., *Ruminations from the Bench: Brief Writing and Oral Argument in the Fifth Circuit*, 70 Tul. L. Rev. 187, 204 (1995).

(k)   *Taking your seat as a good use of time.* "Sit down when you are through even though you have not used all your allotted time. That is the best use of your allotted time." Ben W. Palmer, *Courtroom Strategies* 208 (1959).

(l)   *Stopping while you're ahead.* "[D]o not feel you must use all the allotted time. Appellees, in particular, should counter the opponent's arguments briefly, answer our questions and then sit down, even if the clock has not run. Seeking more questions often backfires. Sit down while you are ahead." Hon. Paul R. Michel, *Effective Appellate Advocacy*, 24 Litig. 19, 22 (Summer 1998).

(m)   *Less as more.* "Don't pad your argument to use your full time. The court will appreciate your consideration of it, you will be able to finish your argument on a completed thought, and your refusal to use your full time shows a desirable confidence in your position which may well, unconsciously perhaps, influence the court in your favor." Owen Rall, *Effective Oral Argument on Appeal*, 48 Ill. B.J. 572, 586 (1960).

(n)   *Moving on.* "As soon as you perceive that the judges understand your point, move to the other one, or at the most, the other two. And when you perceive that they understand these arguments, *sit down*. I cannot emphasize too much the necessity to quit while you're ahead. . . . Do not think that talking for a few more minutes can't hurt. It *will* hurt." Hon. Ruggero J. Aldisert, *Winning on Appeal* 329 (1992).

(o)   *Avoiding contagious loquacity.* "Do not let the fact that your adversary is given to prolixity cause you to fail to adhere to the rule of brevity." Hon. William B. Carswell, *The Briefing and Argument of an Appeal*, 16 Brooklyn L. Rev. 147, 154 (Apr. 1950).

(p) *Finishing early.* "Some lawyers seem to talk to rest their brains; some lawyers seem — now, please don't suspect the speaker of originality in this statement — some lawyers seem inspired by an ambition to make their speeches immortal by making them eternal." S.N. Owen, *Courtroom Oratory,* 60 Albany L.J. 324, 327 (1899).

(q) *Contra: avoiding the curtness that mystifies.* "What counsel has to aim at is not so much keeping his observations short as giving the impression that he is doing so — in other words, carrying on until he has rammed his point home so firmly that it cannot be dislodged, while at the same time conveying the impression of terseness and brevity. This is a high and mysterious art, but an important one because it happens not infrequently that you lose a case by allowing yourself to be bullied or jockeyed into compressing what you have to say." C.P. Harvey, *The Advocate's Devil* 43 (1958).

60. Stop when you're out of time, taking no more than a few seconds to finish your sentence.

If your time expires while a judge is asking or has just finished asking a question, ask the presiding judge, "My time has expired. May I respond, Your Honor?" If your thought will take more than a few seconds to complete, you may ask the presiding judge for enough time to finish. If you're allowed to go on, wrap it up in no more than 15–30 seconds.

(a) *Classic statement 1.* "When the red light goes on, counsel should thank the Court and sit down. However, one may finish answering a question from the Court, and may answer any new question presented by the Court, after the red light has flashed on." Stephen M. Shapiro, *Oral Argument in the Supreme Court of the United States,* 33 Catholic U. Am. L. Rev. 529, 549 (1984).

(b) *Classic statement 2.* "[I]f you still are talking when time runs out, ask for permission to finish your sentence or the point you were making (e.g., 'I see that my time is up. May I finish what I was saying?'), or simply ask for permission to conclude, which generally means stating your request for relief.... If you were in the middle of answering a question, ask permission to finish your answer. Do not ignore the stop sign, and never use the permission granted by the court as an opportunity to continue your argument for a minute or more. It is especially bad to try to use the grace period to make a new point. The panel may decide to cut you off altogether, and that can be embarrassing." Michael D. Murray & Christy H. DeSanctis, *Adversarial Legal Writing and Oral Argument* 273–74 (2006).

(c) *Antagonizing the judges.* "When the red light comes on, immediately close your argument in 30 seconds or so; don't antagonize the judges by prolonging the discussion when your time has expired. . . . When the red light goes on, or you are told that your time is up, and you are in the middle of a sentence or a thought or a response to a question, it is good practice to ask the presiding judge for a brief moment to conclude. Then wrap it up in 15 to 20 seconds." Hon. Ruggero J. Aldisert, *Winning on Appeal* 331 (1992).

(d) *Stopping immediately.* "When the red light comes on, terminate your argument *immediately* and sit down. If you are answering a question from a Justice, you may continue your answer and respond to any additional questions from that Justice or any other Justice. . . . Do not, however, continue your argument after the red light comes on." *Guide for Counsel in Cases to Be Argued Before the Supreme Court of the United States,* 5 (October Term 2006) (accessed at www.supremecourtus.gov/oral_arguments/guideforcounsel.pdf).

(e) *Taxing the Court's patience.* "It is better to stop in the middle of a word than to tax the patience of the court by remaining beyond your allotted time or attempting to do more than finish one sentence when the time is up." Owen Rall, "Persuasive Oral Argument," in *Lawyer's Encyclopedia* 1019, 1034 (1963).

(f) *Embarrassing logorrhea.* "Some of the most painful courtroom scenes in living memory have been the result of lawyers insisting on talking when they had no right to do so and when the court had already indicated that it did not desire to hear them." Frederick Bernays Wiener, *Briefing and Arguing Federal Appeals* § 127, at 338 (2d ed. 1967).

(g) *Running the red light.* "Don't run the stop sign. Treat the red light on the lectern as a red light at an intersection. While the Supreme Court does not cite and ticket advocates for running the red light, the violation will be just as apparent. Effective advocates will begin their conclusion and summary when the yellow light goes on and will conclude their oral arguments before the red light is turned on." Robert M. Roach Jr., "Oral Argument," in *Texas Supreme Court Practice Manual 2005* 16-17 (Richard R. Orsinger ed.).

61. If time permits, close by saying, "Thank you." Then pause briefly. Don't rush from the lectern.

Just as "May it please the Court" is the traditional opening to oral argument, so is a polite acknowledgment of the court's attention a less formal but just as traditional closing.

(a) *Classic statement 1.* "It is O.K. to thank the court for its courteous attention to your cause. Surprisingly, few lawyers do." Hon. Arthur L. Alarcon, "Points on Appeal," in *Appellate Practice Manual* 95, 101 (Priscilla Anne Schwab ed., 1992).

(b) *Classic statement 2.* "[O]bserve the customary ending: 'Thank you, your honors.' Even if they have made life very difficult for you by their questions, retain the respectful posture until the end. Some judges test theories by severe questioning, and you should not take it personally. Be amenable and helpful." John T. Gaubatz & Taylor Mattis, *The Moot Court Book* 101 (3d ed. 1994).

(c) *A final pause.* "You should say your last sentence with emphasis, let the words ring in the air, pause as you look at the [judges] with serious expression, and then pick up your notes and slowly walk back to your seat." Celia W. Childress, *Persuasive Delivery in the Courtroom* 486 (1995).

Responding to the Bench

62. Rejoice at questions. Accept that you may have no chance to speak other than in answer to questions.

You must appreciate the role that questions and answers play in oral argument. Questions are opportunities to elicit your views on points that concern the judges. Advocates' answers are opportunities to persuade the court that their arguments should prevail. Judges' questions aren't stumbling blocks thrown in your path to keep you from getting through what you want to say. They're prime opportunities to clinch the case.

(a) *Classic statement.* "Rejoice when the court asks questions. . . . If the question does nothing more it gives you assurance that the court is not comatose and that you have awakened at least a vestigial interest. Moreover a question affords you your only chance to penetrate the mind of the court, unless you are an expert in face-reading, and to dispel a doubt as soon as it arises. This you should be able to do if you know your case and have a sound position." John W. Davis, *The Argument of an Appeal,* 26 ABA J. 895, 897 (Dec. 1940).

(b) *Justice John M. Harlan's view.* "For some reason that I have never been able to understand, many lawyers regard questioning by the court as a kind of subversive intrusion. And yet, when one comes to sit on the other side of the bar, he finds very quickly that the answer made to a vital question may be more persuasive in leading the court to the right result than the most eloquent of oral arguments." Hon. John M. Harlan, *What Part Does the Oral Argument Play in the Conduct of an Appeal?,* 41 Cornell L.Q. 6, 9 (1955).

(c) *Justice Ruth Bader Ginsburg's view.* "[I]n the most essential way, oral argument at the Supreme Court is what it is generally in federal and many state appellate tribunals — an occasion for an exchange of ideas about the case, a dialogue or discussion between knowledgeable counsel and judges who have done their homework, a 'hot bench,' as appellate advocates say. Some lawyers, I have been told, resent interruption of an oral argument carefully planned as a lecture, and some judges ask few questions. . . . But it seems to me a waste of precious opportunity to use oral argument to recapitulate the briefing instead of uncovering what is in the decision-makers' minds." Hon. Ruth Bader Ginsburg, *Remarks for American Law Institute Annual Dinner, May 19, 1994,* 38 St. Louis L.J. 881, 885 (1994).

(d) *Essence of oral argument.* "Answering questions is what oral argument is all about; everything else is secondary. You should welcome questions. Questions show the court is interested in your case." Henry D. Gabriel, *Preparation and Delivery of Oral Argument in Appellate Courts,* 22 Am. J. Trial Advoc. 571, 585 (1999).

(e) *Some fatherly advice.* "Rejoice when the Court asks you questions. It indicates that you are arguing, not before morons, but before judges eager to be informed. . . . It has been well said that the Judge knows where his doubts lie, at which point he wishes to be enlightened; it is he whose mind must be made up, no one can do it for him, and he must take his own course of thought to accomplish it." Hon. Horace Stern, *Letters from a Judge to His Lawyer Son,* 21 Temple L.Q. 1, 22 (1947).

(f) *Opportunity for your best work.* "Questions from the court present the opportunity for the advocate to get in some of his best work. He should welcome them; he should meet them fairly and squarely." Hon. Herbert F. Goodrich, *A Case on Appeal — A Judge's View* 28 (1952).

(g) *Manna from heaven.* "In an assemblage where the purpose is to inform and persuade, it is like manna from heaven for the potential persuadee to say to the persuader: 'Here is what troubles me about the subject on which you are trying to convince me.' This opening into the mind of the listener is the most valuable piece of information the persuader can get." Hon. John Godbold, *Twenty Pages and Twenty Minutes — Effective Advocacy on Appeal,* 30 Sw. L.J. 801, 818 (1976).

(h) *Best chance to persuade the court.* "Lawyers should not be afraid of questions from the bench. Treat the question as an opportunity to clarify what the judge is thinking now, rather than later when you receive the opinion or decision. If the question indicates you are prevailing, you can fortify your position. If you are losing, you know where your problem lies and can attempt to change the court's mind." Hon. Patti S. Kitching, *The Last Word,* S.F. Daily J., 30 July 1999, at 6.

(i) *What questioning can mean.* "Questions from the bench may indicate that (a) the court knows nothing about the case, (b) not enough about the case, or (c) too much about the case. If the question involves the first two, counsel can provide enlightenment; if it involves the third, counsel may have salvaged a near miss. These questions may be the only indication you will have of what the court regards as important and decisive, and it is a golden opportunity to present the best side of your client's case then and there." Hon. Frank R. Kenison, *Some Aspects of Appellate Arguments*, N.H.B.J., Jan. 1959, at 5, 8.

(j) *Staying flexible.* "Flexibility in an oral argument is the fruit of resourcefulness and hard work. It is absolutely indispensable. A fixed or prepared written argument is doomed. Your argument must adjust to the questioning of the court as well as your opponent's presentation. I must warn you that, without that adaptability, your opportunity for persuasion will be a failure and neither you nor the court will learn anything of value from the exercise." Hon. Irving R. Kaufman, *Appellate Advocacy in the Federal Courts*, 79 F.R.D. 165, 171–72 (1978).

(k) *Neophytes vs. veterans.* "There is no greater difference between the novice and the veteran oral advocate than in the way they respond to questioning from the bench. The former is almost put off that the court would dare intrude on his or her time by interrupting, or is visibly nervous by the interchange from the court. The latter, however, views questions from the court as a godsend because he or she knows that questions are windows on the court's concerns about the issues in the case, and that every question carries with it an invitation to persuade the court that your position, and not your opponent's, is the one that should prevail." Hon. Brian Wice, *Oral Argument in Criminal Cases: 10 Tips for Winning the Moot Court Round*, Tex. B.J., Mar. 2006, at 224, 228.

(l) *Chance to make your best points.* "[Y]ou should always view questions as an opportunity to make your own affirmative points. The best advocates can turn almost any question to their own advantage. The best approach is not to regard a question as an attack on your position, but rather as an opportunity for you to score points. If you have thought through your case, you should be able to come up with adequate responses to most questions the court is apt to ask." Hon. William J. Bauer & William C. Bryson, "The Appeal," in *Master Advocates' Handbook* 261, 281 (D. Lake Rumsey ed., 1986).

(m) *Chance to address judges' concerns.* "People walk out of the Court and say, 'That was unbelievable. I got up there with five brilliant points that I just had to make, and those guys just kept interrupting me. They would not let me say two words.' . . . [O]ne should realize that that was the greatest opportunity. You now have a perfect window into the minds of the Justices. They are telling you exactly what is bothering them. But if your attitude is that you have all these other points that you want to make, and you do not really want to take the time to have to deal with whatever seems to be in the Justices' brains, then you are in trouble." Carter G. Phillips, *Advocacy Before the United States Supreme Court*, 15 T.M. Cooley L. Rev. 177, 190 (1988).

(n) *Letting go of your talking points.* "I hear it all the time: 'Look, I came up here; I had my fifteen minutes to tell you something, and you guys started asking questions, and you never stopped. You took all my time.' I'll tell you why you shouldn't worry about it. The judges have read your briefs, and they've read what the trial court did. They understand the case, and you should consider questions as totally friendly. Do the best job you can in answering them, but don't worry about anything you didn't have a chance to mention." Hon. Robert R. Baldock et al., *What Appellate Advocates Seek from Appellate Judges and What Appellate Judges Seek from Appellate Advocates*, 31 N.M.L. Rev. 265, 276 (2001).

(o) *Fundamental misunderstanding of questions.* "Many lawyers, particularly inexperienced ones, view questions as an annoyance, a distraction, and an interruption from their carefully prepared presentation. It is understandable that lawyers want to discuss each and every point they believe to be important in a methodical, scripted way. But this attitude represents a fundamental misunderstanding of the opportunity that a question presents." Hon. Douglas S. Lavine, *Responding to Questions*, Nat'l L.J., 1 Jan. 2007, at 20.

(p) *Dialogue replacing monologue.* "In certain courts of appeal, the questioning by the judges is so intensive that the lawyer must be ready to accept — without expressing frustration — that all his or her meticulous preparation of the argument will remain in the advocate's outline or mind and, instead of the attorney's intended monologue, the argument will be a dialogue between the judges and counsel." Roberto Aron et al., *Trial Communication Skills* § 14.07, at 14-4 (1996).

(q) *Eliciting a question.* "If [the lawyer] sees that one of the judges seems to want to talk but isn't going to get a chance, he must try to get that judge to say something. Because if the judge has a question and he doesn't get to ask it, he's going to think about that question anyway. Therefore, it's better to try to get it out. Find out what it is and then you can answer it." Hon. Stephen Breyer, interviewed by Bryan A. Garner (6 Nov. 2006).

(r) *Shaping the argument.* "[J]udges exercise considerable control during oral argument, and it is the goal of the astute appellate practitioner to shape the argument nonetheless, through his or her answers to questions." Jennifer S. Carroll, *Appellate Specialization and the Art of Appellate Advocacy*, 74 Fla. B.J. 107, 109 (June 2000).

(s) *Inflexibility as a disservice to client.* "Lawyers who are determined to stick to their prepared remarks, or who are unprepared to adapt to the Court's concept of oral argument, are likely to have a very unsatisfactory experience. They also will accomplish little for their clients." Charles A. Rothfeld, *Avoiding Missteps in the Supreme Court: A Guide to Resources for Counsel*, 7 J. App. Prac. & Proc. 249, 252 (Fall 2005).

(t) *Tuning the cymbals.* "While it may be true, in the trenchant phrase of Bacon, that 'an overspeaking judge is no well-tuned cymbal,' it is not for you as appellate counsel to criticize the talkativeness of the court but rather to seize the chance offered by his question to get into the judge's mind and quell his doubts or satisfy his curiosity." Ralph M. Carson, *Conduct of the Appeal — A Lawyer's View* 36, 84 (1952).

(u) *Danger of announcing eagerness.* "While questions from the bench should be welcomed, it is hardly necessary to make such a pronouncement. If a lawyer announces at the outset that the court may ask him questions, he is invading the province of the court, which will ask questions or not as it wishes." Owen Rall, "Persuasive Oral Argument," in *Lawyer's Encyclopedia* 1019, 1031 (1963).

(v) *Demonstrating confidence.* "[C]apable advocates welcome the opportunity to clarify matters the judges consider important but which are unclear to them. Is it not fair to suggest that counsel whose preference it is that judges keep their questions to themselves have little confidence in their persuasive abilities?" T.W. Wakeling, *The Oral Component of Appellate Work*, 5 Dalhousie L.J. 584, 597 (1979).

(w) *Questioning may be lopsided.* "[I]n the *Briggs* school-desegregation case argued along with *Brown* [*v. Board of Education*], John Davis, defending segregation, was interrupted only 11 times, but Thurgood Marshall was interrupted 127 times." Stephen L. Wasby, *The Supreme Court in the Federal Judicial System* 162 (1978). "Marshall invited questioning; Davis discouraged it." *Id.* at 163.

(x) *Sometimes just two sentences.* "It took two sentences before Justice Scalia threw me my first curve, and we were off my outline and on to the Justices' questions. They came quickly and from all sides. And at some point, to my amazement, it began to feel more like a lively dinner-table conversation than an argument before the highest court in the land." Christina M. Tchen, *Still Grateful After All These Years*, 5 J. App. Prac. & Proc. 157, 160 (Spring 2003).

63. Never talk at the same time as a judge. Yield the floor.

If you're speaking and a judge interrupts, stop talking immediately and listen. When a judge asks you a question, wait for the entire question before answering. Because there is no parity in the right to speak, you must show forbearance.

(a) *Classic statement 1.* "The court rightly considers the argument to be for its own purpose only and feels entirely within its power and jurisdiction to interrupt, propose questions, make comments, or shorten or even abruptly terminate the argument. As a result an attorney unprepared for such an emergency may suffer from mental confusion and be unable to extricate himself or reconstruct his plans so as to be in any sense effective." Jesse Franklin Brumbaugh, *Legal Reasoning and Briefing* 597–98 (1917).

(b) *Classic statement 2.* "The most malicious thing a judge can do to a lawyer is to let him talk on without interrupting him when he is talking uselessly or to the detriment of his client." Piero Calamandrei, *Eulogy of Judges* 40 (1936; John Clarke Adams & C. Abbott Phillips Jr. eds, 1942; repr. 1992).

(c) *Classic statement 3.* "The court is entitled to interrupt the attorney; the attorney is not entitled to interrupt the court." Alan D. Hornstein, *Appellate Advocacy in a Nutshell* 253 (1984).

(d) *Giving your full attention.* "Never under any circumstance interrupt a Justice who is addressing you. Give your full time and attention to that Justice — do not look down at your notes and do not look at your watch. If you are speaking and a Justice interrupts you, cease talking immediately and listen." Michael B. Tigar & Jane B.

Tigar, *Federal Appeals: Jurisdiction and Practice* § 10.09, at 519–20 (3d ed. 1999).

(e) *Rules of engagement.* "Interrupting a judge during argument is always a very bad idea. Fair or not, the rules of engagement permit judges to interrupt lawyers while they are arguing, but the reverse is not true.... The acumen with which you handle interruptions and stay focused and in control sends unmistakable signals about your skill as an advocate." Hon. Douglas S. Lavine, *New Year, New Approach*, Nat'l L.J., 14 Jan. 2008, at 14.

(f) *Stopping in midsyllable.* "Learn to shut up; if one of the justices starts asking a question, stop in midsyllable if necessary." William J. Boyce, *Reflections on Going to the Show*, 17 App. Advocate (report of the State Bar of Texas Appellate Section), Summer 2004, at 21, 23.

(g) *Waiting for the whole question.* "Not only should you stop immediately when a judge begins a question, you need to wait until the judge finishes the question before you start your answer. There are two points here. First, *listen* to the entire question. Do not anticipate based on just a few words and then tune out the balance of the question while you consider your answer. You may end up answering the wrong question. Second, do not interrupt the judge either to finish the question yourself or to begin your answer before the judge finishes articulating every word. Given the extent of your preparation you may know immediately the point the judge is trying to make and you may be able more quickly to articulate it, but doing so is rude and will gain you no points. As painful as it may be on occasion, let the judge get every word of the question out before you presume to be able to answer it." Bradley G. Clary et al., *Advocacy on Appeal* 122 (2d ed. 2004).

(h) *Winning attitude.* "I once began a question with an apology for interrupting counsel's argument. He turned to me and said that he was happy to answer it, since whatever interested the court interested him. That is a winning attitude." Hon. Michael J. Wilkins, *Remember, for Every Case Won at Oral Argument, the Other Side Loses*, Utah B.J., Sept. 2004, at 36, 37.

(i) *Listening carefully, answering clearly.* "The lawyer should stop talking as soon as the court interrupts, listen carefully to the question and try to answer as clearly and persuasively as possible." Ursula

Bentele & Eve Cary, *Appellate Advocacy: Principle and Practice* 370 (1998).

(j) *No exceptions.* "When a judge asks a question, you must immediately stop talking. There is no exception. I have seen lawyers from both sides of the aisle lose the attention and respect of the court by talking over a judge, or, worse, arguing with a judge." Hon. Brian Wice, *Oral Argument in Criminal Cases: 10 Tips for Winning the Moot Court Round*, Tex. B.J., Mar. 2006, at 224, 228–29.

(k) *Not your competitor.* "The Court is not your competitor. When one of the justices wants center stage, give it up. No matter how brilliant or how telling the point you are making, when one of the justices says something, you should stop talking and start listening." Rex E. Lee, *Oral Argument in the Supreme Court*, 72 ABA J. 60, 61 (June 1986).

(l) *Being respectful, not obsequious.* "[G]raciously stop speaking if interrupted by a judge. After all, he is giving you a hint of a concern he has, and your job is to convince him, not to out-talk or overwhelm him. You need not be obsequious, but you must be respectful." John T. Gaubatz & Taylor Mattis, *The Moot Court Book* 103 (3d ed. 1994).

64. Listen carefully to every question — just as you would advise a deponent to do.

Advocates sometimes misunderstand exactly what a judge has asked. The lawyer might then answer only part of the question, or perhaps answer a different question altogether — one the lawyer thought was being asked or wished had been asked. To prevent this common failing, focus hard on the judges' questions.

(a) *Classic statement 1.* "I stress how important it is to listen to the questions. What I find — and this is perhaps the biggest mistake lawyers make — is that they do not listen. Lawyers are notorious for not listening. They are too anxious to speak. The judge begins to ask a question and the lawyer assumes he knows where the judge is going and the automatic pilot kicks in and he starts answering — often in the middle of the question." Hon. Alex Kozinski (interview), Jeffrey Cole, *My Afternoon with Alex: An Interview with Judge Kozinski*, 30 Litig. 6, 18 (Summer 2004).

(b) *Classic statement 2.* When asked what he would do differently if he were an advocate again, Chief Justice John Roberts answered that he would "listen a little more carefully to what the questions are." Hon. John Roberts, at the Ninth Circuit Judicial Conference, 13 July 2006.

(c) *Not a time for oratory.* "Appreciate that oral argument is not an occa-sion for speech-making. Not in a court like this, and it certainly wasn't so on the D.C. Circuit. These are hot benches; the judges are prepared to the hilt. You will do best if you concentrate on the questions you are being asked and not resent them as distract-ing you from your prepared lecture." Hon. Ruth Bader Ginsburg, interviewed by Bryan A. Garner (13 Nov. 2006).

(d) *"The question within the question."* "What makes for the best oral arguments? Not 'argument' at all, but answers to the questions that resolve in your client's favor the doubts of the panel members. It can be useful to listen for the 'question within the question.' Usually, something specific is bothering the inquiring judge. Lis-ten closely to the question that was asked. But listen, too, for the question that was only implied, and try to answer it as well." Hon. Paul R. Michel, *Effective Appellate Advocacy*, 24 Litig. 19, 22 (Sum-mer 1998).

(e) *Avoiding partial answers.* "If you are going to be able to intelligently answer a question, you must first *listen* to the question. . . . [I]t is surprising how often appellate advocates, just like many people in private conversation, seem to hear only part of the question, and respond to the part of it that they heard even though the answer they give may not be an adequate response to the entire question. Whether the question is hostile or friendly, first understand the question, and then give the best answer you can for the purpose of advancing your cause." Hon. William H. Rehnquist, *Oral Advocacy*, 27 S. Tex. L. Rev. 289, 302 (1986).

(f) *Seeking clarification.* "Be sure you understand the questions before you answer them. If you are unsure exactly what the question is, ask for a clarification. Some questions are friendly. It is to your advantage to spot them!" Henry D. Gabriel, *Preparation and Deliv-ery of Oral Argument in Appellate Courts*, 22 Am. J. Trial Advoc. 571, 585 (1999).

(g) *Justice Stephen Breyer's advice.* "Listen to the question. It's what you tell a witness. Listen to the question, think about it for a second, and answer that question. That judge is worried about something, so answer it." Hon. Stephen Breyer, interviewed by Bryan A. Garner (6 Nov. 2006).

(h) *Devoting full attention.* "The only purpose of oral argument is to provoke and encourage questions from the bench. If you do not believe this or cannot cope with this, let someone else argue the case or waive oral argument. If you can cope, then listen carefully to the questions and stop your thought even in the middle of a sentence if a judge leans forward in a questioning posture." Hon. Abner J. Mikva, "Taking an Appeal," in *Appellate Advocacy* 4–5 (28 Oct. 1994).

65. If you speak second, listen closely to what the judges say in questioning your opponent.

If you carefully register the questions that the judges pose to your adversary, you can tailor your responses to the judges' stated concerns and clarify any points they seem to have misunderstood. Most questions to your opponent you might advantageously treat as questions to *you*.

(a) *Classic statement 1.* "The attorney for the appellee should pay special attention to the initial argument by counsel for the appellant and to the Court's questions during that argument, because sometimes it is more important for the appellee's attorney to address what seems to be troubling the Court than it is to get into his or her prepared presentation." Hon. Andrew D. Christie (as quoted in Hon. Ruggero J. Aldisert, *Winning on Appeal* 306 (1992)).

(b) *Classic statement 2.* "If you're the respondent or appellee, you should listen closely to the questions fired at your opponent. If the court seems to agree with your position, you're frequently better off saying nothing. But if the judges appear confused or mistaken on a point, or they haven't disclosed a solid view, you can say, 'I heard the court to have concerns about . . . . Let me respond briefly.'" Jason Vail, *Oral Argument's Big Challenge: Fielding Questions from the Court*, 1 J. App. Prac. & Proc. 401, 407–08 (Summer 1999).

(c) *Addressing each point.* "[T]he respondent must listen carefully to the other side's conversation with the panel and address each of the specific points raised there with clear, brief, pithy responses that incorporate the respondent's salient points, preferably in the context of the controlling precedent, statute, or standard of review. The respondent should be careful to put its strongest points first but to respond to each of the other side's points made during argument, particularly if the panel has signaled its interest in one or more of them." Catherine Valerio Barrad, *Successful Oral Arguments Do Not Involve Any Arguing*, S.F. Daily J., 4 Aug. 2004, at 5, 6.

(d) *Answering questions asked of your opponent.* "Listen to questions judges ask the other side, and be ready to answer them when you argue. If the subject is important enough, answer even if it isn't asked again." Edward L. Lascher, *Oral Argument*, 7 Cal. Litig. 16, 20 (Winter 1994).

66. Willingly answer hypotheticals.

Appellate courts are concerned not only with the outcome of your case but also with how their ruling will affect the law generally. Understandably, the judges want to know how far their ruling might extend. So they often ask hypothetical questions about how the ruling an advocate seeks would play out under different sets of facts. Part of your preparation must include fathoming the broader implications of the ruling you seek.

(a) *Classic statement 1.* "Be prepared for hypothetical questions designed to determine the extent to which a case is cited. What, if any, are the policy implications of a particular argument? How will the court's decision affect future cases? Answer the questions thoroughly and directly." Hon. Judith W. Rogers (as quoted in Hon. Ruggero J. Aldisert, *Winning on Appeal* 306 (1992)).

(b) *Classic statement 2.* "The inexperienced advocate too often responds to a hypothetical with, 'That's not this case,' which has to rank among the most insulting answers possible to a question from the bench. The questioner knows the hypothetical is not this case, but nonetheless wants to know how a case farther out from the core of the rule suggested by a party would come out under that party's theory." David C. Frederick, *Supreme Court and Appellate Advocacy* 102 (2003).

(c) *Avoiding narrow answers.* "Be careful when you answer a hypothetical question posed by a Justice. A 'yes' or 'no' answer might be suitable for a narrow question. Nevertheless, your answer should be carefully tailored to fit the question. A simple 'yes' or 'no' in response to a broad question might unintentionally concede something that produces a follow-on question, the answer to which is damaging to your position." Michael B. Tigar & Jane B. Tigar, *Federal Appeals: Jurisdiction and Practice* § 10.09, at 519 (3d ed. 1999).

(d) *Anticipating hypotheticals.* "Hypothetical questions, of course, must be addressed when posed. There is no justification for not being ready to answer such questions. The identification of potential hypothetical questions must be part of your oral-argument preparation." Gaele McLaughlin Barthold, *Questions by Appellate-Court Jurists: A Threat or an Opportunity?*, Certworthy (Defense Research Inst. App. Advocacy Comm. newsletter), Winter 2001, at 4.

(e) *Purpose of hypotheticals (1).* "The biggest mistake you can make in oral argument is to not answer the question. If a Justice gives you a hypothetical, do not say, 'Well, that is not this case.' Of course that is not this case: that is why it is called a hypothetical." Carter G. Phillips, *Advocacy Before the United States Supreme Court*, 15 T.M. Cooley L. Rev. 177, 192 (1988).

(f) *Purpose of hypotheticals (2).* "Judges often ask hypothetical questions to test the application of the rule you are advocating against different sets of facts. Do not fight the hypothetical. Answer the question, and, if necessary, tell the panel why your case is different. Remember the court is not only deciding your case, which is your primary concern, but is establishing rules for future cases, which is the court's primary concern." Rex S. Heinke & Tracy L. Casadio, *Oral Argument in the Federal Circuit Courts*, 16 Cal. Litig. 36, 40 (No. 2, 2003).

(g) *The wrong responses.* "When you are asked a question, do not duck it, filibuster it, ignore it, or refuse to answer." Hon. Eugene M. Premo, *The Art of Oral Argument*, 15 Cal. Litig. 45, 48 (No. 3, 2002).

(h) *The worst response.* "Because of the Court's need to take a broad and long-run view, Justices frequently ask hypothetical questions going well beyond the facts of the case before them. Very seldom is it wise to say to the Court, in answer to a question, 'The Court need not reach that question in this case.' More than once a Justice has replied, 'I do need to reach it.'" Hon. Simon H. Rifkind, "Appellate Courts Compared," in *Counsel on Appeal* 163, 183 (Arthur A. Charpentier ed., 1968).

67. Answer questions directly at the outset, with a yes or no, or perhaps "Yes, with two qualifications" or "No, Your Honor, but the point has some subtleties."

A judge who asks a question expects a memo-style short answer first, and perhaps a clarification or qualification after that. The judge will probably feel impatient with a lawyer who begins with a discussion before saying yes or no.

(a) *Classic statement 1.* "The advocate need only train herself to *first* respond with a clear expression of agreement or disagreement with the point of the question. Only *after* this clear 'Yes' or 'No' should any necessary explanation be advanced. The failure to do so may merely reflect the advocate's fear of taking a firm position without being certain of where that position may lead. The answer to such trepidation, however, is thorough preparation. If the advocate has thoroughly immersed herself in her case, she should be sufficiently confident of her instincts that even an unanticipated question can be responded to unambiguously — certainly after a brief pause to consider the import of the question and the consequences of various responses." Alan D. Hornstein, *Appellate Advocacy in a Nutshell* 301 (1984).

(b) *Classic statement 2.* "Oral argument preparation should include practicing the use of two words. They are the two most needed words in the advocate's arsenal. One of those words is 'yes,' and the other is 'no.' In general, answers to oral argument questions are too long, and many are needlessly evasive. I have observed that this can be irritating to the questioner and to other members of the Court. Evasive answers also tend to bring more questioners into the fray, and questions that result from prior evasive answers usually are not helpful to your case. . . . [W]hen a yes or no question is asked, the first word that comes from your mouth should be a yes or no. Departing from this little gem of wisdom is probably the most frequent reason Supreme Court oral arguments come unhinged." Rex E. Lee, *Oral Argument in the Supreme Court*, 72 ABA J. 60, 60–61 (June 1986).

(c) *Classic statement 3.* "Even if the question hurts your position, answer it directly. The angriest I have ever seen a state appellate-court justice was with an attorney who refused to give a direct answer to the court's question. Even with a hostile question, use it as a device to persuade the court." Bob Foster, *Oral Advocacy at the Supreme Court of the United States*, Fed. Law. (Sept. 2002), at 23, 23.

(d) *Yea or nay.* "Some advocates need coaching before they understand that when justices ask a yes-or-no question, they want a direct answer. An advocate can go on to explain that answer . . . but must first answer the question with 'yes' or 'no.'" Gregory J. Langlois, *Dress Rehearsal: The Moot Court Program at Georgetown Law Center's Supreme Court Institute*, 7 J. App. Prac. & Proc. 231, 245 (Fall 2005).

(e) *The courage of directly answering damaging questions.* "Questions from the bench should be answered . . . directly and without equivocation. Where a question requires an answer harmful to the advocate's contention, he should courageously give the answer and acknowledge its effect. Where he does not know the answer, he should graciously and frankly say so." Abraham L. Freedman, *On Advocacy*, 1 Vill. L. Rev. 290, 308 (1956).

(f) *No meandering.* "Be responsive. Answer the question directly. Some first-time advocates have a tendency, particularly early in the argument, to give long, rambling answers that cover much more ground than the question requires. Such an answer may obscure the point you need to make and may bore or confuse your listeners." Karen K. Porter et al., *Introduction to Legal Writing and Oral Advocacy* § 16.05, at 175 (1989).

(g) *The cowering pugilist.* "Too often, I have observed lawyers damage their case by dodging the question asked or bobbing and weaving like a boxer when a straight answer would suffice. . . . Beginning your answer with a 'yes' or 'no,' and then embellishing or redirecting the thrust of the question is a useful technique because once the questioner hears the word 'yes' or 'no,' he or she believes his or her concerns are being addressed." Hon. Douglas S. Lavine, *Responding to Questions*, Nat'l L.J., 1 Jan. 2007, at 20.

(h) *Fomenting impatience.* "Don't delay your answer. If you delay it even a few sentences, you may get an unfavorable listener reaction. 'Will he ever come to the point?' is an unuttered question [that] forms quickly in impatient minds." Richard C. Borden, *Public Speaking as Listeners Like It* 26 (1935).

(i) *Let the ceiling fall.* "An advocate should regard having the chandelier fall on him as vastly preferable to failing to respond to a question from the bench. That is the one absolute 'don't' in an enterprise [that] is highly personalized, individualistic, and resourceful by nature. The question must be answered." Edward L. Lascher, *Oral Argument for Fun and Profit*, Cal. St. B.J., Jul./Aug. 1973, at 398, 402.

(j) *The futility of dodging.* "Counsel can never dodge questions. First, dodging questions will anger the judge. Second, it will make you appear unsure of your case. Third, the court will corner you into answering the question anyway." Henry D. Gabriel, *Preparation and Delivery of Oral Argument in Appellate Courts*, 22 Am. J. Trial Advoc. 571, 585 (1999).

(k) *The alienating dodger.* "I know of no greater way to alienate an appellate bench than to try to 'dance around' a direct answer." Bob Foster, *Oral Advocacy at the Supreme Court of the United States*, Fed. Law., Sept. 2002, at 23.

(l) *Handling qualifications.* "Virtually all great advocates answer questions with simple, dispositive answers. If a question calls for a yes or no answer, they give it. But the great advocates also perceive and appreciate when a member of the court is badgering them into making a yes or no concession that will be used in an incomplete and distorted way. There are a number of different approaches to dealing with this problem. First, if the advocate has answered a series of questions with a yes or a no, he can realistically expect the court to give him some leeway if he suddenly puts a qualifier in the answer before saying yes or no. Another approach is to say, 'Yes, but not in all cases and here is why.' Or, 'Generally, yes.' That method softens the harsh effect that can sometimes be produced with a yes or no answer." David C. Frederick, *Supreme Court and Appellate Advocacy* 233 (2003).

(m) *Getting the time out of joint.* "Respond to each question when it is asked. Avoid references forward to arguments you had intended to defer to a later time in your presentation. . . . By similar token, resist the temptation to respond with, 'As I said a moment ago . . . .' The implication is that the questioner may not have been listening attentively." Hon. Hugh R. Jones, *Appellate Advocacy, Written and Oral*, J. Mo. Bar, June 1991, at 297, 303.

(n) *Mislaid hearing aid as a poor excuse.* "In another case, a lawyer from Arkansas — as a matter of fact, a former state Supreme Court Judge — absolutely refused to respond to questions during his oral argument. Finally, my colleague, Senior Judge (then Chief Judge) Matthes, literally screamed, 'Counsel, why don't you respond to questions.' The attorney responded, 'When I come to St. Louis, I leave my hearing aid at home.'" Hon. Myron H. Bright, *The Changing Nature of the Federal Appeals Process in the 1970's*, 65 F.R.D. 496, 507 (1975).

68. After your prompt response, explain your answer more fully if necessary. Never postpone an answer until you've explained something else.

Judges get especially irritated when an advocate answers a question with something like, "I'll get to that in a moment." The judge's understandable instinct is to believe that the advocate is either unprepared or evasive. And the judge who asked the question is likely to become skeptical. Finally, the delay raises the risk that, as often happens, the advocate never will get around to answering.

(a) *Classic statement 1.* "Do not postpone the answering of a question, for if you do the judge will be thinking of nothing but whether you are going to get back to him. Until you do, he will not be a good auditor, and unless you do, he will have a mark against you on his book." Hon. Frank G. Hamley, *Appellate Advocacy*, 12 Ark. L. Rev. 129, 137 (1957).

(b) *Classic statement 2.* "A competent advocate offers an immediate, direct, and satisfactory answer to a judge's question. Delay is dangerous. Delay suggests a lack of preparation, evasion of the truth, or contempt for the questioner. If the search for clarity prompts the question, delay promotes ambiguity, the appellate advocate's enemy. If boredom prompts the question, delay impedes attentiveness. If sympathy prompts the question, delay disappoints an important ally. If egotism prompts the question, delay is a personal offense. Although the motivation for any particular question remains obscure, the need to answer promptly and directly is apparent." Hon. Steven D. Merryday, *Florida Appellate Practice Handbook* § 17.13 (2003).

(c) *No question-ducking.* "Immediately and directly answer the question posed. Do not duck, do not tell the justice you will get to that point, do not refer to the briefs — answer the question!" Bob Foster, *Oral Advocacy at the Supreme Court of the United States*, Fed. Law., Sept. 2002, at 23, 23.

(d) *Straight answers now.* "When courts ask questions, they want straight answers and they want them *now.* One of the worst mistakes you can make as an oral advocate is to respond to a question by saying, 'I'm getting to that,' or 'I'll address that problem later in my argument.'" William J. Bauer & William C. Bryson, *The Appeal: Part II*, Docket, Spring 1987, at 16, 19.

(e) *A Ginsburg vignette.* "A few sittings ago, to take an example still vivid in my mind, an advocate won no friends at court when he responded to a judge's question: 'Forgive me, Your Honor, but I really don't want to be derailed onto that trivial point.'" Hon. Ruth Bader Ginsburg, "Remarks for U. Va. Student Legal Forum Dinner" 7 (1990; repr. in *Appellate Advocacy* (28 Oct. 1994)).

(f) *The true meaning of "later."* "Questions from the bench should be answered when they are asked and not met with the answer, 'I'll come to that later.' 'Later,' alas, too often proves to be too late!" Hon. Harry Ellis Kalodner (as quoted in Hon. John Biggs Jr. et al., "In the Matter of Oral Argument" (1955), in *Advocacy and the King's English* 233, 237 (George Rossman ed., 1960)).

(g) *The greatest blunder of all.* "A lawyer can make no greater mistake, I assure you, in answering questions by the court than to attempt to preserve the continuity of his argument by saying, 'Judge, I have dealt with that in my brief' or by telling the judge who asks the question that he will come back to it 'later' — usually he never does. Even if the lawyer does come back to the question later on, the force of his answer, if it is a good one, and often also of his argument in other aspects where he perhaps is in a stronger position, is usually lost — at least upon the judge who has asked the question." Hon. John M. Harlan, *What Part Does the Oral Argument Play in the Conduct of an Appeal?*, 41 Cornell L.Q. 6, 9 (1955).

(h) *The macabre result of postponing.* "[I]t is fatal to postpone by saying, 'I will come to it later.' Even if you don't forget, the coming to it may be too late. For without the answer to that question everything that you may say thereafter may be left suspended in the air like a levitated body or more likely a corpse — the corpse of your dead case." Ben W. Palmer, *Courtroom Strategies* 205 (1959).

(i) *Weighing answers and nonanswers.* "All answers are weighed — as are nonanswers. If anything, nonanswers get even more weight. They tell us you have no satisfactory answer. Always give the best answer you can. Attempts to change the subject usually are obvious and will be seen as evasions. That cannot help your case." Hon. Paul R. Michel, *Effective Appellate Advocacy*, 24 Litig. 19, 22 (Summer 1998).

(j) *Unkept promises.* "Don't say, 'I'll get to that,' in response to a question. Many attorneys who answer that way never fulfill their promises. Although this is a well-known rule, it is broken more frequently than one would expect. Just a few weeks ago, a leading New York City attorney, arguing an important corporate takeover case, responded to one of my questions by saying, 'I'll get to that, Your Honor.' He never did." Hon. Roger J. Miner, "The Don'ts of Oral Argument," in *Appellate Practice Manual* 263, 265 (Priscilla Anne Schwab ed., 1992).

(k) *Sign of unpreparedness.* "The judges' questions must be answered promptly; delaying the response, even with a polite 'If Your Honor permits, I will reply to your question at the end of my presentation' can give the impression of absence of preparation or ignorance of how to reply to the question." Roberto Aron et al., *Trial Communication Skills* § 14.08, at 14-16 (1996).

(l) *Seeming evasiveness.* "Who has not heard counsel when faced with a difficulty endeavour to postpone the evil day by the time-worn phrase 'I'm coming to that'! You know and the judge knows that he never will, if he can help it. There was one very eminent counsel who is said to have emitted more promissory notes of this kind than any counsel before him and to have redeemed fewer of them. The better course is to deal at once with the point put to you." Rt. Hon. Lord Macmillan, "Some Observations on the Art of Advocacy" (1933), in *Law and Other Things* 200, 211-12 (1937).

(m) *The answer first, then details.* "[Q]uestions are most effectively dealt with when asked, not later on. If the question requires a detailed explanation that the lawyer was planning to give subsequently, the question may be answered briefly when asked, with the statement that it will be discussed in detail later." Hon. Daniel M. Friedman, *Winning on Appeal*, 9 Litig. 15, 60 (Spring 1983).

(n) *Addressing a judge's immediate interest.* "Questions from the bench indicate the judges' interest in a particular point. A lawyer should not evade or postpone the opportunity to satisfy that curiosity by answering, for example: 'I intend to deal with that a little later in my argument, your Honor.'" Alfred L. Scanlan, *Effective Appellate*

Advocacy in the Court of Appeals of Maryland, 29 Md. L. Rev. 126, 137 (1969).

(o) *Value of a prompt answer.* "Above all, oral argument calls for flexibility. If the court indicates that it is familiar with the facts and issues and desires to question me, I respond at once. I know how disconcerting it is to discard a carefully thought out argument, and how tempting it is to tell the court that you will take up those questions later. But I urge, don't postpone; answer at once. Thereby you do not antagonize the court; you may succeed in setting at rest a notion that troubles a judge and you at once exhibit your complete command of the case." Hon. Milton B. Pollack, *Some Practical Aspects of Appellate Advocacy*, N.Y. St. B. Bull., Feb. 1959, at 81, 87.

(p) *Answering when asked.* "Answer the question when it is asked. Even if you get an invitation like, 'Feel free to give me the answer later in your argument if you prefer,' don't accept the invitation. First, you may never get to page 5. Second, your job is not to add to the world's inventory of logical prose." Rex E. Lee, *Oral Argument in the Supreme Court*, 72 ABA J. 60, 61 (June 1986).

(q) *What judges expect.* "Inexperienced attorneys frequently antagonize the Court by evading questions — responding, for example, by saying 'that presents a different case,' or 'that really isn't what this case is about.' The Court is well aware that its questions call for analysis of a point different from the point counsel is pressing. It nonetheless expects a direct answer." Stephen M. Shapiro, *Oral Argument in the Supreme Court of the United States*, 33 Catholic U. Am. L. Rev. 529, 543 (1984).

(r) *Answering as best you can.* "[I]f the judge wants to know something, it is highly advisable for counsel to tell him the answer as well as he can. He should not postpone answering his judicial questioner and he certainly should not evade." Hon. Herbert F. Goodrich, *A Case on Appeal — A Judge's View* 28 (1952).

(s) *Visualizing a door opening.* "We have all too often heard the appeasing formula of counsel tied to his outline, 'I will come to that later' and have noted the dissatisfaction of the inquiring judge who wanted the matter disposed of while it was fresh in his mind.... The best way, if your preliminary preparation has so saturated you with the case that you can deal with it extemporaneously, is to reorganize your argument from the point of view of the question, and make your entry into the court's mind through the door it has opened." Ralph M. Carson, *Conduct of the Appeal — A Lawyer's View* 36, 85 (1952).

(t) *Risks of delaying.* "The psychological time to answer is now. It is the time when the court's interest in that particular point is keenest and the time when the court will probably be most receptive to an intelligent attempt to satisfy its curiosity. Delay in answering risks loss of the inquiring judge's attention, which may be diverted to something far afield or concentrated on another point by the time the answer is belatedly given. Delay in answering risks loss of the interrogating judge's attention in subsequent parts of your argument while he sits and ponders the problem posed by his question, which you have not answered. Delay in answering risks the possibility that the judges will gain the impression that it is futile to seek your help in informing them on matters [that] are troubling them and will sit back through the balance of your argument without attempting to elicit further information from you by way of questions no matter how puzzled they may be." Roy L. Steinheimer Jr., *Winning on Appeal*, 20 Mich. St. B.J. 16, 22 (Oct. 1950).

69. If you don't understand a question, say so with due modesty.

There's no shame or embarrassment in asking a judge to explain a question. It's far better to ask for help than to try to answer a question that you don't understand. Now *that's* a recipe for shame and embarrassment.

(a) *Classic statement 1.* "If you can't answer the question, say so, and if the question defies understanding, or at least you can't understand it, *say so.* Usually the judge will rephrase it, preferably in a more understandable form." Hon. William J. Bauer & William C. Bryson, "The Appeal," in *Master Advocates' Handbook* 261, 281 (D. Lake Rumsey ed., 1986).

(b) *Classic statement 2.* "[T]he defining point in the argument came during an exchange with Justice White. He asked me a question — directed a comment at me, really — that I just didn't understand. The moment presented me with a terrible dilemma. Should I start babbling and hope that I'd say something responsive? Or should I announce in front of the world that I just didn't get it, thereby confirming that I had no business being there in the first place? I paused for a moment and then calmly said, 'Your honor, I regret to say that I do not understand your point.' It was no big deal. Justice White simply rephrased what he was trying to say. More than one person came up to me afterwards to say that they didn't know what he was getting at either." J. Richard Cohen, *Pretender in Paradise*, 5 J. App. Prac. & Proc. 87, 88 (Spring 2003).

(c) *Prompting a rephrased question.* "[I]f counsel entertains any doubts about a question, the proper course is to seek a restatement, a request the court will honor, if the matter is significant." T.W. Wakeling, *The Oral Component of Appellate Work*, 5 Dalhousie L.J. 584, 599 (1979).

(d) *No mind games.* "[Y]ou should realize that Justices do not play games with your mind. It is not like most moot courts, where people come in and just ask questions to see how smart you are, and whether you are going to faint during the procedure. That is not what the Justices are there for. They really are trying to figure out the answer to the question. Thus, they will ask you questions that are designed to help them understand." Carter G. Phillips, *Advocacy Before the United States Supreme Court*, 15 T.M. Cooley L. Rev. 177, 194 (1988).

(e) *A suggested response.* "When a question seems unclear to counsel, it is proper to say, 'Your Honor, I am sorry that I have not understood the question.' Counsel, however, should not invoke this response too often since it may be interpreted as a dilatory tactic." Hon. Edward D. Re, *Brief Writing and Oral Argument* 200 (6th ed. 1987).

(f) *Asking for clarification.* "If you are unclear about what the judge is asking, so indicate." Hon. Daniel M. Friedman, *Winning on Appeal*, 9 Litig. 15, 60 (Spring 1983).

(g) *Example of an incomprehensible question from Justice Frankfurter.* "Mr. Butler, why aren't the two decisions of this court, the first one, which laid down as a Constitutional requirement that this court unanimously felt compelled to agree upon, and the second opinion recognizing that this was a change of what had been supposed to be the provisions of the Constitution, and recognizing that and the kind of life that has been built under the contrary conception said, as equity also has said, you must make appropriate accommodation to the specific circumstances of the situation instead of having a procrustean bed where everybody's legs are cut off or stretched to fit the length of the bed, and who is better to decide that than the local United States Judges, why isn't that a national policy?" Hon. Felix Frankfurter (as quoted in H.S. Thomas, *Felix Frankfurter, Scholar on the Bench* 356 (1960) (citing a press report of the stenographic record)).

70. If you don't know the answer to a question, say so and offer to submit a supplemental brief on the point.

There are times when no matter how thorough the preparation, a question will stump the advocate. The best approach is to be frank in admitting that you don't know the answer. If the court is amenable, you might offer to answer the question in a short supplemental brief.

(a) *Classic statement 1.* "Do not hesitate to admit lack of information, if the court interrupts with a question for which you do not have the answer." Neva B. Talley-Morris, *Appellate Civil Practice and Procedure Handbook* 220 (1975).

(b) *Classic statement 2.* "If a lawyer does not know the answer to a question, he should not try to bluff his way through it. He is likely to get caught and be seriously embarrassed. There is nothing wrong with saying 'I don't know' — provided you do not have to say it too often." Hon. Daniel M. Friedman, *Winning on Appeal*, 9 Litig. 15, 60 (Spring 1983).

(c) *Classic statement 3.* "If you do not know the answer, avoid 'winging it.' That can only lead to trouble. It is better to admit frankly that you do not know, and offer to submit a postargument brief on that point. Attempts to evade a question are usually transparent." David G. Knibb, *Federal Court of Appeals Manual* § 26.5, at 320 (1990).

(d) *Instant analysis.* "Legal, hypothetical, or policy questions must be answered on the spot to the best of one's ability. It is permissible to say 'I have not considered that variant of our situation,' but counsel then should proceed to indicate what factors are pertinent and give his best analysis of the proper outcome." Stephen M. Shapiro, *Oral Argument in the Supreme Court of the United States*, 33 Catholic U. Am. L. Rev. 529, 546 (1984).

(e) *No bluffing.* "Do not bluff or wing it if a judge asks you a question that you cannot answer. If the question goes to the heart of your case, ask for leave to file a supplemental brief. At the same time, do not be gun-shy, or give the impression of disingenuousness or lack of candor by refusing to make unavoidable concessions. You do not have to worry too much about conceding your case away on oral argument. Judges will not hold lawyers to concessions made in the heat of the argument unless they have decided to resolve the case against the lawyer who made the concession anyway, and will merely use the concession to strengthen the opinion." Hon. Richard A. Posner, *Convincing a Federal Court of Appeals*, 25 Litig. 3, 63 (Winter 1999).

(f) *Handling an "undigested difficulty."* "Counsel should always respond to the question directly, either by answering it or by conceding a present unreadiness to answer. . . . [I]f a question raises an 'undigested difficulty,' it is preferable to admit that counsel has not thought of that matter, rather than weaken or detract from the high caliber of a well-reasoned argument by a poor answer. This is especially true if the question is only tangential to the issue. Counsel may also offer to submit a supplemental memorandum on that particular point." Hon. Edward D. Re, *Brief Writing and Oral Argument* 199–200 (6th ed. 1987).

(g) *Understanding the theory of your case.* "If you understand what theory you have to win on and what theory you most want to win on, hypotheticals should not be that frightening. It takes a second to make sure you understand a hypothetical — where it fits into your view of the world, given the legal issue that's in front of you — and then you can either give it up or you can't give it up." Carter G. Phillips (as quoted in Gregory J. Langlois, *Dress Rehearsal: The Moot Court Program at Georgetown Law Center's Supreme Court Institute*, 7 J. App. Prac. & Proc. 231, 246 (Fall 2005)).

(h) *Weighing the penalties.* "If you don't know the answer, admit it; the penalty for not having an answer at your fingertips is less severe than the penalty for trying to fake it, getting caught, and giving the court an opportunity to bat you around like a cat playing with a ball of yarn." William J. Boyce, *Reflections on Going to the Show*, 17 App. Advocate (report of the State Bar of Texas Appellate Section), Summer 2004, at 21, 22–23.

(i) *Difficulty of admitting ignorance.* "Don't bluff. Don't be afraid to tell the court you do not know the answer. This is hard to do. It is embarrassing not to know something the judge considers important." Jason Vail, *Oral Argument's Big Challenge: Fielding Questions from the Court*, 1 J. App. Prac. & Proc. 401, 405 (Summer 1999).

(j) *Dangers of not admitting ignorance.* "Admit it when you do not know the answer. Do not try to talk around it. It makes you look cagey, and the court will wonder what you are hiding. If you just say, 'I don't know,' the court has no choice but to move on. A quick follow up with 'I will be glad to look that up or brief that point and have an answer to the clerk's office by lunch' is often the best approach, as you not only do the best you can for your case, but you also appear professional. Why you did not know the answer is something to worry about later. Right then, get on with your argument." Henry D. Gabriel, *Preparation and Delivery of Oral Argument in Appellate Courts*, 22 Am. J. Trial Advoc. 571, 586–87 (1999).

(k) *A graceful way of moving on.* "If a point [that] you had not antici-pated comes up in the course of the argument, you may explain that you have not had a chance to research the point and ask for the opportunity to submit a supplemental memorandum. . . . This device should not be used too often, but it is a graceful way to deal with a legal issue brought up for the first time by one of the judges during oral argument." Hon. William J. Bauer & William C. Bryson, "The Appeal," in *Master Advocates' Handbook* 261, 282 (D. Lake Rumsey ed., 1986).

(l) *Evasion leading to misstatements.* "Why do some lawyers make fac-tual or legal misstatements? It is not always because they seek an unfair advantage. Often, it is simply due to inadvertence or lack of preparation. Sometimes, it is due to a fear of looking unprepared or ignorant. It is always better, however, to simply state, 'I don't know the answer, Your Honor,' or 'I don't have the answer now, Judge, but I will try to get it for you' than to speculate." Hon. Douglas S. Lavine, *Responding to Questions*, Nat'l L.J., 1 Jan. 2007, at 20.

(m) *Value of supplemental brief.* "No matter how thoroughly you prepare, there always is the possibility that the court will focus on some point that you may not have seen at all or have chosen to believe was unimportant. I believe humility is a great thing, and if I feel I am not really able to cope with the problem, I have no reluctance to say, 'May it please the Court, I should like to file a supplemental brief on this subject.' I believe that if the court presses you to the point at which you feel you must offer to file a supplemental brief, the judges are really interested in the question and that you don't have to worry about their reading the brief after it is filed." Samuel E. Gates, "Hot Bench or Cold Bench: When the Court Has Not Read the Brief Before Oral Argument," in *Counsel on Appeal* 107, 136 (Arthur A. Charpentier ed., 1968).

(n) *A win–win offer.* "[I]f you do not know the answer to a question, offer to submit a letter or supplemental brief. If the court refuses, you are no worse off. If it accepts, you can provide a proper answer after reflecting on it. This also can save you precious time that could easily be wasted while you fumble around looking for an answer that you may not find." Rex S. Heinke & Tracy L. Casadio, *Oral Argument in the Federal Circuit Courts*, 16 Cal. Litig. 36, 41 (No. 2, 2003).

(o) *Frank admission.* "If you do not understand a question, frankly admit it and ask for a clarification. A frank admission is better than answering a question you do not understand." Hon. Hugh R. Jones, *Appellate Advocacy, Written and Oral,* J. Mo. Bar, June 1991, at 297, 303.

71. **After answering, transition back into your argument smoothly. Look for opportunities to use the answer as a segue to your next important point.**

A core skill in effective oral advocacy is steering the discussion away from tangential issues and back to your central points. Doing this requires finesse. The key is tying your answer to some aspect of the next point you want to make. It's important to be familiar enough with your argument that you can be flexible about how you present it. Practicing the argument in every possible order for the points you need to make can help you make smooth transitions.

(a) *Classic statement 1.* "The advocate must have clearly in mind the main points that must be presented no matter how intense the questioning becomes. And, with a little dexterity, the questions from the Court can be used as stepping stones to make these essential points. For example: 'The answer to Your Honor's question is ———. And in this connection, I would emphasize . . . .'" Stephen M. Shapiro, *Oral Argument in the Supreme Court of the United States*, 33 Catholic U. Am. L. Rev. 529, 545 (1984).

(b) *Classic statement 2.* "The highest and best use of questions requires simultaneously answering what is asked without equivocation and using the question as a springboard to make points the advocate hopes will be decisive." Richard A. Givens, *Advocacy*, vol. 1, § 18.01, at 581 (1992).

(c) *Shuffling the deck.* "I don't care how complicated your case is, it usually reduces to at most four or five major points. [He would put them on index cards.] Here's the key precedent, here's the key language, here's the key regulation, here are the key consequences. . . . When I'm practicing giving the argument, I'll go through it, and then I'll shuffle those cards without knowing what they are. Then I'll start again and I'll look down. Okay, my first point is going to be C, and then I'm going to move to point E, and then to point A. You develop practice on those transitions. . . . You can't guarantee the first question you're going to get is going to be on your first point. It may be on your third point. . . . If you've practiced giving that argument [on your] third point and then to the first point and then to whatever, you can make those transitions, and it's much smoother. . . . It conveys a greater degree of confidence on your part in your presentation that you're not pausing and saying, 'I'll go back to something else.' It prevents the argument from seeming disrupted, and it makes the argument look fluid no matter what questions you get or what order the points come out." Hon. John Roberts, interviewed by Bryan A. Garner (2 Mar. 2007).

(d) *Direct answer, then transitional answer.* "Sometimes, a judge will persist with a series of questions that does not seem relevant. Disengaging and returning to your central points can be tough. Aldisert recommends saying, 'If the court please, I have two responses to make to that question.' Give a direct answer to the question as your first response, then before the judge can fire off a follow-up, say, 'For my second response, I would add . . .' and find a link to rush back to your main point." Jason Vail, *Oral Argument's Big Challenge: Fielding Questions from the Court*, 1 J. App. Prac. & Proc. 401, 407 (Summer 1999).

(e) *Controlling the argument.* "Although the advocate should never appear to control the court, the best advocates in fact maintain a very high level of control over the argument and even over the bench; but they do so in a way that is entirely unobtrusive, always maintaining the proper attitude of deference and respect." Alan D. Hornstein, *Appellate Advocacy in a Nutshell* 284 (1984).

(f) *The relentless judge.* "Beware the relentless judge. Sometimes a judge will not let go of a point. However, you must move on. Give your best answer and then politely but firmly steer the argument back on course." Andrew L. Frey, *Preparing and Delivering Oral Argument*, http://www.appellate.net/articles/prepdel799.asp (accessed 26 January 2007).

(g) *Chief Justice Charles Evans Hughes's attitude.* "If counsel moved expeditiously from one main point to another, with neither oratory nor evasiveness, [Chief Justice Charles Evans] Hughes was likely to sit and drink it in. But few lawyers made that kind of argument." M.J. Pusey, *Charles Evans Hughes*, vol. 2, 674 (1951).

(h) *Getting back on track.* "The most difficult questions are those that tend to sidetrack the conversation into irrelevant detours. But the oral advocate is never as effective as when she responds to the judge's question by extending her answer to incorporate the salient and essential points of her argument." Catherine Valerio Barrad, *Successful Oral Arguments Do Not Involve Any Arguing*, S.F. Daily J., 4 Aug. 2004, at 5, 6.

72. Be sensitive to the judges' body language.

With study and practice, you should be able to gauge the judges' general responses to the arguments and the answers to their questions. What should be especially easy is spotting signs that a judge wants to ask a question.

(a) *Classic statement 1.* "Watch the judges' expressions and body language. Any good salesperson will tell you that the customer will signal pleasure or displeasure by facial expressions, eye movement, and body language. Watch for fidgeting, tense mouths, puzzled eyes, and the like. These signals will tell you whom to concentrate [on] in your arguments and what arguments are being accepted." John T. Gaubatz & Taylor Mattis, *The Moot Court Book* 84–85 (3d ed. 1994).

(b) *Classic statement 2.* "[Y]our first task as an advocate is to listen carefully to the judges' questions and comments and take careful note of their demeanor and body language with an eye to determining a question's meaning and purpose. Although discerning the underlying purpose of a question may be akin sometimes to reading tea leaves, by doing so, you can focus your argument to deal with the concerns of the judges who may be unfavorably inclined toward your case." Hon. Margaret M. Grignon, *The Dynamics of Appellate Oral Argument*, Certworthy (Defense Research Inst. App. Advocacy Comm. newsletter), Summer 2006, at 31, 31.

(c) *Subtly inviting questions.* "Occasionally when discussing a point you will see a judge fidget a bit as though about to ask you a question and appear in doubt as to whether he should. In this situation, you can without any ostentation say something like this before leaving the particular subject: 'If the court has no questions to ask on this part I will now pass on to my next point.' This will give the fidgeting judge his chance." Owen Rall, *Effective Oral Argument on Appeal*, 48 Ill. B.J. 572, 584 (1960).

73. Recognize friendly questions for what they are.

Judges don't always ask confrontational questions. Sometimes they're trying to help you. They may ask friendly questions. So don't assume that questioning is necessarily an act of hostility.

(a) *Classic statement 1.* "When counsel apparently has nothing particular in mind to discuss, no arrangement of argument, no clear view of what the questions in the case are, I have an irresistible urge to make him help us in spite of himself, and suggest topics, in the form of enquiries, for him to express his views on." Hon. E. Barrett Prettyman, *Some Observations Concerning Appellate Advocacy*, 39 Va. L. Rev. 285, 300 (1953).

(b) *Classic statement 2.* "Do not assume that the question is hostile. Many are. But some are neutral, and some are helpful. One example of a helpful question is a statement [that], while framed as a question ('Is it your position that?' or 'Is it not true that?') is actually a more persuasive argument than has come to your unassisted mind. Some questions are analogous to a lifeline extended to a drowning person." Rex E. Lee, *Oral Argument in the Supreme Court*, 72 ABA J. 60, 60 (June 1986).

(c) *Questioners' varied motives.* "Hostile-sounding questions often come from favorably inclined judges who are trying to educate a hesitant colleague. Or they may want your help so they can answer your opponent's toughest argument during the conference or when they write an opinion holding for your client. And seemingly friendly questions can be as lethal to advocates as 'friendly fire' is to soldiers. Therefore, avoid overinterpreting our questions. Better to concentrate on good answers than to guess about votes." Hon. Paul R. Michel, *Effective Appellate Advocacy*, 24 Litig. 19, 22 (Summer 1998).

(d) *The danger of misinterpreting motives.* "Judges may well ask friendly questions — that will support the inquiring judge's agreement with her or to support a position that may have been insufficiently developed. When the advocate erroneously responds to such a question as if it were a hostile challenge, she not only forgoes the opportunity presented by the question but also displays her lack of understanding of her position or her inattention to the bench or both." Alan D. Hornstein, *Appellate Advocacy in a Nutshell* 295 (1984).

(e) *Biting the helping hand.* "The attorney must be 'tuned in' to the question and its real purpose. If the questioner's attitude, and the sense of the question, seem favorable, a very brief, congenial response is appropriate. Above all, counsel should avoid becoming combative with a judge whose question is helping the cause. All too often, an attorney bites the helping hand." Hon. Jim R. Carrigan, "Some Nuts and Bolts of Appellate Advocacy," in *Appellate Practice Manual* 102, 109 (Priscilla Anne Schwab ed., 1992).

(f) *Goading you to expound.* "Do not assume that all questions from the bench are hostile. Some may be designed to probe and push you to explore and justify your argument. Others may even be intended to assist you in articulating or developing your argument. Some members of the court may use questions to counsel as a means of educating and communicating with colleagues on the bench!" Hon. Hugh R. Jones, *Appellate Advocacy, Written and Oral*, J. Mo. Bar, June 1991, at 297, 303.

(g) *Becoming a mouthpiece in an intra-court debate.* "Friendly questions. These are the soft pitches judges throw lawyers to enable them to cast their positions in a favorable light. Sometimes the judge will even restate your position for you. Such questions from an appellate judge can mean that she is using the lawyer as a mouthpiece in a debate with her colleagues on the panel." Jason Vail, *Oral Argument's Big Challenge: Fielding Questions from the Court*, 1 J. App. Prac. & Proc. 401, 403 (Summer 1999).

(h) *The judge as devil's advocate.* "Do not automatically assume that a question from a judge whom you believe is antagonistic to your position is going to be a hardball. Sometimes judges just want to play devil's advocate to see if your position is intractable. The worst mistake you can make is to fail to detect a softball question and hit it out of the park." Hon. Brian Wice, *Oral Argument in Criminal Cases: 10 Tips for Winning the Moot Court Round*, Tex. B.J., Mar. 2006, at 224, 229.

74. **If the judge is downright hostile and expresses a clear indication that you're wrong, consider an appeal to humility. But you can't be hostile in return: be firm and confident and friendly.**

Judges ask hostile questions for different reasons. The questioner may strongly disagree with your position, may have an overaggressive personality, may be irritated at the other judges, or may have a different motive altogether. You must politely stand firm against hostile questions without directly challenging the judge.

(a) *Classic statement 1.* "The lawyer who is rash enough to criticize the judge while pleading a case acts as unwisely as does the scholar who criticized the professor during an oral examination." Piero Calamandrei, *Eulogy of Judges* 17 (1936; John Clarke Adams & C. Abbott Phillips Jr. eds., 1942; repr. 1992)

(b) *Classic statement 2.* "Hostility frequently is a sign of frustration that the questioner is in the minority. Counsel should remember that, while one or more Justices may seem dissatisfied with his positions or answers, a majority of the Court may well be on his side. In dealing with hostile questions, counsel should give a polite but firm response and get back to his main contentions." Stephen M. Shapiro, *Oral Argument in the Supreme Court of the United States*, 33 Catholic U. Am. L. Rev. 529, 543 (1984).

(c) *Classic statement 3.* "In the long run, the court will respect counsel who politely stand their ground rather than being pummeled by questions from the court." Hon. Arthur A. McGivern (as quoted in Hon. Ruggero J. Aldisert, *Winning on Appeal* 307 (1992)).

(d) *The problem stated.* "On some occasions . . . the Justices make little pretext of having doubt about the proper outcome but simply pound the advocate with questions — often nothing more than the same question posed in different ways — that can in no circumstances be answered to the Justices' satisfaction." Andrew L.

Frey, *Tilting at Windmills*, 5 J. App. Prac. & Proc. 117, 120 (Spring 2003).

(e) *Philosophical differences.* "Hostile questions. Some judges will come at you in a tough, often unfriendly way. This isn't necessarily because they dislike you or your client (although that's possible). Usually it happens because the judge is philosophically at odds with your position." Jason Vail, *Oral Argument's Big Challenge: Fielding Questions from the Court*, 1 J. App. Prac. & Proc. 401, 403 (Summer 1999).

(f) *Standing ground.* "[D]on't be timorous or overawed. Maintain a position of respectful equality. Don't be disturbed or pushed around simply because a judge disagrees with your position. Stand your ground firmly but with courtesy and dignity." Hon. Ruggero J. Aldisert, *Winning on Appeal* 330 (1992).

(g) *Justices' priorities.* Chief Justice Roberts has said that "being advocate-friendly is not a major priority." Hon. John Roberts, at the Ninth Circuit Judicial Conference, 13 July 2006.

(h) *No grounds for disrespect.* "[W]hatever the nature of the questions, the lawyer should retain his poise and composure and under no circumstances lose his temper or become impertinent or disrespectful. Whatever the aggravation and however unfair the question may seem to be, there is no possible justification for impertinence or disrespect." Hon. Harold R. Medina, *The Oral Argument on Appeal*, 20 ABA J. 139, 143 (1934).

(i) *No grounds for groveling.* "The appropriate attitude is one of respect but not one of groveling. Thus, it is entirely appropriate, should the occasion demand it, to disagree with the bench. It is never appropriate, however, to treat the bench condescendingly or flippantly or disrespectfully. That the advocate may know more about the case or even about the law than does the judge, that the judge displays her ignorance, even her ineptitude, is no excuse for the advocate to exhibit anything less than responsible professional behavior." Alan D. Hornstein, *Appellate Advocacy in a Nutshell* 252 (1984).

(j) *A model response.* "When the judge says, 'Counsel, that argument is simply ridiculous,' the response could be, 'Your Honor, I respectfully disagree, and I have offered legitimate reasons why it is not. My hope is only that Your Honor, on reflection, will change your mind.'" Hon. Ruggero J. Aldisert, *Winning on Appeal* 339 (1992).

(k) *The wrong response.* "A Justice may abruptly indicate conclusions [that] tempt a lawyer to reply as one did long ago in a local court in the country where I practiced. He had barely stated his contention when the judge said: 'There is nothing to your proposition — just nothing to it.' The lawyer drew himself up and said: 'Your Honor, I have worked on this case for six weeks and you have not heard of it twenty minutes. Now, Judge, you are a lot smarter man than I am, but there is not that much difference between us.'" Hon. Robert H. Jackson, *Advocacy Before the Supreme Court: Suggestions for Effective Case Presentations*, 37 ABA J. 801, 862 (Nov. 1951).

(l) *Responding politely.* "Judges treat lawyers in overtly hostile ways very seldom, but it's awfully unpleasant when it happens, probably because it is so rare. Ignore it as best you can and, if anything, become even more meticulously polite; you'll win points with the offender's colleagues, at least." Edward L. Lascher, *Oral Argument*, 7 Cal. Litig. 16, 20 (Winter 1994).

(m) *Persistent assertiveness.* "Anyone may feel anxious dealing with people who are brusque and domineering. The reasonably assertive person controls her anxiety and, without showing hostility, persists in advancing ideas that she considers reasonable." Jesse S. Nirenberg, *How to Sell Your Ideas* 169 (1984).

(n) *Professionalism.* "Being fastidiously polite in the presence of a boor isn't easy; but this is what professionalism is all about — doing something expertly — and fastidious politeness is utterly essential when dealing with the difficult judge. As it happens, politeness comes easily when dealing with one of the good judges, so the rule is a very simple one: with both good and bad judges, it is in your interest, and in the interests of your clients, to maintain fastidious politeness and an undiminished attitude of respect. Even if you think your judge is a rude, ill-educated boor, behave towards him or her with perfect courtesy. You'll accomplish nothing if you don't." Keith Evans, *The Language of Advocacy* 75–76 (1998).

(o) *Potential ally.* "Do not get angry at the judge who attacks your position. He may be your best supporter on the appeal." Hon. Arthur L. Alarcon, "Points on Appeal," in *Appellate Practice Manual* 95, 101 (Priscilla Anne Schwab ed., 1992).

(p) *Empirical study suggesting that hostile questions signal disagreement.* "Many of the Justices [of the U.S. Supreme Court] pose hostile or argumentative questions to both sides, but it seems that more often they go easy on the lawyer for the party they support and only play devil's advocate to the lawyer for the party they oppose. Essentially, whether they do it by asking more questions or by asking questions that are more hostile in content, the Justices simply give the side they disagree with a harder time." Sarah Levien Shullman, *The Illusion of Devil's Advocacy*, 6 J. App. Prac. & Proc. 271, 292 (Fall 2004).

75.   Avoid overtly taking issue with the judge.

Remember that judges' questions are usually well-intentioned. A judge who challenges you is trying to understand why you see things differently. Your most counterproductive response to such a challenge is to show any hint of impatience or belligerence.

(a) *Classic statement 1.* "[D]o not argue with the judge. Answer all questions calmly and thoughtfully. Do not raise your voice, and even if you are frustrated, don't let it show. If one line of argument isn't working and the point is essential to your case, try another, and if that line doesn't work, try still another." Laurel Currie Oates & Anne Enquist, *Just Briefs* 192 (2003).

(b) *Classic statement 2.* "There are other ways to slip into an adversarial relationship with a member of the Court. You should not attribute a position with which you disagree to one of the justices, even one who has just stated it. Rather than, 'I disagree with you,' attribute the position to your real opponent. 'The appellee's argument to that effect is wrong for two separate reasons,' or, 'the lower court's holding is based on that position, which is squarely rejected by the language and history of the statute.'" Rex E. Lee, *Oral Argument in the Supreme Court*, 72 ABA J. 60, 60 (June 1986).

(c) *The classic British view.* "[R]emember that however genuine your contempt for the Court may be, you conceal it until you get outside." Edward Abbott Parry, *Judgments in Vacation* 218 (1911).

(d) *Lord Denning's view.* "Treat every court with the utmost respect: express what you have to say, if justified, firmly but with patience." Lord Denning's practice notes (as quoted in Edmund Heward, *Lord Denning* 24 (1990)).

(e) *The modern British view.* "The quickest way to lose respect is by being quarrelsome with the judge, or with the opposition, by taking dull points . . . , by being high-handed with witnesses, condescending to juries, pointed, irritated, arrogant, slightly sneering, and pompous. Strangely, this really does happen." Iain Morley, *The Devil's Advocate: A Short Polemic on How to Be Seriously Good in Court* 59 (2005).

(f) *No being flabbergasted.* "Counsel never should express exasperation with the Court for persistent examination. And if it is necessary to disagree at the end of a colloquy, counsel should do so courteously: 'With great deference, Your Honor, we see that case in a very different light. In our view, ...'" Stephen M. Shapiro, *Oral Argument in the Supreme Court of the United States*, 33 Catholic U. Am. L. Rev. 529, 548 (1984).

(g) *No loin-girding.* "The task of the attorney is to induce conviction, to advocate, and to persuade. At no point does he gird his loins to do battle with the court itself." John Alan Appleman, "Tactics in Appellate Briefs," in *Advocacy and the King's English* 440, 460 (George Rossman ed., 1960).

(h) *Futility of arguing.* "Don't argue with the judge. Attempting to convince a judge that his or her entire line of reasoning is wrongheaded will rarely be productive. Instead, acknowledge the court's areas of concern and demonstrate why those areas should be resolved in your favor. Try to work within the court's analytical framework, not demolish it." Michael Paul Thomas, *The Rites and Rights of Oral Argument*, Cal. Law., Sept. 2004, at 40, 42.

(i) *Avoiding red-flag phrasings.* "'With all due respect, Your Honor.' This is well-known trial lawyer's code for 'You are obviously stupid, Your Honor, so I will now educate you.' Anyone with a whiff of emotional intelligence should know to avoid such a red flag. Instead, lawyers should try, 'Has the court considered . . .' or 'Would the court prefer some briefing on that point?'" Douglas G. Carnahan, *The Top Ten List of Things You Shouldn't Say in Court*, S.F. Daily J. Extra, 8 Sept. 2003, at 9, 9.

76. Stand firm when you need to. Know what you can and can't concede.

Judges will often seek concessions. In preparing for argument, you should anticipate what you may be asked to concede and prepare a response. Whether or not you concede a point, you should respond respectfully and with as little harm to your case as possible.

(a) *Classic statement 1.* "The skillful advocate always keeps his hand upon the pulse of his tribunal; and the moment he feels that his argument is not in accord with it, retires to deliver his attack from another point of view. But cases occur in which a collision and open war are inevitable, and in which it is the advocate's duty not to flinch from withstanding the judge. Such cases are, however, rare." Hon. F.C. Moncreiff, *The Wit and Wisdom of the Bench and Bar* 140 (1882).

(b) *Classic statement 2.* "Any concession you make should have been well thought out ahead of time. In fact, if you can volunteer your concession before being asked to do so, this will show that you are reasonable and in control of your case." Myron Moskovitz, *Winning an Appeal* § 4.3 at 63 (3d ed. 1995).

(c) *Classic statement 3.* "A skillfully made concession . . . can make the advocate more credible to the court by demonstrating the reasonableness of the advocate's position. In determining just how much an advocate can concede and still win, the advocate must be conscious of how best to draw the lines around her position and how to express the limiting principles that cabin the proposed rule in a manner that most accurately conveys how the court should articulate its ruling." David C. Frederick, *Supreme Court and Appellate Advocacy* 101 (2003)

(d) *Defending crucial territory.* "Lawyers often do not adequately come to grips with the realization that you can lose on a number of issues and still win. Lawyers need to figure out what is the smallest piece of territory they need to defend and then defend that piece to the limit. But everything else, they can give up, if necessary, and still win." Hon. Alex Kozinski (interview), Jeffrey Cole, *My Afternoon with Alex: An Interview with Judge Kozinski*, 30 Litig. 6, 18 (Summer 2004).

(e) *Conceding too much.* "Based on what I have observed of Supreme Court arguments, more cases have been lost by counsel seeking to be agreeable and conceding points they should not, than by their standing firm. The Justices seem to agree." David J. Bederman, *A Chilly Reception at the Court*, 5 J. App. Prac. & Proc. 51, 57–58 (Spring 2003).

(f) *Valorous discretion.* "The oral advocate must so understand the case and the law that concessions can be made where appropriate, to avoid the appearance that the principle argued would cause absurd results (or that the advocate does not understand what he or she is talking about). But even where the judges are hostile to the point being made, the lawyer must sometimes 'hold 'em' and stand fast or the case will either be damaged or lost." Timothy A. Baughmann, *Effective Appellate Oral Advocacy: "Beauty Is Truth, Truth Beauty,"* 77 Mich. B.J. 38, 39 (Jan. 1998).

(g) *No placating a judge.* "You must never yield to the temptation to give the judge the answer he seems to want just because that will apparently please him. In the first place, he may be leading you on to see just how far you will go, and he may then turn on you. This is a honeyed approach [that] some judges use to test the lawyer's intellectual honesty." Owen Rall, "Persuasive Oral Argument," in *Lawyer's Encyclopedia* 1019, 1032 (1963).

(h) *Avoiding careless concessions.* "Do not make careless concessions at oral argument on the spur of the moment. They may come back to haunt you." Hon. Ruggero J. Aldisert, *Winning on Appeal* 336 (1992).

(i) *Concessive phrasing.* "You must know when to concede and, more important, how to concede. A traditional and effective approach is often, 'I think that . . . ; however, even if the court disagrees, it is still [fallback position].'" Henry D. Gabriel, *Preparation and Delivery of Oral Argument in Appellate Courts*, 22 Am. J. Trial Advoc. 571, 586 (1999).

(j) *Narrowing the rule to win (1).* "[B]e prepared to make necessary or unavoidable concessions. The wise advocate prefers to win the case on the narrowest possible principle rather than lose the appeal by arguing for a broad new rule of law." Catherine Valerio Barrad, *Successful Oral Arguments Do Not Involve Any Arguing*, S.F. Daily J., 4 Aug. 2004, at 5, 6.

(k) *Narrowing the rule to win (2).* "[D]o not concede arguments that you need not concede, and do not fall victim to questions that lead logically to the slippery slope of defeat. Be especially careful in your answers if the question attempts to take you in the direction of some grand policy or sweeping principle. These are the most dangerous inquiries: Remember the wisdom of presenting your case on the narrowest principle that allows your client to prevail. If the court wants to use your case to announce some new broad rule of law, it does not need your argument to do so. Unless you must, never insist on a great change to justify a decision for your client." Talbot D'Alemberte, *Oral Argument: The Continuing Conversation*, 25 Litig. 12, 15 (Winter 1999).

(l) *Conceding vs. distinguishing facts.* "One cannot run away from concessions that must be made. This is particularly true of factual matters. For example, if a Justice inquires 'isn't it true that your client testified ——,' an answer must be given in the affirmative if that is the case. In dealing with a question calling for a concession, it is essential to *first answer the question*, and only then to explain why the conceded matter is not dispositive. If a Justice is disturbed that you are not making a concession that you must make, simply say 'I do acknowledge Your Honor's point. The record shows ——. That, however, is not dispositive here because . . . .'" Stephen M. Shapiro, *Oral Argument in the Supreme Court of the United States*, 33 Catholic U. Am. L. Rev. 529, 546–47 (1984).

(m) *Factual vs. legal concessions.* "There is a difference between factual and legal concessions. If the record facts are against you, concede their existence, but hasten to argue that this concession does not destroy your case. Be very careful, however, of legal concessions. If you realize, usually on the way home from the courthouse, that you have made an improvident concession on a point of some significance, all is not lost. I believe it is appropriate to file a supplemental brief by letter, which refers to the question and your response and clarifies it. Be certain to serve your adversary with a copy. There is no guarantee that all judges would accept it. I would." Hon. Ruggero J. Aldisert, *Winning on Appeal* 337 (1992).

(n) *Acknowledgment plus explanation.* "Don't concede a point merely because a judge thinks you should. If a judge believes you should concede a point but you do not, say, 'I acknowledge Your Honor's point, but it does not dispose of the issues here . . . .'" Andrew L. Frey, *Preparing and Delivering Oral Argument*, http://www.appellate. net/articles/prepdel799.asp (accessed 26 Jan. 2007).

(o) *A Scottish exemplar of a necessary virtue.* "[J. Condie Sandeman, K.C.] was the embodiment of courage. If he believed in a proposition, he would fight for it unflinchingly, no matter what opposition or criticism came from Bench, or Bar." Archibald Crawford, *Public Speaking* 86 (1935).

77. Never ask whether you've adequately answered a question — and never pose any other substantive question to the bench except to elicit clarification of a judge's question.

Judges ask the questions from the bench. They don't answer them except when issuing orders and opinions. Beyond seeking to clarify what a judge has asked, questions from advocates are inappropriate in oral argument.

(a) *Classic statement 1.* "Don't answer a question with a question. Sometimes a judge's inquiry needs clarification, and you shouldn't hesitate to ask for it. Otherwise, questions, even rhetorical ones, should be avoided. One of my senior colleagues put a question to a young lawyer during oral argument and received this reply: 'Why do you ask that, Your Honor?' That sort of reply is not well received. Of course, it is far better than the following reply received by a judge in the Eighth Circuit: 'You wouldn't want to know that, Your Honor.'" Hon. Roger J. Miner, *The Don'ts of Oral Argument*, 14 Litig. 3, 4 (Summer 1988).

(b) *Classic statement 2.* "[D]on't answer by asking the judge a question. In oral argument, it is inappropriate to question a judge." Laurel Currie Oates & Anne Enquist, *Just Briefs* 192 (2003).

(c) *Good and bad rebuttals.* "Rebuttal is difficult. Few do it well. Merely restating the opening argument is useless. Launching new attacks is unfair (and also useless). Refuting each of appellee's arguments is impossible in the time permitted. Saying nothing is unsettling to counsel and the client, although saying nothing is preferable to saying something badly. . . . In most cases counsel should pronounce the single theme on which the case depends most strongly and briefly deflect any severe error or obvious ambiguity that endangers the case's essential theme, and then should sit down graciously and confidently." Hon. Steven D. Merryday, "Oral Argument," in *Florida Appellate Practice* § 17.17, at 17–27 (4th ed. 1997).

(d) *What not to ask.* "[D]on't interrogate the judge as to what questions he or she might want to ask. Don't ask the court 'have you read the briefs,' or 'what questions do you have,' or 'how do you want me to proceed.' Such questions are not calculated to place the court in the best of good humor. If the judge has no immediate questions and seems willing to let you proceed in the manner you have prepared, by all means go forward and present your well structured and organized argument. If the judge expresses a tentative point of view, by all means without delay present your 'correct' view of things. If the judge does have questions, don't be annoyed and do answer promptly and directly." Hon. J. Thomas Greene, *Don't Forget Your Orals*, 183 F.R.D. 289, 293 (1999).

(e) *Inappropriate questions.* "The advocate ought never voluntarily surrender control of the argument. Thus, for example, asking the court if it wishes to hear the facts is inappropriate; if the court is familiar with the facts and does not wish them formally presented, it is the court's place to advise the advocate; it is not her place to ask. In addition to surrendering control, the initiation of questions on the part of the advocate may make for awkwardness in the argument." Alan D. Hornstein, *Appellate Advocacy in a Nutshell* 254 (1984).

(f) *A case study.* "One of my favorite exchanges in oral argument arose in the case of *NCAA v. Tarkanian.* . . . Justice Stevens asked the following hypothetical: 'Let us assume that we are talking about O'Hare Airport (which is a municipal authority), and let us assume that United Airlines (which is the largest airline at O'Hare) came to the municipal authority and said, "You have got to fire Joe Smith, and if you do not, we are going to yank all our planes out of here and put them in Midway Airport."' Justice Stevens then asked whether United Airlines would be a state actor under Tarkanian's counsel's theory of the case. . . . Tarkanian's counsel did not make a verbal response. He was silent and stayed that way for a good solid minute. Coming to Tarkanian's counsel's aid and comfort, Justice Scalia said, 'The answer you're looking for to that question is "No."' Tarkanian's counsel, quick on his feet, immediately said, 'No.' Justice Stevens, in response, asked, 'Why?' At that point, Tarkanian's counsel looked to his savior, Justice Scalia [who] said, 'You are on your own now.' The argument sort of disintegrated from that point on." Carter G. Phillips, *Advocacy Before the United States Supreme Court*, 15 T.M. Cooley L. Rev. 177, 193 (1988).

(g) *Inviting adversity.* "While you must understand the question before you start to answer, it is a mistake to probe the adequacy of your answer before you move on. If your questioner wants more, he or she will tell you so. Asking puts the justice in the unwanted position of having to evaluate your answer. Worse, it can inadvertently lead the questioner into an adversarial frame of mind, by requiring him or her to focus on and articulate just why it is that your answer is inadequate." Rex E. Lee, *Oral Argument in the Supreme Court*, 72 ABA J. 60, 60 (June 1986).

(h) *The delusional advocate.* "Here is another example of what should be avoided. We have all seen it happen. A judge on the bench asks the advocate what he considers a very pertinent question. The latter, instead of undertaking to answer the query, says: 'Your Honor, let me ask *you* this question.' Personally, I think that is the most classic of all 'famous last words.' For an attorney to honestly believe that by such conduct in an oral argument he is still on the objective track of persuasion is fantastic." Watson Clay, "Presenting Your Case to the Court of Appeals" (1952), in *Advocacy and the King's English* 330, 332 (George Rossman ed., 1960).

Rebutting

78. Never waive rebuttal beforehand.

If you're the appellant, reserve two minutes or so to answer your adversary's points. Even if you end up not needing the time, just having it gives you a tactical advantage.

(a) *Classic statement 1.* "Very rarely will you need more than two or three minutes for rebuttal, but you should save it if only because of the effect its existence may have on your opponent's willingness to stray from objectivity." Rex E. Lee, *Oral Argument in the Supreme Court*, 72 ABA J. 60, 62 (June 1986).

(b) *Classic statement 2.* "Never waive rebuttal in advance, which means always be sure you have enough time left to rebut; otherwise, the appellee's lawyer may try to pull the wool over the judge's eyes knowing that you will not be able to correct his misstatements. But if, having reserved time for rebuttal, you find that you have nothing to say, perhaps because it is obvious that your opponent has said nothing to move the judges, then waive rebuttal rather than wasting the judges' time." Hon. Richard A. Posner, *Convincing a Federal Court of Appeals*, 25 Litig. 3, 62 (Winter 1999).

(c) *Keeping it concise.* "Reserve time for rebuttal, and use the time to make only a couple of important points, simply and concisely. Then sit down." Catherine Valerio Barrad, *Successful Oral Arguments Do Not Involve Any Arguing*, S.F. Daily J., 4 Aug. 2004, at 5, 6.

(d) *Making a clear request.* "If you are the appellant in a court that permits rebuttal, make certain that you save time for it. I have found it very useful to go to the clerk, the marshal, or whoever is keeping time for the court, and to make a clear request for rebuttal time. That also gives me a chance to make certain that I understand what the lights on the podium or other signals indicate. If you do not plan accordingly, you may find that the red light that comes on during your principal argument has actually signaled the expiration of your entire time, and that you have lost your opportunity for rebuttal." Talbot D'Alemberte, *Oral Argument: The Continuing Conversation*, 25 Litig. 12, 67 (Winter 1999).

(e) *Advantages of rebuttal.* "Not only does [rebuttal] permit a reply to otherwise unanswered and possibly misleading assertions by the opponent, it gives you the advantage of the last or next-to-last word, which the tribunal is more likely to remember than the bulk of earlier argument." Richard A. Givens, *Advocacy*, vol. 1, § 18.01, at 583 (1992).

79. Take notes for rebuttal, and then refute the more important points with rifle shots.

Your rebuttal time is best used by addressing the judges' concerns that your adversary couldn't adequately respond to. While your adversary argues, prepare brief notes for this purpose.

(a) *Classic statement 1.* "[R]ebuttal can be very useful, if you do it right. What you should do is copy every question that any judge asks the other side. Just make a note of what judge it is and what question it is. Surely, if your argument has been at all effective, one of the judges will ask a question which your opponent will want to duck. The reason he will want to duck it is that the answer favors you. So for your rebuttal, just get up and say, 'Mr. Chief Justice, you asked Mr. Jones such and such a question. I think if Your Honor will turn to page 88 of the record, folio 264, in the middle of that folio you will see the testimony of the witness Zimmerman.' Then pause, let him get the book — never tell a judge what is in the record until he has it in front of him. Then you say, 'The witness Zimmerman said thus and thus. I think that is the answer to Your Honor's question.' Then sit down." Hon. Whitman Knapp, *Why Argue an Appeal? If So, How?*, 14 Record N.Y.C.B.A. 415, 430 (1959).

(b) *Classic statement 2.* "When listening to the opponent's argument, take notes — though not so copiously that they are worthless as a reference for rebuttal. Leave a space on the paper to 'star' or 'highlight' points that require rebuttal. Select one or two (rarely more) items from this list . . . to use on rebuttal." Michael B. Tigar & Jane B. Tigar, *Federal Appeals: Jurisdiction and Practice* § 10.11, at 524 (3d ed. 1999).

(c) *Knowing what to rebut.* "[D]uring your opponent's argument you take notes of matters that he is misstating or as to which he is wrong, and that you can usefully reply to and correct. . . . By the time the opponent's argument is drawing to a close, you should have a pretty good idea of the points that are significant enough to warrant mentioning in a reply — and any doubts should be resolved in favor of elimination." Frederick Bernays Wiener, *Briefing and Arguing Federal Appeals* § 134, at 349 (2d ed. 1967).

(d) *Persuasive follow-ups.* "Know your opponent's arguments and listen when your opponent is talking and being questioned. Follow up with this on your rebuttal. Address points that your opponent could not answer adequately for the judges; follow up with arguments the judges were making from the bench and be sure to point out any misstatements of law or fact by your opponent. This way, rebuttal can be a very persuasive weapon in your arsenal." Ronald J. Rychlak, *Effective Appellate Advocacy: Tips from the Teams*, 66 Miss. L.J. 527, 544–45 (1997).

(e) *Planning during the argument, not before.* "The rebuttal should be planned during the course of respondent's argument; it never should be prepared in advance. No matter how much time is left over for rebuttal, counsel should make only three or four important points. It is not appropriate to compile a long list of your opponent's errors and then touch upon every one of them during rebuttal." Stephen M. Shapiro, *Oral Argument in the Supreme Court of the United States*, 33 Catholic U. Am. L. Rev. 529, 549 (1984).

80. Rebut only as necessary, and stick to major points.

Your rebuttal time is wasted if you just rehash your arguments. Instead, you might give a short, forceful presentation of one or two of your best points — in light of what your adversary has just said.

(a) *Classic statement 1.* "Nearly always the time spent in rebuttal is not very well spent. Lawyers are inclined to get down to small points, so small that half an hour later the court will not have the faintest recollection of what was said." Hon. Herbert F. Goodrich, *A Case on Appeal — A Judge's View* 28 (1952).

(b) *Classic statement 2.* "Courts are generally restless by the time of the rebuttal, so make it short and very punchy. The best approach is to have two or three specific points to make and to announce that you want to discuss only those points. Do not linger on any point — speak your piece and sit down. By all means do not stand up and start correcting minor errors in the appellee's presentation. The court will quickly become impatient with such nonsense, and you will lose more than you gain. The most effective rebuttals last less than one minute." Hon. William J. Bauer & William C. Bryson, "The Appeal," in *Master Advocates' Handbook* 261, 282 (D. Lake Rumsey ed., 1986).

(c) *Weighing whether to rebut.* "When deciding whether and how to use your rebuttal time, consider whether: (1) your opponent made a critical misstatement of law or fact that cannot go uncorrected; (2) there is an obviously weak or mishandled part of your opponent's presentation that you can exploit to your advantage; or (3) you need an opportunity to correct or supplement a weak answer you gave during your opening presentation." Bradley G. Clary et al., *Advocacy on Appeal* 130 (2d ed. 2004).

(d) *The wisdom of refraining.* "When it comes to rebuttal, it is often wise to make none. If you do make a rebuttal argument, don't repeat your main argument. Just correct any misstatements of fact, or distinguish an important case or principle which your opponent has relied upon, or briefly refute an argument [that] you believe has impressed one or more judges." Hon. John C. Bell Jr., *Oral Arguments Before the Supreme Court of Pennsylvania*, 24 Pa. B. Assn. Q. 133, 136 (1953).

(e) *Insipid nitpicking deplored.* "An insipid, note-cluttered, nitpicking rebuttal statement is far worse than none at all." Prentice H. Marshall, "Oral Argument," in *Illinois Civil Practice After Trial* 9-1, 9-25 (1976).

(f) *Introducing the rebuttal.* "Because time is so limited, most advocates begin their rebuttal by telling the court how many points they plan to make: 'I would like to make two points.' This introduction tells the court what to expect. The advocate then makes his or her first point and supports it and, unless interrupted by a question, moves to the second point. Most advocates close by quickly repeating their request for relief." Laurel Currie Oates & Anne Enquist, *Just Briefs* 193 (2003).

(g) *No more than one or two points.* "[L]imit your rebuttal to a single point, if possible, and in any event to no more than two points. The purpose of rebuttal is to attack misstatements and glossed-over or avoided weaknesses in the appellee's presentation. No appellee makes more than one or two such errors without getting caught by the court. Therefore, you need no more than one or two points of attack." John T. Gaubatz & Taylor Mattis, *The Moot Court Book* 97 (3d ed. 1994).

(h) *Only if it's important.* "One thing is certain; do not rebut unless you have something really important and telling to say, and unless you say it vigorously and effectively." Hon. Daniel M. Friedman, *Winning on Appeal*, 9 Litig. 15, 60 (Spring 1983).

(i)   *A poor example.* "One of the most outstandingly poor rebuttals I have ever heard anywhere began with the announcement that 'Petitioner's counsel has been guilty of a misstatement.' The courtroom waited expectantly — and then the mountain brought forth this mouse: 'He said petitioner was president of the corporation when the record plainly shows that he was simply its vice-president.'" Frederick Bernays Wiener, *Briefing and Arguing Federal Appeals* § 133, at 349 (2d ed. 1967).

81.   Waive rebuttal if your opponent hasn't scored any points.

Sometimes the strongest rebuttal is none at all. By waiving your rebuttal time, you're telling the court that you're confident that yours is the stronger case and that you needn't impose any further on the court's precious time.

(a)   *Classic statement 1.* "When counsel for the appellant rises at the close of respondent's argument and confines himself to a terse statement that he sees no occasion for rebuttal, he gives an impression of confidence that reinforces his opening argument. Such a statement may be a superior rebuttal." Hon. George Rossman, "Appellate Practice and Advocacy" (1955), in *Advocacy and the King's English* 241, 255 (George Rossman ed., 1960).

(b)   *Classic statement 2.* "[I]n some cases, the way to use rebuttal to the best tactical advantage is simply to say, 'Unless the Court has questions, I have nothing further.' The risks in waiving rebuttal are obvious. The principal advantage is that it can be a rather effective way of saying that the case for judgment in your favor is so strong that nothing more need be said on the subject." Rex E. Lee, *Oral Argument in the Supreme Court*, 72 ABA J. 60, 62 (June 1986).

(c)   *A signal that nothing merits a response.* "Although counsel for appellant should always reserve a brief time for rebuttal (assuming you are not in a jurisdiction where time is given automatically), waive your time if nothing truly critical remains. The act of waiving rebuttal itself tells the court your opponent said nothing deserving of response." Bradley G. Clary et al., *Advocacy on Appeal* 130 (2d ed. 2004).

(d) *Rebuttal rarely if ever determinative.* "As a judge, I have never seen an appellant's counsel use rebuttal effectively, and I have never seen the decision turn on anything said in rebuttal." Hon. James L. Robertson, "Reality on Appeal," in *Appellate Practice Manual* 119, 127 (Priscilla Anne Schwab ed., 1992).

Final Thoughts

82. Remember the importance of continual improvement.

Don't ever assume that you've mastered your full potential as an advocate. You'll never do that. So continue honing your skills — everything from strengthening client communications to analytical thinking to powerful speaking techniques. Stock your mind. And practice.

(a) *Communications with the client.* "Following the argument, the attorney should send a letter to the client, providing him or her with the attorney's impressions of the oral argument, including specific concerns expressed by the judges and a rough estimate of the anticipated time before decision." Robert M. Tyler Jr., *Practices and Strategies for a Successful Appeal*, 16 Am. J. Trial Advoc. 617, 691 (1993).

(b) *Duty of constant preparation.* "[D]o not let your preparation wait upon a retainer. There is not time to become an advocate after the important case comes to you. Webster, when asked as to the time he spent in preparing one of his arguments, is said to have replied that his whole life was given to its preparation. So it is with every notable forensic effort." Hon. Robert H. Jackson, *Advocacy Before the Supreme Court: Suggestions for Effective Case Presentations*, 37 ABA J. 801, 863 (Nov. 1951).

(c) *Accepting every invitation to speak.* "A good rule for a young lawyer is never to decline an invitation to speak — schools, service clubs, community drives, Sunday School, political meetings — anywhere on any subject. In learning to teach a Bible lesson to a Sunday School class of high school students, one learns much of value for pleading a case to a jury, arguing a point to a court, stating a proposition to a conference, or maintaining a position in a negotiation. Speaking effectively in our day is an art acquired only by hard work. The 'gift of gab' is a hindrance rather than a help. Glib talk sounds well, but it is not effective in this middle of the Twentieth Century. A lawyer should speak as often as he can. He will learn something new about the art of speaking every time he speaks." Hon. E. Barrett Prettyman, *Some Observations Concerning Appellate Advocacy*, 39 Va. L. Rev. 285, 302 (1953).

(d) *The artistry of getting points across.* "The art of transmitting ideas must be learned by long years of study and then a lifetime of practice." Hon. Edward S. Dore, "Expressing the Idea" (1954), in *Advocacy and the King's English* 810, 811 (George Rossman, ed. 1960).

(e) *Mountaintops and valleys.* "Instead of considering each lawsuit as the crisis of your career at the bar, learn to take your inevitable victories gracefully and modestly. Also learn to take your inevitable defeats with understanding . . . . A lawyer's life is not all spent on the invigorating mountaintop; there are valleys and deserts through the head and depression of which he has had to make his way. He has had to traverse impassable jungles and climb rock formations where there was hardly a foot or hand hold. Even when he has arrived at the mountaintop, it is not all a series of unbroken successes from that point onward. Big or little, young or old, fledgling or experienced advocate, we must all learn to take it in our stride. . . . Learn to learn from your defeats. Thus you have turned a loss into a profit. A lawyer can be reasonably happy if he has once learned the philosophy that at the bar we cannot all win, all the time." A.S. Cutler, *Successful Trial Tactics* 300, 301–02 (1949).

(f) *An improvable skill.* "Of all our faculties, probably that of effective public speech is the most susceptible of growth and development, and, like other faculties, it is best cultivated by use and imitation." Roger A. Pryor, *On Forensic Oratory*, 1 Nat'l L. Rev. 309, 312 (1888).

(g) *Fearless judiciousness.* "To earn the good opinion of the Bench should, from the first, be an object of the beginner; and it can be — and is in fact, I am sure — obtained, by earnest, straightforward fearless and judicious conduct of your cases, without ever imperiling the interests of your clients, which it is, of course, your duty to safeguard." David Dundas, *Observations on the Art of Advocacy*, 3 Can. L. Rev. 171, 179 (1904).

(h) *Excellence requiring hard work.* "[T]he chief reason of the absence of eloquence is a neglect of the means to acquire the habit of graceful and fluent elocution. It is indeed extraordinary that so little pains should be taken by men to qualify themselves for success in speaking. . . . [W]hy should we imagine that the art of oratory is exempt from the necessity of toil, any more than painting or sculpture, poetry or music? No one expects excellence in these, except from men who have devoted themselves with untiring assiduity to a study of the principles of their art." William Forsyth, *Hortensius: An Historical Essay on the Office and Duties of an Advocate* 345 (3d ed. 1879).

Bibliography of Works Cited

Alarcon, Arthur L. "Points on Appeal," in *Appellate Practice Manual* 95 (Priscilla Anne Schwab ed., 1992).

Aldisert, Ruggero J. *Winning on Appeal* (1992).

Anderson, Hu C. "Briefs and Arguments That Help the Court" (1943), in *Advocacy and the King's English* 312 (George Rossman ed., 1960).

Appleman, John Alan. "Tactics in Appellate Briefs," in *Advocacy and the King's English* 440 (George Rossman ed., 1960).

Aron, Roberto, et al. *Trial Communication Skills* (1996).

Ayres, Joe & Janice Miller. *Effective Public Speaking* (1983).

Baldock, Robert R., et al. *What Appellate Advocates Seek from Appellate Judges and What Appellate Judges Seek from Appellate Advocates*, 31 N.M.L. Rev. 265 (2001).

Barrad, Catherine Valerio. *Successful Oral Arguments Do Not Involve Any Arguing*, S.F. Daily J., 4 Aug. 2004, at 5.

Barthold, Gaele McLaughlin. *Questions by Appellate-Court Jurists: A Threat or an Opportunity?*, Certworthy (Defense Research Inst. App. Advocacy Comm. newsletter), Winter 2001, at 4.

Bauer, William J. & William C. Bryson. "The Appeal," in *Master Advocates' Handbook* 261 (D. Lake Rumsey ed., 1986).

Bauer, William J. & William C. Bryson. *The Appeal: Part II*, Docket, Spring 1987, at 16.

Baughmann, Timothy A. *Effective Appellate Oral Advocacy: "Beauty Is Truth, Truth Beauty,"* 77 Mich. B.J. 38 (Jan. 1998).

Baxter, Maurice G. *Daniel Webster and the Supreme Court* (1966).

Beck, James M. *May It Please the Court* (O.R. McGuire ed., 1930).

Bederman, David J. *A Chilly Reception at the Court*, 5 J. App. Prac. & Proc. 51 (Spring 2003).

Bell, John C., Jr. *Oral Arguments Before the Supreme Court of Pennsylvania*, 24 Pa. B. Assn. Q. 133 (1953).

Bentele, Ursula & Eve Cary. *Appellate Advocacy: Principle and Practice* (1998).

Berman, Kenneth R. *Snatching Victory: Arguing to Win*, 21 Litig. 18 (Winter 1995).

Bigelow, S. Tupper. *Legal Etiquette and Courtroom Decorum* (1955).

Biggs, John, Jr., et al. "In the Matter of Oral Argument" (1955), in *Advocacy and the King's English* 233 (George Rossman ed., 1960).

Birkett, Norman. "The Art of Advocacy: Character and Skills for the Trial of Cases" (1948), in *Advocacy and the King's English* 919 (George Rossman ed., 1960).

Birkett, Norman. "Advocacy" (1954), in *Advocacy and the King's English* 3 (George Rossman ed., 1960).

Birkett, Norman. *Six Great Advocates* (1961).

Blair, Paxton. "Appellate Briefs and Advocacy" (1949), in *Advocacy and the King's English* 788 (George Rossman ed., 1960).

Board of Student Advisers at Harvard Law School. *Introduction to Advocacy* (7th ed. 2002).

Borden, Richard C. *Public Speaking as Listeners Like It* (1935).

Boyce, William J. *Reflections on Going to the Show*, 17 App. Advocate (State Bar of Texas Appellate Section), Summer 2004, at 21.

Breitel, Charles D. "A Summing Up," in *Counsel on Appeal* (Arthur A. Charpentier ed., 1968).

Brennan, William J. *Harvard Law School Occasional Pamphlet No. 9* (1967).

Bright, Myron H. *The Changing Nature of the Federal Appeals Process in the 1970's*, 65 F.R.D. 496 (1975).

Bright, Myron H. *The Power of the Spoken Word: In Defense of Oral Argument*, 72 Iowa L. Rev. 35 (1986).

Bright, Myron H. *The Ten Commandments of Oral Argument*, 67 ABA J. 1136 (1981).

Bright, Myron H. & Richard S. Arnold. *Oral Argument? It May Be Crucial!*, 70 ABA J. 68 (Sept. 1984).

Brinkmann, Beth S. *A First Argument in the Tradition of Many*, 5 J. App. Prac. & Proc. 61 (Spring 2003).

Brooks, Keith. *Practical Speaking for the Technical Man* (1958).

Bruce, Andrew A. *The American Judge* (1924).

Brumbaugh, Jesse Franklin. *Legal Reasoning and Briefing* (1917).

Buehler, E.C. *You and Your Speeches* (1949).

Burger, Warren E. *The Special Skills of Advocacy*, 42 Fordham L. Rev. 227 (1973).

Butler, Charles Henry. *A Century at the Bar of the Supreme Court of the United States* (1942).

Calamandrei, Piero. *Eulogy of Judges* (1936; John Clarke Adams & C. Abbott Phillips Jr. eds, 1942; repr. 1992).

Carnahan, Douglas G. *Courtroom Clod: Learn How to Talk to a Judge*, S.F. Daily J., 24 Nov. 2000.

Carnahan, Douglas G. *The Top Ten List of Things You Shouldn't Say in Court*, S.F. Daily J. Extra, 8 Sept. 2003, at 9.

Carrigan, Jim R. "Some Nuts and Bolts of Appellate Advocacy," in *Appellate Practice Manual* 102 (Priscilla Anne Schwab ed., 1992).

Carrington, Paul D, et al. *Justice on Appeal* (1976).

Carroll, Jennifer S. *Appellate Specialization and the Art of Appellate Advocacy*, 74 Fla. B.J. 107 (June 2000).

Carson, Hampton L. *John G. Johnson: A Great American Lawyer*, 3 Cornell L.Q. 100 (1918).

Carson, Ralph M. *Conduct of the Appeal — A Lawyer's View* (1952).

Carswell, William B. *The Briefing and Argument of an Appeal*, 16 Brooklyn L. Rev. 147 (Apr. 1950).

Carter, Orrin N. "Preparation and Presentation of Cases in Courts of Review" (1917), in *Advocacy and the King's English* 296 (George Rossman ed., 1960).

Cartwright, James H. *The Briefs and Argument That Help the Court*, 19 Ill. St. B.J. 15 (1896).

Childress, Celia W. *Persuasive Delivery in the Courtroom* (1995).

Cicero. *Cicero on Oratory and Orators* (45 B.C.; J.S. Watson trans., 1986).

Clary, Bradley G., et al. *Advocacy on Appeal* (2d ed. 2004).

Clay, Watson. "Presenting Your Case to the Court of Appeals" (1952), in *Advocacy and the King's English* 330 (George Rossman ed., 1960).

Coates, Timothy. *I Couldn't Wait to Argue*, 5 J. App. Prac. & Proc. 81 (Spring 2003).

Coffin, Frank M. *A Lexicon of Oral Advocacy* (1984).

Coffin, Frank M. *On Appeal: Courts, Lawyering and Judging* (1994).

Cohen, J. Richard. *Pretender in Paradise*, 5 J. App. Prac. & Proc. 87 (Spring 2003).

Cole, Jeffrey. *An Interview with Judge Randolph*, 2 Litig. 16 (Winter 1999).

Cole, Jeffrey. *My Afternoon with Alex: An Interview with Judge Kozinski*, 30 Litig. 6 (Summer 2004).

Collodel, Douglas J. *Oral Argument — California Style?*, Certworthy (Defense Research Inst. App. Advocacy Comm. newsletter), Fall 1998, at 11.

Coxe, Alfred C. "Is Brief-Making a Lost Art?" (1908), in *Advocacy and the King's English* 338 (George Rossman ed., 1960).

Craven, Charles W. *Chili Palmer and the Art of Appellate Oral Argument*, Committee News (App. Advocacy Comm. newsletter of the ABA Sec. Tort, Trial, and Ins. Prac.), Summer 2005, at 1.

Craven, Charles W. "Posttrial and Appellate Oral Argument: A Curmudgeon's Perspective," in *A Defense Lawyer's Guide to Appellate Practice* 221 (2004).

Crawford, Archibald. *Public Speaking* (1935).

Crispe, Thomas Edward. *Reminiscences of a K.C.* (1910).

Currie, George R. *Some Aspects of Appellate Practice Before the Wisconsin Supreme Court*, 1955 Wis. L. Rev. 554.

Cutler, A.S. *Successful Trial Tactics* (1949).

D'Alemberte, Talbot. *Oral Argument: The Continuing Conversation*, 25 Litig. 12 (Winter 1999).

Davis, John W. *The Argument of an Appeal*, 26 ABA J. 895 (Dec. 1940).

Dempsey, David J. *Legally Speaking* (2002).

Denning, Alfred Thompson. *The Discipline of Law* (1979).

Denning, Alfred Thompson. *The Family Story* (1981).

Dershowitz, Alan. *Letters to a Young Lawyer* (2001).

Deutsch, Samuel & Simon Balicer. *How to Take an Appeal* (1931).

Donovan, J.W. *Tact in Court* (6th ed. 1915).

Dore, Edward S. "Expressing the Idea" (1954), in *Advocacy and the King's English* 810 (George Rossman ed., 1960).

Douglas, William O. *The Court Years, 1939–1975* (1980).

Du Cann, Richard. *The Art of the Advocate* (1964).

Dundas, David. *Observations on the Art of Advocacy*, 3 Can. L. Rev. 171 (1904).

Dworsky, Alan L. *The Little Book on Oral Argument* (1991).

Elster, Charles Harrington. *The Big Book of Beastly Mispronunciations* (2d ed. 2006).

English Justice (1932).

Evans, Keith. *The Language of Advocacy* (1998).

Fest, Thorrel B. *Oral Aspects of Appellate Argument*, 22 Rocky Mtn. L. Rev. 273 (1950).

Files, Gordon L. *Oral Argument: Before or After the Decision?*, 54 Cal. St. B.J. 88 (1979).

Fitzgerald, Henry St. John & Daniel Hartnett. *Effective Oral Argument*, 18 Prac. Law. 51 (April 1972).

Foley, Edward B. *Learning (and Teaching) from Doing*, 5 J. App. Prac. & Proc. 107 (Spring 2003).

Fontham, Michael R., et al. *Persuasive Written and Oral Advocacy in Trial and Appellate Courts* (2002).

Forsyth, William. *Hortensius: An Historical Essay on the Office and Duties of an Advocate* (3d ed. 1879).

Foster, Bob. *Oral Advocacy at the Supreme Court of the United States*, Fed. Law., Sept. 2002, at 23.

Fournet, John B. *The Effective Presentation of a Case to the Supreme Court in Brief and Argument*, 3 La. B.J. 95 (Jan. 1956).

Frank, John P. *Lincoln as a Lawyer* (1961).

Frederick, David C. *Supreme Court and Appellate Advocacy* (2003).

Freedman, Abraham L. *On Advocacy*, 1 Vill. L. Rev. 290 (1956).

Frey, Andrew L. *Preparing and Delivering Oral Argument*, http://www.appellate. net/articles/prepdel799.asp (accessed 26 Jan. 2007).

Frey, Andrew L. *Tilting at Windmills*, 5 J. App. Prac. & Proc. 117 (Spring 2003).

Friedman, Daniel M. *Winning on Appeal*, 9 Litig. 15 (Spring 1983).

Fuess, Charles M. *Rufus Choate: The Wizard of the Law* (1928).

Gabriel, Henry D. *Preparation and Delivery of Oral Argument in Appellate Courts*, 22 Am. J. Trial Advoc. 571 (1999).

Garner, Bryan A. *A Dictionary of Modern Legal Usage* (2d ed. 1995).

Garner, Bryan A. *Garner's Modern American Usage* (2d ed. 2003).

Garth, Leonard I. *How to Appeal to an Appellate Judge*, 21 Litig. 20 (Fall 1994).

Gates, Samuel E. "Hot Bench or Cold Bench: When the Court Has Not Read the Brief Before Oral Argument," in *Counsel on Appeal* 107 (Arthur A. Charpentier ed., 1968).

Gaubatz, John T. & Taylor Mattis. *The Moot Court Book* (3d ed. 1994).

Ginsburg, Ruth Bader. *Remarks for American Law Institute Annual Dinner, May 19, 1994*, 38 St. Louis L.J. 881 (1994).

Ginsburg, Ruth Bader. *Remarks for U. Va. Student Legal Forum Dinner* (1990; repr. in *Appellate Advocacy* (28 Oct. 1994)).

Givens, Richard A. *Advocacy* (1992).

Godbold, John. *Twenty Pages and Twenty Minutes — Effective Advocacy on Appeal*, 30 Sw. L.J. 801 (1976).

Goodrich, Herbert F. *A Case on Appeal — A Judge's View* (1952).

Goodrich, Herbert F. "In the Matter of Oral Argument" (1955), in *Advocacy and the King's English* 233 (George Rossman ed., 1960).

Gould, Milton S. *Oral Argument Losing Its Appeal*, Nat'l L.J., 23 Mar. 1981, at 15.

Greene, J. Thomas. *Don't Forget Your Orals*, 183 F.R.D. 289 (1999).

Grignon, Margaret M. *The Dynamics of Appellate Oral Argument*, Certworthy (Defense Research Inst. App. Advocacy Comm. newsletter), Summer 2006, at 31.

Griswold, Erwin N. *Appellate Advocacy with Particular Reference to the United States Supreme Court*, N.Y. St. B.J., Oct. 1972, at 375.

Gurfein, Murray I. "Appellate Advocacy, Modern Style," in *Appellate Practice Manual* 256 (Priscilla Anne Schwab ed., 1992).

Hamley, Frank G. *Appellate Advocacy*, 12 Ark. L. Rev. 129 (1957).

Harlan, John M. *What Part Does the Oral Argument Play in the Conduct of an Appeal?*, 41 Cornell L.Q. 6 (1955).

Harris, Richard. *Hints on Advocacy* (17th ed. 1937).

Harvey, C.P. *The Advocate's Devil* (1958).

Hatchett, Joseph W. & Robert J. Telfer III. *The Importance of Appellate Oral Argument*, 33 Stetson L. Rev. 139 (2003).

Hay, Peter. *The Book of Legal Anecdotes* (1989).

Heinke, Rex S. & Tracy L. Casadio. *Oral Argument in the Federal Circuit Courts*, 16 Cal. Litig. 36 (No. 2, 2003).

Herrmann, Mark. *The Curmudgeon's Guide to Practicing Law* (2006).

Heward, Edmund. *Lord Denning* (1990).

High, James L. *Advocacy v. Oratory*, 1 Advocate 190 (1888).

Hoff, Ron. *Say It in Six* (1996).

Hogan, Christine. *May It Please the Court*, 27 Litig. 8 (Summer 2001).

Honigman, Jason L. *The Art of Appellate Advocacy*, 64 Mich. L. Rev. 1055 (1966).

Hornstein, Alan D. *Appellate Advocacy in a Nutshell* (1984).

Hughes, Charles Evans. *The Supreme Court of the United States* (1928).

Hyde, H. Montgomery. *Norman Birkett: The Life of Lord Birkett of Ulverston* (1964).

Jackson, Robert H. *Advocacy Before the Supreme Court: Suggestions for Effective Case Presentations*, 37 ABA J. 801 (Nov. 1951).

Jacobs, Robert Lee. *The Judge's View*, 42 Pa. B.Q. 119 (1970).

Janner, Greville. *Janner's Complete Speechmaker* (1981).

Jefferson, Thomas. 21 May 1816 letter to Francis Eppes, in 19 *The Writings of Thomas Jefferson* 242 (memorial ed., 1903).

Jennings, Newell. "The Argument of an Appeal from the Judge's Point of View" (1946), in *Advocacy and the King's English* 551 (George Rossman ed., 1960).

Joiner, Charles W. "The Trial Brief" (1955), in *Advocacy and the King's English* 45 (George Rossman ed., 1960).

Jones, Hugh R. *Appellate Advocacy, Written and Oral*, J. Mo. Bar, June 1991, at 297.

Karlen, Delmar. *Appellate Courts in the United States and England* (1963).

Kaufman, Irving R. *Appellate Advocacy in the Federal Courts*, 79 F.R.D. 165 (1978).

Kenison, Frank R. *Some Aspects of Appellate Arguments*, N.H.B.J., Jan. 1959, at 5.

Kerr, James M. *Hints on Advocacy*, 1 Colum. L.T. 141 (1888).

Kester, Randall B. *Tailoring Appellate Arguments*, 43 Or. L. Rev. 135 (1964).

Kitching, Patti S. *The Last Word*, S.F. Daily J., 30 July 1999, at 6.

Knapp, Whitman. *Why Argue an Appeal? If So, How?*, 14 Record N.Y.C.B.A. 415 (1959).

Knibb, David G. *Federal Court of Appeals Manual* (1990).

Kozinski, Alex. *In Praise of Moot Court — Not!*, 97 Colum. L. Rev. 178 (1997).

Kozinski, Alex. *The Wrong Stuff*, 1992 B.Y.U. L. Rev. 325.

Langlois, Gregory J. *Dress Rehearsal: The Moot Court Program at Georgetown Law Center's Supreme Court Institute*, 7 J. App. Prac. & Proc. 231 (Fall 2005).

Larkins, John K., Jr. "Oral Argument on Motions," in *The Litigation Manual: Pretrial* 107 (1999).

Lascher, Edward L. *Oral Argument*, 7 Cal. Litig. 16 (Winter 1994).

Lascher, Edward L. *Oral Argument for Fun and Profit*, Cal. St. B.J., Jul./Aug. 1973, at 398.

Lavine, Douglas S. *New Year, New Approach*, Nat'l L.J., 14 Jan. 2008, at 14.

Lavine, Douglas S. *Responding to Questions*, Nat'l L.J., 1 Jan. 2007, at 20.

Lazarus, Edward. *Closed Chambers* (1999).

Lee, Rex E. *Oral Argument in the Supreme Court*, 72 ABA J. 60 (June 1986).

Levin, Jay M. *The Importance of the Opening in an Appellate Argument: A Case Study*, Certworthy (Defense Research Inst. App. Advocacy Comm. newsletter), Winter 2000, at 13.

Levy, Herbert Monte. *How to Handle an Appeal* (3d ed. 1990).

Lewis, Anthony. *The Supreme Court and How It Works* (1966).

Llewellyn, Karl N. *A Lecture on Appellate Advocacy*, 29 U. Chi. L. Rev. 627 (1962).

Llewellyn, Karl N. *The Common Law Tradition: Deciding Appeals* (1960).

Loughran, John T. "The Argument in the Court of Appeals" (1943), in *Advocacy and the King's English* 570 (George Rossman ed., 1960).

Loughran, John T. *The Argument of an Appeal in the Court of Appeals*, 12 Fordham L. Rev. 1 (1943).

Lummus, Henry T. "How Lawyers Should Argue Cases on Appeal" (1943), in *Advocacy and the King's English* 348 (George Rossman ed., 1960).

Macmillan, Hugh Pattison. "Some Observations on the Art of Advocacy" (1933), in *Law and Other Things* 200 (1937).

Marshall, Prentice H. "Oral Argument," in *Illinois Civil Practice After Trial* 9-1, (1976).

Marshall, Thurgood. "The Federal Appeal," in *Counsel on Appeal* 139 (Arthur A. Charpentier ed., 1968).

Martineau, Robert J. *Fundamentals of Modern Appellate Advocacy* (1985).

Marvell, Thomas B. *Appellate Courts and Lawyers* (1978).

Mazengarb, O.C. *Advocacy in Our Time* (1964).

McAmis, Luke M. *The Lawyer and the Court of Appeals*, 24 Tenn. L. Rev. 279 (1956).

McBurney, James H. & Ernest J. Wrage. *Guide to Good Speech* (2d ed. 1960).

McEwen, Stephen A. *Preparing Yourself for Oral Argument*, L.A. Law., June 2002, at 10.

Medina, Harold R. *The Oral Argument on Appeal*, 20 ABA J. 139 (1934).

Merryday, Steven D. *Florida Appellate Practice Handbook* § 17 (2003).

Merryday, Steven D. "Oral Argument," in *Florida Appellate Practice* § 17 (4th ed. 1997).

Michel, Paul R. *Effective Appellate Advocacy*, 24 Litig. 19 (Summer 1998).

Mikva, Abner J. *Counsel Lack Selectivity in Appellate Advocacy*, Legal Times, 15 Nov. 1982.

Mikva, Abner J. "Taking an Appeal," *Appellate Advocacy*, 28 Oct. 1994, at 4.

Miner, Roger J. *The Don'ts of Oral Argument*, 14 Litig. 3 (Summer 1988).

Minnick, Wayne C. *The Art of Persuasion* (2d ed. 1968).

Mitchell, Ewan. *The Lawyer and His World* (1962).

Molo, Steven F. & Paul P. Biebel Jr. "Preparing for Oral Argument," in *Appellate Practice Manual* 244 (Priscilla Anne Schwab ed., 1992).

Moncreiff, F.C. *The Wit and Wisdom of the Bench and Bar* (1882).

Morison, H. Graham. *Oral Argument of Appeals*, 10 Wash. & Lee L. Rev. 1 (1953).

Morley, Iain. *The Devil's Advocate: A Short Polemic on How to Be Seriously Good in Court* (2005).

Moore, O. Otto. *Some Observations on Oral Argument*, 33 Rocky Mntn. L. Rev. 30 (1960).

Mosk, Stanley. *In Defense of Oral Argument*, 1 J. App. Prac. & Proc. 25 (Winter 1999).

Moskovitz, Myron. *Winning an Appeal* (3d ed. 1995).

Munkman, John H. *The Technique of Advocacy* (1951).

Murray, Michael D. & Christy H. DeSanctis. *Adversarial Legal Writing and Oral Argument* (2006).

Nelson, John E., III. "Building a Brief," in *Appellate Practice Manual* 228 (Priscilla Anne Schwab ed., 1992).

Nirenberg, Jesse S. *How to Sell Your Ideas* (1984).

Nizer, Louis. *My Life in Court* (1963).

Nizer, Louis. *Thinking on Your Feet* (1940).

Norvell, James R. *The Case on Appeal*, 1 So. Tex. L.J. 229 (1954).

Oates, Laurel Currie & Anne Enquist. *Just Briefs* (2003).

On Some Common Errors in Advocacy, 10 Va. L.J. 710 (1886).

Oral Argument Before Courts of Error, 2 Cent. L.J. 550 (1875).

"Oral Argument — Through the Looking Glass," in *Appellate Practice for the Maryland Lawyer* (Paul Mark Sandler & Andrew D. Levy eds., 2001).

Oratory and the Law — A Plea, 7 W. Va. Bar 219 (1900).

Owen, S.N. *Courtroom Oratory*, 60 Albany L.J. 324 (1899).

Page, Leo. *First Steps in Advocacy* (1943).

Palmer, Ben W. *Courtroom Strategies* (1959).

Pannick, David. *Advocates* (1992).

Parry, Edward Abbott. *Judgments in Vacation* (1911).

Parry, Edward Abbott. *My Own Way: An Autobiography* (1932).

Parry, Edward Abbott. *What the Judge Thought* (1922).

Paterson, Alan. *The Law Lords* (1982).

Payler, Frederick. *Law Courts, Lawyers and Litigants* (1926).

Perdue, Jim M. *The Art of Demonstrative Evidence*, Trial, May 2005, at 46.

Phillips, Carter G. *Advocacy Before the United States Supreme Court*, 15 T.M. Cooley L. Rev. 177 (1988).

Pierce, Lawrence W. *Appellate Advocacy: Some Reflections from the Bench*, 61 Fordham L. Rev. 829 (1993).

Pollack, Milton B. "The Civil Appeal," in *Counsel on Appeal* 29 (Arthur A. Charpentier ed., 1968).

Pollack, Milton B. *Some Practical Aspects of Appellate Advocacy*, N.Y. St. B. Bull., Feb. 1959, at 81.

Pope, Jack. *Argument on Appeal*, 14 Prac. Law. 33 (1968).

Porter, Karen K., et al. *Introduction to Legal Writing and Oral Advocacy* (1989).

Posner, Richard A. *Convincing a Federal Court of Appeals*, 25 Litig. 3 (Winter 1999).

Pound, Roscoe. *Appellate Procedure in Civil Cases* (1941).

Pregerson, Harry. *The Seven Sins of Appellate Brief Writing and Other Transgressions*, 34 UCLA L. Rev. 431 (1986).

Premo, Eugene M. *The Art of Oral Argument*, 15 Cal. Litig. 45 (No. 3, 2002).

Prettyman, E. Barrett. *Some Observations Concerning Appellate Advocacy*, 39 Va. L. Rev. 285 (1953).

Prettyman, E. Barrett, Jr. *Supreme Court Advocacy: Random Thoughts in a Day of Time Restrictions*, 4 Litig. 16 (Winter 1978).

Pryor, Roger A. *On Forensic Oratory*, 1 Nat'l L. Rev. 309 (1888).

Pusey, M.J. *Charles Evans Hughes* (1951).

Quintilian. *Quintilian on the Teaching of Speaking and Writing: Translations from Books One, Two, and Ten of the Institution Oratoria* (ca. A.D. 95; James J. Murphy trans., 1987).

Rall, Owen. *Effective Oral Argument on Appeal*, 48 Ill. B.J. 572 (1960).

Rall, Owen. "Persuasive Oral Argument," in *Lawyer's Encyclopedia* 1019 (1963).

Re, Edward D. *Brief Writing and Oral Argument* (6th ed. 1987).

Rehnquist, William H. *From Webster to Word-Processing*, 1 J. App. Prac. & Proc. 1 (Winter 1999).

Rehnquist, William H. *Oral Advocacy*, 27 S. Tex. L. Rev. 289 (1986).

Rehnquist, William H. *Oral Advocacy: A Disappearing Art*, 35 Mercer L. Rev. 1015 (1984).

Rehnquist, William H. *The Supreme Court: How It Was, How It Is* (1987).

Rhetorica ad Herrenium (1st century B.C.; Harry Caplan trans., 1954).

Riback, Stuart M. *First Argument Impressions of the Supreme Court*, 5 J. App. Prac. & Proc. 146 (Spring 2003).

Rifkind, Simon H. "Appellate Courts Compared," in *Counsel on Appeal* 163 (Arthur A. Charpentier ed., 1968).

Roach, Robert M., Jr. "Oral Argument," in *Texas Supreme Court Practice Manual 2005* (Richard R. Orsinger ed.).

Roach, Robert M., Jr. & Kevin Dubose. Texas Bar CLE Presentation, *Eight Commonly Made Mistakes in Appellate Oral Argument* (Austin, Tex.; 9 Jan. 1998).

Roberds, W.G. *Some Suggestions as to Oral Arguments and Written Briefs in the Supreme Court of Mississippi*, 29 Miss. L.J. 403 (1958).

Robertson, James L. "Reality on Appeal," in *Appellate Practice Manual* 119 (Priscilla Anne Schwab ed., 1992).

Rosenberg, Lawrence D. *Using the Lessons of Aristotle to Present Outstanding Oral Arguments: Part II*, ABA App. Prac. J., Spring 2006, at 15.

Robinette, John J. *A Counsel Looks at the Court*, 53 Can. B. Rev. 558 (1975).

Rossman, George. "Appellate Practice and Advocacy" (1955), in *Advocacy and the King's English* 241 (George Rossman ed., 1960).

Rothfeld, Charles A. *Avoiding Missteps in the Supreme Court: A Guide to Resources for Counsel*, 7 J. App. Prac. & Proc. 249 (Fall 2005).

Rutledge, Wiley B. *The Appellate Brief*, 28 ABA J. 251 (1942).

Rychlak, Ronald J. *Effective Appellate Advocacy: Tips from the Teams*, 66 Miss. L.J. 527 (1997).

Sasso, Gary L. *Appellate Oral Argument*, 20 Litig. 27 (Summer 1994).

Savage, David G. *Say the Right Thing*, 83 ABA J. 54 (Sept. 1997).

Scalia, Antonin & Bryan A. Garner. *Making Your Case: The Art of Persuading Judges* (2008).

Scanlan, Alfred L. *Effective Appellate Advocacy in the Court of Appeals of Maryland*, 29 Md. L. Rev. 126 (1969).

Schaefer, Walter V. *Appellate Advocacy*, 23 Tenn. L. Rev. 471 (1954).

Schloff, Laurie & Marcia Yudkin. *Smart Speaking* (1991).

Shapiro, Stephen M. *Oral Argument in the Supreme Court of the United States*, 33 Catholic U. Am. L. Rev. 529 (1984).

Shapiro, Stephen M. *Questions, Answers, and Prepared Remarks*, 15 Litig. 33 (Spring 1989).

Shepherd, John C. & Jordan B. Cherrick. *Advocacy and Emotion*, 139 F.R.D. 619 (1991).

Shullman, Sarah Levien. *The Illusion of Devil's Advocacy*, 6 J. App. Prac. & Proc. 271 (Fall 2004).

Schweitzer, Sydney C. *Trial Guide* (1948).

Silberman, Laurence H. *Plain Talk on Appellate Advocacy*, 20 Litig. 3 (Spring 1994).

Spearman, Jean Johnson. "General Communication Skills," in *Master Advocates' Handbook* 285 (D. Lake Rumsey ed., 1986).

Spears, Franklin. *Presenting an Effective Appeal*, Trial, Nov. 1985, at 95.

Spence, Garry. *How to Argue and Win Every Time* (1995).

Steinberg, Harris B. "The Criminal Appeal," in *Counsel on Appeal* 1 (Arthur A. Charpentier ed., 1968).

Steinheimer, Roy L., Jr. *Winning on Appeal*, 20 Mich. St. B.J. 16 (Oct. 1950).

Stern, Horace. *Letters from a Judge to His Lawyer Son*, 21 Temple L.Q. 1 (1947).

Stern, Robert L. *Appellate Practice in the United States* (1981).

Stern, Robert L., et al. *Supreme Court Practice* (8th ed. 2002).

Stolley, Scott Patrick. *Consult Your Talking Mirror*, Certworthy (Defense Research Inst. App. Advocacy Comm. newsletter), Spring 1998, at 14.

Stryker, Lloyd Paul. *The Art of Advocacy* (1954).

Taft, Henry W. *Legal Miscellanies: Six Decades of Changes and Progress* (1941).

Talley-Morris, Neva B. *Appellate Civil Practice and Procedure Handbook* (1975).

Tate, Albert, Jr. *The Appellate Advocate and the Appellate Court*, 13 La. B.J. 107 (Aug. 1965).

Tate, Albert, Jr. *Federal Appellate Advocacy in the 1980s*, 5 Am. J. Trial Advoc. 63 (1981).

Tate, Albert, Jr. *On Questions from the Bench*, 7 La. B.J. 128 (Aug. 1959).

Tchen, Christina M. *Still Grateful After All These Years*, 5 J. App. Prac. & Proc. 157 (Spring 2003).

Thomas, H.S. *Felix Frankfurter, Scholar on the Bench* (1960).

Thomas, Michael Paul. *The Rites and Rights of Oral Argument*, Cal. Law., Sept. 2004, at 40.

Tigar, Michael B. & Jane B. Tigar. *Federal Appeals: Jurisdiction and Practice* (3d ed. 1999).

Townsend, Roger D. *Browsing the Bookshelf*, Certworthy (Defense Research Inst. App. Advocacy Comm. newsletter), Summer 2005, at 47.

Turner, Paul. *Oral Argument and the Judson Welliver Society*, 14 Cal. Litig. 16 (No. 1, 2001).

Tyler, Robert M. *Practices and Strategies for a Successful Appeal*, 16 Am. J. Trial Advoc. 617 (1993).

Vail, Jason. *Oral Argument's Big Challenge: Fielding Questions from the Court*, 1 J. App. Prac. & Proc. 401 (Summer 1999).

Vanderbilt, Arthur T. *Forensic Persuasion* (1950).

Wakeling, T.W. *The Oral Component of Appellate Work*, 5 Dalhousie L.J. 584 (1979).

Ward, Raymond P. *The Importance of Earnest Oral Argument*, Certworthy (Defense Research Inst. App. Advocacy Comm. newsletter), Summer 1999, at 12.

Wasby, Stephen L. *The Supreme Court in the Federal Judicial System* (1978).

Weiss, Samuel. *How to Try a Case* (1930).

Wellman, Francis L. *Day in Court: Or, the Subtle Arts of Great Advocates* (1910).

White, Byron. *The Work of the Supreme Court: A Nuts and Bolts Description*, N.Y. St. B.J., Oct. 1982, at 346.

Wice, Brian. *Oral Argument in Criminal Cases: 10 Tips for Winning the Moot Court Round*, Tex. B.J., Mar. 2006, at 224.

Wiener, Frederick Bernays. *Briefing and Arguing Federal Appeals* (2d ed. 1967).

Wiener, Frederick Bernays. *Oral Advocacy*, 62 Harv. L. Rev. 56 (1948).

Wiener, Jacques L., Jr. *Ruminations from the Bench: Brief Writing and Oral Argument in the Fifth Circuit*, 70 Tul. L. Rev. 187 (1995).

Wilcox, Henry S. *Foibles of the Bar* (1906).

Wilkins, Michael J. *Remember, for Every Case Won at Oral Argument, the Other Side Loses*, Utah B.J., Sept. 2004, at 36.

Wilkins, Raymond S. "The Argument of an Appeal" (1947), in *Advocacy and the King's English* 277 (George Rossman ed., 1960).

Williams, Glanville. *Learning the Law* (A.T.H. Smith ed., 12th ed. 2002).

Wilson, John F. & Carroll C. Arnold. *Public Speaking as a Liberal Art* (1964).

Witkin, B.E. *Manual on Appellate Court Opinions* (1977).

Wolff, Michael A. *From the Mouth of a Fish: An Appellate Judge Reflects on Oral Argument*, 45 St. Louis Univ. L.J. 1097 (2001).

Words of Advice to Attorneys from Members of Appellate Courts of Alabama, 4 Ala. L. Rev. 207 (1952).

Wright, Thomas J. & Perry H. Piper. *Oral Advocacy — Some Reminders*, Tenn. B.J., Nov./Dec. 1994, at 28.

Index